PACKAGING 3
PACKUNGEN 3
EMBALLAGES 3

AN INTERNATIONAL SURVEY OF PACKAGE DESIGN

EIN INTERNATIONALES HANDBUCH DER PACKUNGSGESTALTUNG

UN RÉPERTOIRE INTERNATIONAL DES FORMES DE L'EMBALLAGE

Edited by: / Herausgegeben von: / Réalisé par:

Walter Herdeg

GRAPHIS

Walter Herdeg, The Graphis Press, Zurich

Distributed in the United States by

Hastings House

Publishers
10 East 40th Street, New York, N.Y. 10016

Editor and Art Director: Walter Herdeg
Editorial Staff: Project Manager: Jack J. Kunz,
Assistant Editors: Stanley Mason, Hans Kuh,
Art Associates: Ulrich Kemmner, Peter Wittwer

PUBLICATION No. 146   [ISBN 8038-2684-2]

Contents   Inhalt   Sommaire

■ This book would be incomplete without a warm word of thanks to those who have contributed to it: first of all to all those packaging designers and agencies who went to the considerable trouble of submitting their often bulky productions, and who have shown great patience throughout the lengthy period of preparation of this book with its detailed captions and credit information; secondly to the many individuals and packaging organizations who have given us their unstinting assistance and support; and finally to those who have made a major personal contribution to it, particularly Jack Kunz, who did most of the compilation work, Karl Fink, writer of the preface, Hans Kuh, Hartmut W. Staats and Irv Koons.

■ Dieses Buch wäre unvollständig ohne ein herzliches Wort des Dankes an all jene, die zum Gelingen dieser Publikation beigetragen haben. Dieses richtet sich hauptsächlich an alle Packungsgestalter und Agenturen, die sich die Mühe nahmen, ihre oft voluminösen Produktionen einzusenden, und die während der sich in die Länge ziehenden Vorbereitungsarbeiten grosse Geduld an den Tag legten; aber auch an alle Packungsspezialisten und -organisationen, auf deren Hilfe und Unterstützung wir angewiesen waren; und nicht zuletzt gebührt all jenen Mitarbeitern herzlicher Dank, die durch persönlichen Einsatz die Herausgabe ermöglichten, hauptsächlich Jack Kunz, der das gesamte Material sammelte und zusammenstellte, Karl Fink, dem Autor des Vorwortes, Hans Kuh, Hartmut W. Staats und Irv Koons.

■ Ce livre serait incomplet sans un «grand merci» adressé à tous ceux qui ont contribué à la réalisation de cette publication. Les remerciements sont destinés en particulier aux emballagistes et agences publicitaires qui ont pris la peine de soumettre leurs productions parfois assez volumineuses et qui ont manifesté une patience extraordinaire pendant la longue période qu'a nécessité le rassemblement des informations pour les légendes et les listes d'artistes; en second lieu à tous les spécialistes et organisations de conditionnement qui nous ont prêté leur assistance précieuse; et enfin à ceux qui, par leur contribution et leur engagement personnels, ont pris une part importante quant à la réalisation, particulièrement Jack Kunz qui a réuni le matériel, Karl Fink, auteur de la préface, Hans Kuh, Hartmut W. Staats et Irv Koons.

The designer of our cover, WALTER BALLMER, is a Swiss who studied at Basle and later set up his own design studio in Milan. He made a name with his exhibitions for Olivetti and has distinguished himself in design programmes and silk-screen posters, winning many awards. His work as a fine artist and sculptor has also been widely exhibited.

Der Umschlaggestalter WALTER BALLMER ist ein Schweizer Graphiker, der in Basel studierte und später sein eigenes Design-Studio in Mailand eröffnete. Er machte sich einen Namen mit seinen Ausstellungen für Olivetti und durch seine Gestaltungsprogramme und Siebdruckplakate, die ihm verschiedene Preise einbrachten. Sein Werk als Künstler und Bildhauer wurde in vielen Ausstellungen gezeigt.

WALTER BALLMER, l'artiste de notre couverture, est un suisse qui a fait ses études à Bâle. Depuis de longues années il a son propre studio de design à Milan. Il s'est fait un nom par ses expositions pour Olivetti et a remporté plusieurs prix pour ses remarquables programmes de design et ses affiches sérigraphiques. Il a eu plusieurs expositions de son œuvre d'art et de ses sculptures.

Walter Herdeg   # Foreword / Vorwort / Avant-propos

While eleven years elapsed between the first and second GRAPHIS books on packaging, this third volume follows only seven years after the second. The intervals mirror the accelerated cadence of change in the packaging industry. New materials and techniques, new aspects of manufacture and merchandizing impose a faster tempo with which the packaging designer must keep pace, and this survey is meant to bring him up to date on the best that has been done in his field in the last few years. This does not mean that the remarks of experts on the various sectors of packaging in our last issue have lost their validity; they are still to the point, and for that reason we have restricted editorial comment in this volume to a single survey by a leading packaging authority. The packages shown in this book are once more a careful selection based on graphic excellence and on the overall conception of the package in technical, functional and aesthetic respects. The complaint sometimes heard that a selection from this basically "artistic" standpoint is an "ivory tower" approach that disregards the dozens of compulsions to which the package designer is exposed by merchandizing necessity will not really stand critical scrutiny. It has repeatedly been demonstrated that the consumer is quite able to appreciate and to react to good design. And the examples reproduced in this book are eloquent proof of the fact that packages satisfying all the requirements of the market can also be attractive to look at and even — in the best of cases — things of beauty.

Während zwischen dem Erscheinen des ersten und zweiten GRAPHIS-Bandes über Packungen elf Jahre lagen, folgt dieser dritte Band schon nach einer Zeitspanne von sieben Jahren. Diese Zeiträume widerspiegeln den immer schnelleren Wechsel auf dem Gebiet der Verpackung. Neue Materialien, neue Techniken, neue Herstellungsmethoden und Absatzanalysen bestimmen das Tempo der Weiterentwicklung, mit welcher der Packungsgestalter Schritt halten muss. Dieser Überblick über die besten Arbeiten, die auf diesem Gebiet in den letzten Jahren realisiert wurden, soll ihn wieder auf den neuesten Stand bringen. Dies will natürlich nicht heissen, dass die Aussagen der Experten, die im letzten Band die verschiedenen Aspekte beleuchteten, heute ihre Gültigkeit verloren haben; sie sind auch heute noch genauso zutreffend, deshalb haben wir uns in diesem Band auf einen einzigen Beitrag eines führenden Packungsspezialisten beschränkt. Die hier wiedergegebenen Packungen wurden sorgfältig ausgewählt aufgrund ihrer hervorragenden graphischen Gestaltung und ihrer Gesamtkonzeption, wobei technische, funktionelle und ästhetische Gesichtspunkte berücksichtigt wurden. Der manchmal gemachte Vorwurf, wonach eine Auswahl vom rein künstlerischen Standpunkt aus die an den Packungsgestalter gestellten kommerziellen Anforderungen und Einschränkungen nicht in Betracht zieht, hält der Kritik nicht in allen Aspekten stand. Es hat sich oft herausgestellt, dass der Käufer sehr wohl gutes Packungsdesign zu schätzen weiss und dementsprechend positiv reagiert. Wie die hier gezeigten Beispiele beweisen, können Packungen, die den gestellten Marktanforderungen vollauf entsprechen, auch sehr attraktiv gestaltet sein.

Alors que les deux premiers volumes GRAPHIS consacrés à l'emballage ont paru à onze années d'intervalle, le troisième suit déjà sept ans plus tard, témoignant ainsi de l'accélération des changements qui interviennent nécessairement dans l'industrie de l'emballage. Matériaux et techniques nouveaux, formes nouvelles de fabrication et de commercialisation imposent leur loi à un rythme toujours plus rapide, auquel l'emballagiste est bien obligé de s'adapter. Le présent panorama veut précisément l'informer du meilleur de ce qui s'est fait à travers le monde dans son domaine spécialisé, ces dernières années. Pourtant, les observations formulées dans le dernier volume par les experts des divers secteurs du design d'emballage gardent toute leur valeur. C'est pourquoi nous nous sommes contenté dans le présent ouvrage d'une seule contribution rédactionnelle, mais celle-là de poids, due à un auteur qui fait autorité en la matière. Une fois de plus, ce volume contient une sélection attentive selon les critères de l'excellence graphique et de la conception globale de l'emballage combinant les aspects technique, fonctionnel et esthétique. On entend parfois dire qu'un choix inspiré de ces principes éminemment «artistiques» risque de passer à côté des nombreuses contraintes de caractère commercial qui s'exercent sur l'emballagiste. Loin de constituer une approche de «tour d'ivoire», notre position tient compte du fait souvent démontré que le consommateur est parfaitement capable d'apprécier le design de qualité et de réagir en conséquence. Et les exemples réunis ici apportent une preuve convaincante de ce que les emballages répondant à toutes les exigences du marché peuvent aussi séduire par leur présentation et même atteindre à la qualité d'objets de beauté.

Introduction

This book of noteworthy packages of the past seven years is, in a sense, a social document. As a group, the packages reveal not only aesthetic growth in a design discipline but a falling away of old design standards and the death of some treasured packaging truisms. This introduction will explore some social changes that have influenced our style of living and the thinking of designers who create packages to suit that life-style.

Packaging's progress towards ephemera

Packaging design once had permanence, unlike more ephemeral commercial arts. Advertisements for a product might come, go and be forgotten but packages were designed for years. Manufacturers of successful products undertook design change with trepidation, fearful of alienating customers by depriving them of a packaging look they trusted and which spoke for the unchanging integrity of the product. Packaging was a somewhat stodgy graphic expression, influenced by cautious marketing experts, approved by conservative management, and directed to loyal consumers.

It might be said that one of today's most important artifacts, packaging, presents a clear reflection of our evolving society. While advertising still directs its appeal to a woman in her kitchen, catering to her man with glittering glassware, tastier dinners and whiter shirts, packaging for household products has adapted to the realities of reaching not only women (single as well as married) but men who do laundry, wash the family dishes and cook for themselves and others.

A new society, new influences

Here in Graphis/Packaging III you will find reflected the significant sociological movements of the 1970's: consumerism, feminism, the breakdown of sex role stereotypes, the recognition that the consumer world is the real world, peopled by many races and economic levels. You can see the rock music beat, with its restless, driving, shifting tempo. Look at the packages. You will see the influence of a generation of young adult consumers, raised on psychedelic colour and the constant visual stimulation of television, bombarded with product messages. It is a generation almost lacking a sense of brand loyalty — a new breed of consumer, to be resold constantly through advertising or at point of sale. The gradual disappearance of that dependable customer for Brand X soup or Brand Y deodorant has diminished the need for the old familiar package and has led to more open, more inventive, more dynamic packaging design.

Young adults as consumers

This generation has grown to maturity in the seven years since the appearance of Graphis/Packaging II. The post-war children who were still finishing their schooling at the start of this decade are now established adults. They are the "young marrieds" whose hunger for household goods warms the hearts of home products manufacturers; the customers for the latest fashions in clothing, home furnishings, automobiles, cameras; the mothers and fathers of the disposable diaper crowd. And they are different customers from any we have known before. Born in the late forties and early fifties, they are products of the sixties, an era of social change as significant as the twenties. These are young men and women who have created an altered social order merely voiced by their elders. Women are living, not just talking, more liberated lives. Innumerable middle-class young people have rejected the professional careers their parents had planned for them in order to pursue less structured, less confining lives. One can see the contrasting directions of contemporary life, the changes in life-style, goals and personal habits that have recast our thinking about what we want our world to look like.

Striving for the natural

Although we seem to have reached an all-time high in the use of packaged products for cleaning, preening and feeding, there is, paradoxically, a trend away from all this convenience into natural foods, cooking from scratch, brown-bagging (carrying one's own food, instead of eating in restaurants). This is partially attributable to a desire to return to a less artificial way of doing things; in part, it is an expression of social conscience — a desire to conserve energy and utilize the world's food supply equitably. It is intensified by economic problems all over the world.

Remembrance of other eras

The back-to-nature trend has aroused new interest in crafts — woodworking, calligraphy, handmade things — as a relief from the goods produced by sophisticated machines. A recent exhibition in New York of Japanese packaging employing traditional handicraft techniques enjoyed immense popularity and is now travelling to other cities. Recall of a more leisured world has stimulated nostalgic awakening to design of other eras — Art Nouveau and Art Déco, for instance — and young audiences applaud the old films and early jazz. But while young adults reach for a return to simpler values and less complex ways of living, the world moves inexorably on. The producers of goods consumed by a constantly increasing part of the world's population recognize that they can serve those idealistic needs only superficially. For they are simultaneously confronted by hard economic and marketing truths which will have a lasting effect on the look of packages.

Contemporary distribution problems

Producers must develop more efficient marketing, warehousing and distribution techniques suited to a retailing structure increasingly dependent on self-service. Retailers are faced with a discouragingly high rate of "stock shrinkage" — less politely, shop-lifting. Petty shop-lifting has achieved a certain éclat, has become sport among an all-too-broad age group that spans the economic spectrum. Pilferage, endemic to self-service stores, has hastened the trend towards carding and blister packing of a wide range of products. There are indications that it and other problems may lead us to a science-fiction type of shopping in which the customer makes selections from display or dummy packages or even colour photographs, receiving the actual merchandise only at the check-out counter or at loading points where packages await claim like (God help us) airline baggage today.

Universal Product Code as a solution

And so we find a trend in sharp contrast to that "natural" look. Breakfast cereal producers, for instance, have indeed adapted to the natural food trend by introducing more nutritious "granola" types of products in graphically nostalgic packages. Simultaneously, their continuing development programmes strive for more sophisticated processing and movement of goods from production line to warehousing, wholesale distribution and the various steps of retail marketing. On one panel of the cosy, old-fashioned cereal package showing the farmyard, sheaves of wheat and crocks of molasses, you will find the new Universal Product Code imprint which will make possible that computer-aided wholesale and retail distribution system. Before too long, our nature-hungry consumer will have to learn new electronic activating techniques in order to implement the purchase of the product.

The Universal Product Code in the United States and its counterparts in other countries are serving to identify a broadening concept of what a package is. Magazines, records and paperbound books, for instance, will carry the UPC imprint, fortifying their role as packages. Already, the world of packaging includes knock-down small furniture, such as occasional tables. Hardware items — 12 nuts and bolts, an electric chain saw or a length of garden hose — are packaged or carded, blister-wrapped and labelled. While this packaging has simplified the operation of hardware stores, it has also extended the sale of many of these products to other types of stores. Because a packaged item can end up in unexpected retail outlets, it must be designed to compete for attention with diverse products. This, again, has influenced the look of packages.

Return to simplicity

Packaging simplicity and forthrightness are now evident, for instance, in cosmetics and toiletries which have traditionally been dominated by costly packaging meant to project a luxury image. The luxury look is still to be seen in quantity, of course, but so is packaging that has a simple, often elegant, laboratory-scientific appearance.

Unselfconscious nomads

Living styles have changed radically in the first half of the seventies. There is less formality in eating habits, in home decoration, entertaining, dress and in the way people comport themselves. They eat in transit — on trains and buses and on the street; they eat at the cinema and at concerts. People carry more. The tote or shoulder bag has been adopted by both sexes as the solution for a kind of nomad approach to each new day. The bags, creels or musettes hold food, cans of hairspray, cosmetics, the indispensible hairbrush and a can or two of Coke or Pepsi or wine. Because the life-style is free and unpredictable, so are the needs.

Packaging trends: Unisex

Of the trends that are influencing packaging's look, one of the strongest is the development of unisex products. These are, of course, manifestations of the breakdown of sex role stereotypes, the growth of feminism, the new acceptance of homosexuality. There is unisex meal preparation and unisex housekeeping. There are unisex clothes, hair styles, hairsprays, deodorants, cosmetics and fragrances, all used interchangeably by both sexes. Colour symbolism standards are breaking down. Purple is no longer a colour for the aged. It is now a gala young colour, ready to vibrate and to clash or to have a psychedelic relationship with reds and cerises, yellows and oranges.

Trends: Information as an influence

The role of the package as a sales device has become more important than ever in our self-service world. Yet the trend is away from advertising-like, postery, hard-sell packaging. A combination of legislation and the demands of the consumer movement has increased the quantity of information on content and product use that package surfaces must carry.

The need for the package to communicate as well as to attract the eye has been intensified by the development of a wealth of products which do new and special things. Package copy must not only explain the often unusual way in which the product should be used but, in some cases, must explain what it is for in the first place. Although the need to cram extensive information into small space has challenged designers, the effect has been better typographic organization. There is clearer, more complete, more honest communication in today's packages.

Packages as décor

Designers have changed their concept of packaging graphics and with it the role that packaging plays in our lives. They have transformed the home product package from a brash container meant to hold merchandise and announce its contents into an acceptable — even welcome — piece of household equipment. Products used continually in our daily lives — on the dining table, the dressing table, in the bathroom or kitchen — are increasingly packaged with taste and discretion so that they can be used openly; they no longer shout their identity or sales messages. The facial tissue and shampoo that once were kept out of sight, the cleanser that was concealed beneath the sink now have a clean, pleasing appearance that makes them acceptable in the open.

Packages as status symbols

Packaging design has matured. It has made peace with the consumer, becoming an ally instead of an intruder, is more and more a positive part of our visual environment. The package has, in fact, become so integral a part of our lives, so socially acceptable, that it has developed snob appeal. The lowly shopping bag, once carried only by those too poor to afford delivery of goods, is now a status symbol. The world's famous shops — Gucci, Fauchon, Bonwit Teller, Mark Cross and others — have seen fit to translate their paper shopping bags into more permanent form, for sale, of course. Fabric tote bags, with the names and familiar graphic styles of retailers proudly emblazoned, are walking advertisements, carried with dignity and pride by men as well as women.

Picnics in packages

Well-known restaurants (New York's Brasserie is typical) have generated take-out food business through the design of elegant packaging in the form of white-faced corrugated picnic boxes with shelves containing components of a fine ready-to-eat meal. These have achieved sufficient status to be used at conferences and stockholders' meetings. They have a certain cachet among executives, who take pride in having them served, in their clearly identified packages, as luncheons at their desks.

Fast foods and take-out foods have spawned a new type of package in the strongly identified boxes that hold ready-to-go hamburgers, pizza, fried chicken, fish and chips and ice cream. The identity is carried on disposable plates and utensils, as well. The gigantic "M" which identifies MacDonald's hamburgers is fast becoming international and promises (or threatens) to become as universally recognizable as Coca Cola.

The new sensuality

Under the influence of our new sexual patterns, package forms and graphics are often clearly suggestive. The blatant appeal of low-cut shirts that expose either cleavage or broad, hairy chests, of tight jeans that outline buttocks, are echoed in sexually suggestive packaging and packaging graphics. The trend is probably most apparent in products for use on the person. Men, newly converted to cosmetics, are confronted with a vast array of products that seem to utilize machismo graphics and phallic shapes to reassure them that these are, indeed, masculine products. In women's perfumes, the discipline of the hard "Chanel" edge has given way to the sensuous, voluptuous curve. The much-admired new Halston perfume bottle is a tactile and visual experience in sensual packaging. It is asymmetric and, in a marketing way, bold, following none of the successful existing perfume containers in its form.

The passing of the packaging cliché

Packaging is losing its graphic clichés, the safe visual forms that lent themselves to permanent adoption — the horizontal band of colour, the colour break across the centre, the oval panel, the blue-red hardware look, the neutral colour pharmaceutical look. They enjoyed easy recognition and were package-like in concept. The face of the package was mostly hand-lettered in styles whose use was limited almost exclusively to packaging. Packages now can and do change, not in gradual steps to escape notice but in drastic reverses in direction, often with upward spurts in sales when the change takes place. No longer afraid of design obsolescence, package designers are becoming bolder, less safe. Design quality is slowly improving. Identity is achieved through simple, subtler means.

Surprises make for fun

With the freedom that the ability to change has brought, packaging has developed a sense of humour. Not the forced humour of bottles in cute animal shapes but the playfulness that only the ephemeral can afford. The L'Eggs panty hose package that suddenly turned up in bright bunny egg colours for Easter is typical. One expression of the new informality is the less organized look in some packaging. There is the trend away from the graphic grid system, away from the well-ordered vertical-horizontal. There is the truncated product name, leaving something to the imagination and having an element of surprise. There are wrap-around identities and brand names on the diagonal. With the advent of typographic photocomposition package-like hand lettering is on the wane, since much of it was used simply to overcome the limitations of metal type shoulders.

The colour palette has opened. Colours are more varied and used more creatively. Standard, basic packaging colours that motivation experts once convinced manufacturers were the ones that would sell have been replaced by other colours and colour combinations — which sell. The weird, the psychedelic have opened our eyes to the off-beat.

Who designs packages? Generalism as a speciality

To grasp the scope of change which is occurring in packaging, look at the names of the men and women working in the field today. Some outstanding items in Graphis/Packaging III are by designer generalists — film makers, exhibit designers, illustrators, book designers, painters, photographers, architects, product designers. If you study today's best packaging you will find that it is done by designers who represent many disciplines and persuasions.

Graphis/Packaging II reported the 1960's, a period of preoccupation with convenience, with gadgetry, with opulence, that catered to laziness and consumed raw materials with wanton disregard for ecology. As a good book should, Graphis/Packaging II raised questions about ecology and conservation. But packaging design of the sixties reflected no such concern; packaging of the first half of the seventies shows only limited improvement.

A note on profligate packaging

It is ironic that at a time when our profligate use of energy and materials is being severely questioned, unit packaging that conserves costly personnel time continues on the rise. Portion-controlled foods, single-use disposable instruments and other unit packages hardly conserve materials but they do conserve the time of the sales person, the nurse, the doctor, the laboratory technician, the waiter — to say nothing of dispensing with the dishwasher.

At the beginning of this article, I said that packaging reflects society. Nowhere is this more apparent than in the continued wasteful use of materials in the face of paper and energy shortages and the need to maintain ecological balance. Manufacturers give lip-service to environmental needs; but many go on squandering resources and producing packages that compound global problems as though there were no tomorrow which, indeed, there may not be.

KARL FINK, a graduate of the Parsons School of Design, set up his own design studio, Karl Fink and Associates, in 1951. He is a founder, fellow, honorary lifetime director and twice past-president of the Package Designers Council and has served on the professional council of The Packaging Institute and on the board of the Inter-Society Colour Council. At present he is in his second term as president of the American Institute of Graphic Arts. He has taught and lectured widely on packaging and graphic design.

Karl Fink

Einleitung

Dieses Buch über beachtenswerte Verpackungen der letzten sieben Jahre ist gewissermassen ein soziales Dokument. Als Gruppe gesehen, zeigen die Verpackungen nicht nur die ästhetische Weiterentwicklung in einem Design-Zweig, sondern auch den Wegfall alter Design-Normen und den Tod einiger liebgewordener Verpackungs-Binsenwahrheiten. Diese Einführung wird einige soziale Veränderungen untersuchen, die unseren Lebensstil und das Denken von Designern beeinflusst haben, die diesem Lebensstil entsprechende Verpackungen kreiert haben.

Entwicklung der Verpackung zur Eintagsfliege

Verpackungs-Design war einst von Dauer, im Gegensatz zu vergänglicheren Formen der Gebrauchsgraphik. Anzeigen für ein Produkt kommen, gehen und werden vergessen; Verpackungen jedoch wurden auf Jahre hinaus entworfen. Hersteller erfolgreicher Produkte unternahmen einen Design-Wechsel nur mit Hangen und Bangen, fürchteten sie doch, sich Kunden abspenstig zu machen, wenn sie ihnen ein Verpackungsgesicht nahmen, dem sie vertrauten und das für die beständige Reinheit des Produktes sprach. Verpackungs-Design war eine etwas schwerfällige graphische Ausdrucksweise, beeinflusst von vorsichtigen Marketing-Experten, gutgeheissen von einem konservativen Management und abgezielt auf loyale Verbraucher.

Man kann wohl sagen, dass einer unserer wichtigsten Gebrauchsgegenstände, die Verpackung, ein klares Spiegelbild unserer sich fortentwickelnden Gesellschaft bietet. Während die Anzeigenwerbung immer noch mit glitzernden Glaswaren, schmackhafteren Gerichten und weisseren Hemden an die ihren Mann umsorgende Frau hinter dem Küchenherd appelliert, hat sich die Verpackung von Haushaltswaren längst der Realität angepasst, nicht nur Frauen (verheiratete und unverheiratete) ansprechen zu müssen, sondern auch Männer, die Wäsche und Familiengeschirr waschen und für sich selbst und andere kochen.

Eine neue Gesellschaft, neue Einflüsse

Hier in Graphis/Packaging III finden Sie die bedeutenden sozialen Bewegungen der siebziger Jahre widergespiegelt: Konsumwelle, Feminismus, Zerfall des Geschlechtsrollen-Klischees sowie die Erkenntnis, dass die Verbraucherwelt die reale Welt darstellt, bevölkert von verschiedenen Menschenarten auf verschiedenen Wirtschaftsebenen. Sie können den Rhythmus der Rockmusik mit seinem rastlosen, treibenden Tempo erkennen. Schauen Sie die Verpackungen an! Sie werden den Einfluss einer Generation junger Verbraucher erkennen, die mit psychedelischem Farbenrausch und der ständigen visuellen Stimulation des Fernsehens, bombardiert mit Produktsendungen, erwachsen geworden sind. Es ist eine Generation, die praktisch keine Markentreue mehr kennt — ein neuer Verbraucherschlag, der sich durch Anzeigenwerbung dauernd weiterverkaufen lässt oder bereit dazu ist. Das stufenweise Verschwinden des verlässlichen Kunden für Suppe X oder Deodorant Y hat die Notwendigkeit für altvertraute Verpackungen verringert und zu einem freieren, einfallsreicheren, dynamischeren Verpackungs-Design geführt.

Junge Erwachsene als Konsumenten

Diese Generation ist in den sieben Jahren seit dem Erscheinen von Graphis/Packaging II herangewachsen. Die Nachkriegskinder, die zu Beginn dieses Jahrzehnts noch ihre Schulbildung beendeten, sind inzwischen etablierte Erwachsene geworden. Sie sind die «Jungverheirateten», deren Hunger auf Haushaltsgüter die Herzen der Hersteller dieser Dinge erwärmt; sie sind die Käufer der letzten Mode in Bekleidung, Möbeln, Automobilen, Kameras; sie sind die Mütter und Väter des unübersehbaren Gewimmels der Wegwerfwindelverbraucher. Und sie sind grundverschieden von allen Kunden, die wir je gekannt haben. Geboren in den späten vierziger und frühen fünfziger Jahren, sind sie das Produkt der sechziger, einer Ära sozialer Veränderungen, die so bedeutend war wie die zwanziger Jahre. Es sind junge Männer und Frauen, die eine veränderte Gesellschaftsordnung geschaffen haben, die von ihren Eltern nur in Worte gefasst wurde. Frauen, die ein freieres Leben führen und nicht nur davon reden. Unzählige junge Leute der Mittelklasse haben den Beruf abgelehnt, den ihre Eltern für sie geplant hatten, um statt dessen ein weniger organisiertes, weniger beengtes Leben zu führen. Man kann die gegensätzlichen Richtungen zeitgenössischen Lebens erkennen, die Veränderungen in Lebensstil, Zielvorstellungen und persönlichen Gewohnheiten, die unser Denken darüber, wie wir uns die Welt wünschen, umgeprägt haben.

Streben nach dem Natürlichen

Obgleich wir anscheinend einen beispiellos hohen Stand im Gebrauch von verpackten Produkten für Reinigung, Körperpflege und Ernährung erreicht haben, führt paradoxerweise ein Trend fort von dieser Bequemlichkeit und hin zu natürlichem Essen, seine Lebensmittel mit sich herumzutragen oder auch selbst zu kochen, statt in Restaurants zu speisen. Dies beruht teilweise auf dem Wunsch nach Rückkehr zu einer weniger künstlichen Lebensweise, teilweise ist es aber auch ein Ausdruck sozialen Gewissens: der Wunsch, Energie zu sparen und die Nahrungsmittelreserven der Welt gerecht zu nutzen. Verstärkt wird dieser Trend noch durch weltweite Wirtschaftsprobleme.

Erinnerung an andere Zeiten

Der Trend «Zurück zur Natur» hat neues Interesse am Handwerk geweckt — an Holzschnitzereien, Kalligraphie, handgearbeiteten Gegenständen —, als Abwechslung zu den von ausgeklügelten Maschinen hergestellten Dingen. Eine New Yorker Ausstellung von japanischen Verpackungen in traditioneller Handarbeit fand kürzlich ungemein rege Beachtung und bereist nun andere Städte. Die Erinnerung an eine weniger betriebsame Welt hat eine nostalgische Besinnung auf das Design anderer Zeiten geweckt — Art Nouveau und Art Déco zum Beispiel —, und junge Menschen finden an alten Filmen und früher Jazzmusik Gefallen. Doch während junge Erwachsene eine Rückkehr zu bescheideneren Werten und einer unkomplizierteren Lebensweise anstreben, schreitet die Welt unerbittlich weiter. Die Produzenten der von einem ständig wachsenden Anteil der Weltbevölkerung konsumierten Waren erkennen, dass sie diese idealistischen Bedürfnisse nur oberflächlich befriedigen können. Denn sie werden gleichzeitig mit harten ökonomischen und absatzpolitischen Notwendigkeiten konfrontiert, die einen nachhaltigen Einfluss auf das Verpackungsgesicht ausüben werden.

Zeitgenössische Vertriebsprobleme

Hersteller müssen leistungsfähigere Marketing-, Lager- und Vertriebsmethoden entwickeln, die einer immer mehr von Selbstbedienung geprägten Einzelhandelsstruktur angepasst sind. Einzelhändler sehen sich einem deprimierend hohen Ausmass von «Lagerschwund» gegenüber, weniger höflich Ladendiebstahl genannt. Kleine Ladendiebereien sind unter gewissem Beifall zum Sport einer viel zu weit gespannten Altersgruppe geworden, die über das gesamte Wirtschaftsspektrum reicht. Lange Finger machen, endemisch für Selbstbedienungsläden, hat den Trend zur Montage auf Karton und Plastiksichtpackung für eine grosse Anzahl von Produkten beschleunigt. Es gibt Anzeichen dafür, dass dieses und andere Probleme uns vielleicht eine Art Science-Fiction-Einkauf bescheren werden, bei dem der Kunde seine Auswahl nach Schaupackungen unter Glas oder Atrappen oder gar Farbphotos trifft und die eigentliche Ware nur noch an der Ausgangsschranke oder an Verladestellen empfangen kann, wo die Pakete wie (Gott bewahre uns davor!) Fluggepäck auf Abholung warten.

Universal Product Code als Lösung

So finden wir hier einen Trend, der in scharfem Gegensatz zu besagtem «Natürlichkeitsstreben» steht. Hersteller von Getreideflocken haben sich zum Beispiel dem Trend zu natürlichem Essen angepasst, indem sie nahrhaftere, «kernige» Produkte in nostalgischen Ver-

packungen anbieten. Gleichzeitig bemühen sie sich in ständigen Entwicklungsprogrammen um verfeinerte Bearbeitungs- und Transportmethoden der Waren vom Fliessband über die Lagerhaltung bis hin zum Grosshandel und den diversen Einzelhandelsstufen. Auf einer Seitenfläche der anheimelnden, altmodischen Getreideflockenpackung mit dem Bild von einem Bauernhof, von Weizengarben und Krügen mit Sirup finden Sie den neuen Universal Product Code (UPC) eingeprägt, der dieses Gross- und Einzelhandels-Vertriebssystem mit Hilfe von Computern ermöglicht. Sehr bald wird unser naturhungriger Konsument mit neuen elektronischen Auslösetechniken umzugehen lernen müssen, um seine Einkäufe ausführen zu können.

Der Universal Product Code in den USA und dessen Gegenstücke in anderen Ländern dienen auch dazu, den Begriff «Verpackung» wesentlich zu erweitern. Zeitschriften, Schallplatten und Taschenbücher werden zum Beispiel den UPC-Aufdruck tragen und so die Rolle der Verpackung verdeutlichen. Verpackt gibt es bereits zerlegbare Kleinmöbel wie etwa Beisetztische. Eisenwaren — ein Dutzend Schrauben und Muttern, eine elektrische Kettensäge oder auch ein fertig montierter Gartenschlauch — werden auf Karton befestigt, in Plastiksichtpackungen versiegelt und etikettiert. Während dieses Verpacken die Arbeitsvorgänge im Eisenwarenladen vereinfacht, hat es ausserdem den Verkauf vieler dieser Produkte auf andere Ladentypen ausgedehnt. Da ein verpackter Gegenstand in unerwarteten Einzelhandelsschleusen enden kann, muss er so beschaffen sein, dass er mit diversen anderen Produkten um Beachtung wetteifern kann. Dies wiederum hat das Verpackungsgesicht beeinflusst.

Rückkehr zur Einfachheit

Einfachheit und Ehrlichkeit der Verpackung sind heute offensichtlich, zum Beispiel bei Kosmetik- und Toilettenartikeln, die traditionell in teuren Verpackungen daherkamen, um den Eindruck des Luxus zu vermitteln. Das luxuriöse Aussehen ist natürlich noch in vielen Fällen geblieben, aber es gibt heute auch viele Verpackungen, die ein schlichtes, oft elegantes, laboratoriumsmässig-wissenschaftliches Gesicht haben.

Unbefangene Nomaden

Der Lebensstil weiter Kreise hat sich in der ersten Hälfte der siebziger Jahre radikal geändert. Essgewohnheiten, Wohnungseinrichtung, Vergnügungen, Kleidung und Auftreten der Menschen sind weniger förmlich und steif. Sie essen unterwegs — im Zug, im Bus und auf der Strasse; sie essen im Kino und im Konzert. Die Leute tragen mehr mit sich herum. Die Einkaufs- oder Schultertasche ist von beiden Geschlechtern als die

Lösung für eine nomadenhafte Einstellung zu jedem neuen Tag übernommen worden. Die Beutel, Weidenkörbe oder Umhängetaschen enthalten Esswaren, Dosen mit Haarspray, Kosmetika, die unentbehrliche Haarbürste und eine oder zwei Dosen Coke oder Pepsi oder Wein. Weil dieser Lebensstil frei und unvoraussagbar ist, sind es auch die Bedürfnisse.

Verpackungstrends: Unisex

Einer der stärksten Trends, die das Verpackungsgesicht beeinflussen, ist die Entwicklung von Unisex-Produkten. Dies ist natürlich eine der sichtbaren Folgen des Zusammenbruchs der Geschlechtsrollen-Klischees, des wachsenden Feminismus, der neu entstandenen Billigung der Homosexualität. Es gibt Unisex-Fertiggerichte und Unisex-Haushaltszubehör; weiterhin Unisex-Kleidung, Haarmoden, Haarsprays, Deodorants, Kosmetika und Parfums, die alle austauschbar von beiden Geschlechtern benutzt werden können. Farbsymbole als Richtlinien haben keine Gültigkeit mehr. Purpur ist nicht mehr eine Farbe für alte Leute. Es ist zu einer festlichen, jungen Farbe geworden, bereit zu vibrieren und disharmonisch zu wirken oder in eine psychedelische Beziehung zu den verschiedenen Schattierungen von Rot, Gelb und Orange zu treten.

Trends: Einfluss der Information

Die Rolle der Verpackung als Verkaufsmittel ist in unserer auf Selbstbedienung ausgerichteten Welt wichtiger geworden denn je. Dennoch geht die Entwicklung weg von der reklamemachenden, plakathaften, aufs Verkaufen um jeden Preis ausgerichteten Packung. Eine Kombination aus Gesetzgebung und Forderungen der Konsumentenverbände hat den Anteil der Information auf der Packung über deren Inhalt und den Gebrauch des darin befindlichen Produktes zwangsläufig erhöht.

Die Forderung, dass die Verpackung neben der Augenfälligkeit auch Information vermitteln muss, ist durch die Entwicklung einer Vielzahl neuer, spezielle Wünsche befriedigender Produkte noch verstärkt worden. Die Beschriftung auf der Packung soll nicht nur die oft ungewöhnliche Anwendungsweise des Produktes erläutern, sondern muss manchmal sogar erst erklären, wozu es überhaupt bestimmt ist. Obschon die Notwendigkeit, umfassende Information auf kleinem Raum zusammenzudrängen, eine Herausforderung für den Designer war, hat sie ausserdem eine bessere typographische Gliederung gebracht. Die heutigen Verpackungen sprechen den Käufer ehrlicher und informativer an.

Verpackung als Schmuck

Die Designer haben ihre Vorstellung von Verpackungsgestaltung und damit von der Rolle, die diese Verpackung in unserem Leben spielt, grundlegend geändert. Sie haben die Verpackung für Haushaltserzeugnisse von einem blossen Behälter (der eine Ware enthalten und sie bezeichnen sollte) zu einem annehmbaren — und sogar gern gesehenen — Teil der Haushaltsausstattung gemacht. Ständig in unserem Alltag gebrauchte Produkte — auf dem Esstisch, dem Toilettentisch, im Bad und in der Küche — werden zunehmend in geschmackvollen und diskreten Packungen angeboten, so dass man sie offen hinstellen kann; sie schreien ihren Sinn und Zweck nicht mehr heraus. Das Gesichtstüchlein und das Shampoo, früher ausser Sicht aufbewahrt, das Putzmittel, früher unter dem Ausguss versteckt, haben heute ein adrettes, gefälliges Aussehen.

Verpackung als Statussymbol

Das Verpackungs-Design ist erwachsen geworden. Es hat seinen Frieden mit dem Konsumenten geschlossen, ist zum Verbündeten anstelle des Eindringlings geworden und mehr und mehr ein positives Detail unserer visuellen Umwelt. Die Verpackung ist in der Tat ein so integrierender Bestandteil unseres Lebens geworden, so gesellschaftlich annehmbar, dass sie einen eigenen Snob Appeal entwickelt hat. Die unansehnliche Einkaufstasche, einst nur von jenen getragen, die sich eine Hauslieferung ihrer Waren nicht leisten konnten, ist jetzt eine Art Statussymbol geworden. Die berühmten Einkaufsgeschäfte der Welt — Gucci, Fauchon, Bonwit Teller, Mark Cross und andere — haben sich veranlasst gesehen, ihre Papierbeutel in eine dauerhaftere Form umzuwandeln — gegen Geld, versteht sich. Einkaufstaschen aus Stoff, stolz geschmückt mit dem Namenszug und dem bekannten, graphisch gestalteten Emblem des jeweiligen Hauses, sind wandernde Reklameschilder, die mit Würde und Stolz von Männern und Frauen herumgeführt werden.

Picknick in Packungen

Bekannte Restaurants (New York's Brasserie ist ein typisches Beispiel) befruchteten ihr Geschäft mit Speisen zum Mitnehmen durch das Design von eleganten Verpackungen in Form von Picknick-Schachteln mit weisser, gerippter Oberfläche und Einzelfächern zur Aufnahme der Bestandteile eines schmackhaften Fertiggerichtes. Sie haben soviel Ansehen gewonnen, dass sie bei Konferenzen und Aktionärsversammlungen gereicht werden. Und sie geniessen eine gewisse Vorzugsstellung bei leitenden Angestellten, die sich etwas darauf einbilden, sie sich in diesen markanten Packungen als Zwischenmahlzeit am Schreibtisch servieren lassen zu können.

Schnellgerichte und Gerichte zum Mitnehmen haben in grosser Zahl neue Verpackungstypen in Form jener sehr deutlich gekennzeichneten Schachteln hervorgebracht, in denen man mitnahmebereite Hamburger, Pizza, Brathühnchen, Fisch und Chips oder auch Eiscreme transportieren kann. Eine identische Kennzeichnung tragen auch Wegwerfteller und -bestecke. Das mächtige «M», Kennzeichen für MacDonald's Hamburger, wird rasch international und verspricht (oder droht) weltweit so bekannt zu werden wie Coca Cola.

Die neue Sinnlichkeit

Unter dem Einfluss unserer neuen Sexualstruktur sind Packungsformen und graphische Darstellungen oft unverhohlen zweideutig. Die deutliche Herausforderung tief ausgeschnittener Hemden, die entweder den weiblichen Busenansatz oder eine breite, behaarte männliche Brust sehen lassen und mit der enge Jeans das Gesäss modellieren, findet ihr Echo in sinnlich-suggestiven Verpackungen und Verpackungsgraphiken. Der Trend zeigt sich wahrscheinlich am deutlichsten bei Produkten zum persönlichen Gebrauch. Männer, die neuerdings zu Kosmetika bekehrt worden sind, sehen sich einer Unzahl von Produkten gegenüber, die anscheinend Machismo-Graphik und phallische Formgebung verwenden, damit es auch ganz sicher ist, dass es sich um wirklich maskuline Produkte handelt. Bei Damenparfums ist die harte «Chanel»-Linie der sinnlich-verführerischen, wollüstigen Rundung gewichen. Die vielbewunderte neue Halston-Parfumflasche ist ein fühl- und sichtbares Erlebnis sinnlichen Verpackungs-Designs; sie ist asymmetrisch und, was das Marketing betrifft, kühn, da sie in der Form keinem der bekannten, erfolgreichen Parfumbehälter ähnelt.

Das Verschwinden des Verpackungsklischees

Die Verpackung streift ihre graphischen Klischees ab — die risikolose, sichtbare Form, die sich zum Dauergebrauch anbot: den horizontalen Farbstrich, die Farbentrennung in der Mitte, das ovale Titelfeld, den blaurothen Eisenwarenhabitus, die neutrale Arzneimittelfarbgebung. Sie boten den Vorteil leichter Erkennbarkeit und entsprachen dem landläufigen Verpackungsbegriff. Die Frontseite der Verpackung wies meist Handsatz und einen Schriftstil auf, der fast ausschliesslich für Verpackungen vorbehalten war. Verpackungen können und dürfen sich heute nicht nur allmählich ändern, damit dies der Beachtung entgeht, sondern auch rasch und in drastisch entgegengesetzter Richtung, was oft sogar einen plötzlichen Verkaufsanstieg zur Folge hat. Ohne länger Angst vor dem langsamen Dahinschwinden des Markenbildes haben zu müssen, werden die Designer kühner und gleichzeitig risikofreudiger. Die Qualität des Designs wird langsam besser. Die Markenidentität wird durch einfachere, subtilere Methoden erreicht.

Überraschung macht Spass

Mit der Freiheit, die mit der Möglichkeit zur Veränderung gekommen ist, hat das Verpackungs-Design einen Sinn für Humor entwickelt. Nicht den gezwungenen Humor von Gefässen in ausgeklügelten animalischen Formen, sondern die Verspieltheit, die sich nur ein Eintagsgeschöpf leisten kann. Die L'Eggs-Damenschlüpferpackung [1], die plötzlich zu Ostern in leuchtend bunten Ostereierfarben erschien, ist ein typisches Beispiel dafür. Ein Ausdruck dieser neuen Zwangslosigkeit ist das weniger systematisch geplante Erscheinungsbild mancher Verpackungen. Da gibt es den Trend weg von dem graphischen Liniensystem, weg von dem wohlgeordneten Horizontal-Vertikal-Rasternetz. Da finden wir den verstümmelten Produktnamen, der ein wenig Raum für die Phantasie lässt und ein Element der Überraschung in sich trägt. Da haben wir Firmenzeichen auf Bauchbinden und diagonal geschriebene Markennamen. Mit dem Aufkommen des Photosatzes in der Typographie ist der verpackungsgerechte Handsatz im Schwinden begriffen, da er grossenteils nur benutzt wurde, um die Beschränkungen der gegebenen Achselfläche im Maschinensatz zu umgehen.

Die Farbenpalette ist voller und vielfältiger geworden. Farben werden abwechslungsreicher und kreativer verwendet. Die üblichen Verpackungsgrundfarben, die den Herstellern einst von Motivationsexperten als die einzig verkaufsfördernden eingeredet wurden, sind von anderen Farben und Farbkombinationen ersetzt worden — die ebenfalls verkaufen! Das geisterhaft Eigenartige, das Psychedelische hat uns die Augen für das Ungewöhnliche geöffnet.

Wer entwirft Verpackungen? Vielfalt als Besonderheit

Um den ganzen Umfang des Wandels zu erfassen, der auf dem Verpackungsgebiet vor sich geht, müssen wir die Namen der Männer und Frauen beachten, die heute hier arbeiten. Einige hervorragende Beiträge in Graphis/Packaging III stammen von vielseitig tätigen Designern — Filmemachern, Ausstellungs-Designern, Illustratoren, Buchgestaltern, Malern, Photographen, Architekten und Produktgestaltern. Wenn Sie die besten Verpackungen von heute betrachten, werden Sie finden, dass sie von Designern entworfen sind, die viele Fachgebiete und Meinungen vertreten.

Graphis/Packaging II berichtete über die sechziger Jahre, eine Periode der Beschäftigung mit der Bequemlichkeit dienenden Vorrichtungen, Erfindungen und Mechanismen, mit dem Überfluss, der die Trägheit befriedigte, und in der Rohstoffe mit verantwortungsloser Missachtung der Ökologie verbraucht wurden. Wie es einem guten Buch geziemt, hat Graphis/Packaging II Fragen nach Ökologie und Umweltschutz gestellt. Aber

[1] Leg = Bein, Hosenbein in Analogie zu Egg = Ei.

das Verpackungs-Design der ersten Hälfte der siebziger Jahre zeigt nur begrenzte Fortschritte zum Besseren.

Eine Bemerkung zu verschwenderischer Verpackung

Es ist eine Ironie unserer den verschwenderischen Verbrauch von Energie und Rohstoffen ernsthaft in Frage stellenden Zeit, dass die teure Arbeitszeit sparende Einzelverpackung immer noch im Vormarsch ist. Lebensmittel-Portionenpackungen, zu einmaligem Gebrauch bestimmte Wegwerfinstrumente und andere Einzelverpackungen sparen zwar kaum Material ein, dagegen aber die Arbeitszeit des Verkäufers, der Krankenschwester, des Arztes, des Laboranten, des Kellners — von einem eventuellen Verzicht auf die Ge-

schirrwaschmaschine wollen wir schon gar nicht reden.

Zu Anfang dieses Artikels habe ich gesagt, dass die Verpackung ein Spiegelbild unserer Gesellschaft darstellt. Nirgendwo ist dies offensichtlicher als in der fortgesetzten Materialverschwendung angesichts von Papierknappheit, Energieverknappung und der Sorge um die Erhaltung des ökologischen Gleichgewichts. Es wird weiter zu aufwendig verpackt. Hersteller geben Lippenbekenntnisse zu den Erfordernissen des Umweltschutzes ab; doch viele verschwenden weiterhin unbekümmert Rohstoffe und produzieren Verpackungen, die ein weltweites Problem noch erschweren, als gäbe es kein Morgen mehr — womit sie in der Tat recht haben könnten.

KARL FINK promovierte an der Parsons School of Design und eröffnete 1951 sein eigenes Design-Studio — Karl Fink & Associates. Er ist Mitbegründer, Mitglied, Ehrendirektor auf Lebzeiten und zweifacher Ex-Präsident des Package Designers Council, gehörte zum Lehrkörper des Packaging Institute und zum Ausschuss des Inter-Society Colour Council. Im Moment ist er Präsident (zweite Amtszeit) des American Institute of Graphic Arts. Er hielt Vorlesungen und Kurse über Pakkungsgestaltung und Graphik-Design.

Karl Fink **Introduction**

Le présent ouvrage consacré aux emballages les plus remarquables de ces sept dernières années constitue en un sens un document social capital. Vus dans l'ensemble, ces emballages ne témoignent pas seulement de la croissance intervenue sur le plan esthétique dans l'une des grandes disciplines du design; ils signalent aussi le déclin de certaines normes anciennes régissant ce domaine, ainsi que la disparition pure et simple de plus d'un précepte éculé de l'emballagisme. La présente introduction entend mettre en évidence certains changements sociaux dont l'impact a transformé notre style de vie et influencé la pensée des artistes appelés à créer les emballages adaptés à cette nouvelle qualité de vie.

L'emballage en route vers l'éphémère

La création d'emballages se distinguait naguère par sa résistance aux modes du jour des réalisations éphémères des autres arts appliqués aux besoins du commerce. Les annonces pour un produit déterminé sombraient vite dans l'oubli, mais les emballages restaient identiques au fil des années. Les fabricants de produits solidement implantés répugnaient à en modifier la présentation, de crainte de s'aliéner la faveur de la clientèle habituée à un conditionnement qui, par sa pérennité même, témoignait de la qualité inchangée du produit. Par la force des choses, un emballage de l'époque respirait le conformisme des prudents experts en marketing qui le tenaient sur les fonts baptismaux, de la direction conservatrice des entreprises et de la frange fidèle des consommateurs.

Les choses ont bien changé. L'un des artefacts les plus importants de l'époque actuelle, l'emballage, reflète nettement cette évolution, qui concerne la société tout entière. Alors que la publicité continue de s'adresser directement à la maîtresse de maison occupée dans sa cuisine à rendre la vie plus agréable à son mari par une vaisselle plus propre, des repas plus savoureux et des chemises plus blanches au sortir de la machine à laver, l'emballage des produits ménagers s'est adapté aux réalités du jour en ne visant plus seulement les femmes mariées ou célibataires, mais aussi les hommes qui ont charge de la lessive, de la vaisselle et de la cuisine pour eux-mêmes et pour autrui.

A société nouvelle, influences nouvelles

Dans le présent volume, Graphis/Packaging III, vous trouverez l'écho de tous les grands mouvements sociologiques représentatifs des années 1970: consommation de masse, féminisme, abandon des rôles stéréotypés impartis aux deux sexes, découverte de la multiplicité de la réalité habitée par des consommateurs issus de races très diverses et occupant des niveaux économiques très divers. Vous verrez pulser dans ces emballages le rock au rythme endiablé, entraînant, heurté. Vous y verrez également l'influence d'une génération de jeunes consommateurs adultes conditionnés par un monde psychédélique de couleurs et les mille et un stimuli visuels de la télévision, et soumis à un bombardement inlassable de messages publicitaires. C'est une génération à qui fait quasiment défaut la loyauté vis-à-vis de marques définies de produits, une nouvelle race de consommateurs qu'il s'agit de captiver en permanence par des actions publicitaires générales et de P.L.V. La disparition progressive du consommateur fidèle aux potages X ou aux désodorisants Y a réduit le rôle mnémonique de l'emballage traditionnel, ouvrant la voie à l'innovation et au dynamisme dans un domaine de création qui retrouvait le rythme de la vie.

Les jeunes consommateurs adultes

Or, cette génération est parvenue à sa maturité dans les sept ans qui se sont écoulés depuis la publication du 2e volume de Graphis/Packaging. Les enfants d'après guerre, qui finissaient leurs études au début de la décennie, sont aujourd'hui des adultes entrés dans la vie active. Jeunes mariés, leur appétit pour les mille et un objets nécessaires à un jeune ménage prospère fait la joie de tout fabricant d'articles ménagers. Ce sont les clients rêvés pour la dernière mode en matière d'habillement, d'ameublement, d'automobiles, d'équipements photo. Jeunes parents, ils consomment entre autres un volume impressionnant de langes à jeter. Et ces consommateurs sont bien différents de tous ceux que nous avons connus à ce jour. Nés à la fin des années 40 et au début des années 50, ils ont été formés pendant les années 60, une décennie qui a vu des changements sociaux aussi importants que ceux intervenus dans les années 1920. Ces jeunes hommes et ces jeunes femmes ont créé l'ordre social rénové que réclamaient leurs aînés. Les femmes ne parlent pas seulement d'émancipation: elles vivent une vie plus libre de contraintes. Un nombre considérable de jeunes des classes moyennes ont rejeté l'idée d'une carrière professionnelle soigneusement planifiée par leurs parents pour opter résolument pour un mode de vie moins structuré, moins contraignant. C'est ainsi qu'apparaissent des tendances contradictoires au sein de la vie contemporaine, des changements d'attitudes, de visées et d'habitudes qui ont modifié notre conception du monde à bâtir.

Le retour à la nature

Bien que nous ayons atteint un niveau record d'utilisation de produits de nettoyage, de mise en valeur et d'alimentation du corps humain sous emballage attrayant, un paradoxe curieux veut qu'une tendance croissante se manifeste en faveur de l'abandon de tous ces éléments de confort et du retour à la nature : alimentation naturelle, cuisine simple, le casse-croûte mangé sur le pouce dispensant de recourir au circuit des restaurants. On peut y voir d'une part le désir de retourner à un mode de vie dépouillé de ses artifices, d'autre part la marque d'une prise de conscience sociale — la volonté de contribuer à la conservation de l'énergie et de limiter la consommation de nourriture dans un monde où une partie des hommes ont faim en permanence. Cette tendance est encore accentuée par les problèmes économiques qui dominent l'actualité internationale.

Le retour aux sources anciennes

Le mouvement du retour à la nature a ravivé l'intérêt pour les formes anciennes de l'artisanat — le travail du bois, la calligraphie, la fabrication manuelle d'objets en petite série qui permet d'échapper à l'anonymat des articles de masse sortant des chaînes de fabrication sophistiquées. A New York, une exposition récente d'emballages japonais réalisés au moyen de techniques artisanales traditionnelles a connu un immense succès ; elle est en train de voyager de ville en ville. La nostalgie d'un monde où ce qui prime, c'est la qualité de vie, a amené la résurgence des principes esthétiques d'époques révolues tels que l'Art Nouveau et l'Art Déco, et les jeunes sont les plus enthousiastes à applaudir les films du bon vieux temps et le jazz old style. Mais tandis que les jeunes adultes regardent en arrière pour retrouver des valeurs plus simples et un mode de vie moins complexe, le monde progresse inexorablement. Les fabricants des marchandises consommées par une fraction toujours plus considérable de la population mondiale réalisent qu'ils ne peuvent satisfaire qu'en surface ces besoins idéalistes. C'est qu'ils ont à affronter en même temps les rigueurs d'une économie assiégée et les réalités inéluctables du marketing, qui risquent d'avoir un effet durable sur la conception des emballages.

Problèmes de distribution à l'époque actuelle

Les fabricants doivent élaborer des techniques de marketing, de stockage et de distribution plus efficaces pour faire face à une structure de vente au détail où le libre-service devient un facteur prépondérant. Les détaillants enregistrent de leur côté un taux incroyablement élevé de perte de stocks par vols à l'étalage. Les menus larcins ont été élevés au rang d'une activité sportive dont on peut tirer gloire par un groupe de consommateurs d'âge varié qui se recrutent dans tous les milieux socio-économiques. Phénomène endémique dans les magasins de libre-service, le chapardage a accéléré le processus d'introduction de la présentation d'une grande variété de produits sous moulage plastique ou agrafés sur carton. Nous semblons bien nous acheminer vers un mode d'achat solutionnant ce problème et divers autres par une approche de science-fiction où le client fera son choix d'après des emballages de présentation ou des emballages factices, voire de simples photos couleurs, et ne prendra livraison de la marchandise qu'une fois arrivé à la caisse ou sur un quai de chargement où les paquets pourront être récupérés comme les bagages dans les halls d'arrivée des aéroports (ce qui n'est guère une perspective réjouissante).

La solution du Code Universel des Produits

Cette tendance est évidemment en opposition nette avec le retour à une présentation «naturelle» des marchandises mises en vente. Ainsi, les fabricants de produits à base de céréales pour le petit déjeuner ont tenu compte de la vogue des produits naturels en lançant force mélanges nutritifs présentés dans des emballages nostalgiquement anachroniques. En même temps, la logique du développement impose de plus en plus des procédés perfectionnés de fabrication et de transport de ces mêmes produits rétro, tout au long de la chaîne qui mène de l'usine à l'entrepôt, puis chez le grossiste et le détaillant. C'est ainsi que l'emballage vieux jeu qui nous replonge dans l'atmosphère douillette de la cuisine de grand-maman en évoquant basse-cour, gerbes de blé et bocaux de mélasse identifiera sur l'une de ses faces les produits céréaliers qu'il contient grâce au nouveau Code Universel des Produits qui est à la base du système de distribution grossistes et détaillants de l'avenir mettant en œuvre des équipements électroniques et des ordinateurs. Dans très peu de temps, notre consommateur désireux de se mettre la nature sous la dent devra se familiariser avec des techniques presse-bouton pour accéder à l'objet de sa convoitise.

Le Code Universel des Produits élaboré aux Etats-Unis et ses équivalents dans les autres pays servent également une conception élargie de l'emballage. Les magazines, disques et livres, pour ne prendre que cet exemple-là, porteront le numéro CUP, attestant ainsi le rôle d'emballages qui est aussi le leur. Le monde de l'emballage comprend déjà les petits meubles en pièces détachées à monter soi-même, tels que les tables démontables. Les articles de quincaillerie — 12 vis avec leurs écrous, une tronçonneuse électrique ou un bout de tuyau d'arrosage — sont emballés ou agrafés sur du carton ou encore présentés sous bulle plastique et étiquetés. Ce mode de présentation n'a pas seulement simplifié le travail des quincailliers, mais aussi permis la mise en vente d'un grand nombre de ces articles dans d'autres types de magasins. Comme un article présenté de la sorte peut fort bien atterrir dans un point de vente auquel le fabricant ne songeait pas, son emballage doit être conçu de manière à accrocher l'attention au sein d'une foule de produits fort divers. Il est inévitable que ce genre de considérations ait influencé à son tour l'aspect visuel des emballages.

Le retour à la simplicité

Le naturel revient au galop dans la conception même des emballages, qui se fait plus simple et plus directe. Cette tendance est manifeste dans les cosmétiques et articles de toilette, traditionnellement acquis aux emballages luxueux visant à projeter une image de confort et de prestige. Ces derniers se rencontrent encore en abondance, bien entendu, mais les emballages rénovés aux lignes simples, souvent élégantes, évoquant la précision scientifique des laboratoires, sont déjà légion.

Le sans-gêne du nomade moderne

Les styles de vie ont subi des changements radicaux en cette première moitié de la décennie 1970. On mange, on s'habille, on décore sa maison, on s'amuse avec bien plus de naturel, et le comportement en public fait foin d'une bonne partie du formalisme traditionnel. On mange sur le tas, dans les trains, dans les autobus, dans la rue, au cinéma et au concert. On transporte bien plus de choses avec soi, dans les sacoches, cabas et musettes que les nomades nouveau genre des deux sexes aiment à porter en bandoulière. On y trouve des provisions, du fixateur pour cheveux, des cosmétiques, l'indispensable brosse à cheveux, des boîtes ou bouteilles de Coca-cola, de Pepsi-cola ou de vin. Le contenu de ces fourre-tout reflète bien l'amour de la liberté et de l'imprévu qui anime les jeunes errants de notre époque.

Le principe directeur de l'unisexe

Parmi les principes directeurs de l'emballagisme contemporain, on trouve au premier plan la mise au point de produits unisexes, qui expriment évidemment l'abandon des rôles stéréotypés impartis aux deux sexes, la poussée du féminisme, l'acceptation sociale de l'homosexualité. Désormais, ni la cuisine ni le ménage ne sont plus des domaines réservés exclusivement aux femmes. On trouve des vêtements, des styles de coiffure, des fixateurs pour cheveux, des désodorisants, des cosmétiques et des parfums convenant aux deux sexes et utilisés indifféremment par les consommateurs et les consommatrices. Même le symbolisme traditionnellement attaché aux couleurs subit le contrecoup de cette évolution. Le mauve n'est plus seulement réservé au troisième âge, mais a envahi la confection pour jeunes gens, où on le fait vibrer et flamboyer dans ses nuances pourprées ou s'assortir sur un mode psychédélique au rouge, au cerise, au jaune et à l'orange.

Le principe directeur de l'information éducative

Le rôle de l'emballage dans la promotion des ventes est aujourd'hui plus important que jamais, étant donné l'avènement d'un monde du libre-service. Ce faisant, le caractère purement publicitaire, affichiste et commercial à tout casser s'efface au profit d'une information accrue sur le contenu et son mode d'emploi, telle que la réclament impérativement la législation nouvelle et les organisations de consommateurs.

Par ailleurs, la tâche de communication qui revient à l'emballage à part son rôle dans l'éveil de l'attention du client potentiel a encore été renforcée par la diffusion d'une foule de produits qui introduisent les consommateurs à des activités nouvelles et spécialisées. Le texte figurant sur l'emballage ne doit alors pas seulement expliquer un mode d'emploi souvent inhabituel, il doit aussi parfois expliquer tout d'abord à quoi le produit est destiné. Il est évident que l'incorporation d'un texte dense n'a pas été sans poser des problèmes, vu les maigres surfaces disponibles. Pourtant, le résultat en a été une disposition typographique plus satisfaisante au service d'une communication plus claire, plus complète et plus honnête.

L'emballage en tant qu'élément de décoration

En transformant leur conception de la présentation des emballages, les designers ont transformé le rôle que l'emballage joue dans notre vie quotidienne. Ils ont fait d'un contenant peu élaboré même dans ses références au contenu un élément parfaitement acceptable, voire bienvenu de l'équipement ménager. Les produits dont nous nous servons continuellement et quotidiennement — sur la table de notre salle à manger, sur notre table de toilette, à la salle de bains, à la cuisine — sont conditionnés avec de plus en plus de goût et de discrétion, ce qui permet de les exhiber sans gêne; ils ne dérangent plus par un attifement tapageur servant à des fins d'identification ou publicitaires. Les serviettes de démaquillage et les shampooings jadis soustraits à la vue des familiers de la maison, les produits de nettoyage naguère rangés sous l'évier ou dans une armoire surgissent au grand air avec un air propre et plaisant qui renforce le confort visuel de l'habitat.

L'emballage en tant que symbole du statut social

Le design d'emballages a acquis ses titres de maturité. Il a fait la paix avec le consommateur, devenant son allié après avoir été un envahisseur, et il s'intègre toujours davantage dans notre environnement visuel où il prend place en tant qu'élément positif. Qui plus est, l'emballage, en se faisant accepter au plan social, est rentré dans le champ de vision des snobs. L'humble cabas en papier réservé jadis à la clientèle trop modeste pour se faire livrer ses achats a aujourd'hui accédé au rang de symbole du statut social. Les magasins les plus prestigieux du monde — Gucci, Fauchon, Bonwit Teller, Mark Cross parmi d'autres — n'ont pas dédaigné donner une forme plus permanente aux sacs en papier qu'ils remettent à leurs clients, pour les mettre en vente séparément. Les sacs en tissu au nom de grands détaillants, ornés de leurs logos et emblèmes familiers, véritable publicité ambulante, font la fierté de leurs heureux propriétaires, hommes et femmes mélangés.

Le pique-nique sous emballage

Des restaurants connus (tels que la Brasserie, à New York) ont développé sensiblement leurs fournitures de ravitaillement à l'emporter en présentant sous un emballage élégant — boîtes de pique-nique à compartiments, en carton blanc micro-ondulé — tous les composants d'un dîner de qualité prêt à être consommé. Le niveau de présentation est tel que ces en-cas ont même trouvé le chemin des salles de conférences et des réunions d'actionnaires. Ils jouissent d'une assez forte popularité parmi les cadres dirigeants, qui trouvent de bon ton de se les faire servir à leur bureau dans leurs emballages clairement identifiables.

Les repas vite faits et les plats à l'emporter ont popularisé un nouveau type d'emballage en boîtes aisément identifiables contenant des hamburgers, de la pizza, du poulet frit, du poisson-pommes frites. La marque du distributeur se répète sur les assiettes et couverts à jeter. Le «M» géant servant à identifier les hamburgers de McDonald's se propage rapidement au plan international et risque d'être bientôt connu dans le monde entier au même titre que le Coca-cola.

Une sensualité nouvelle

La sexualité s'affirmant à cor et à cri dans le monde d'aujourd'hui n'a pas manqué d'influencer la forme et la présentation des emballages, qui s'avèrent plus d'une fois fort suggestifs à cet égard. L'attrait sensuel des chemises à large décolleté révélant le sillon entre les seins ou un torse velu, le sex-appeal des jeans moulant les fesses se retrouvent dans des emballages et des illustrations d'emballages dotés du même pouvoir d'évocation sexualisé. La tendance en question s'affirme le plus nettement dans les produits de beauté et d'hygiène. Les hommes convertis de date récente aux vertus des cosmétiques se voient offrir une vaste gamme d'articles dont la présentation baigne dans une atmosphère de virilité triomphante et de recherche formelle sur un mode phallique propres à dissiper tous les doutes de la clientèle masculine quant à l'utilisation d'artifices jadis jugés féminins. Dans le secteur des parfums pour femmes, la ligne nette et disciplinée de Coco

Chanel a cédé le pas à des courbes sensuelles et voluptueuses. Le nouveau flacon de parfum de Halston, qui fait l'objet de l'admiration générale, est une expérience tactile et visuelle intéressante dans le cadre du renouvellement du conditionnement sous l'égide de la sensualité. Sa conception asymétrique brave les préceptes éprouvés du marketing et jure avec tous les conditionnements de parfum réalisés avec succès à ce jour.

Disparition des caractères distinctifs traditionnels

Les caractères distinctifs traditionnels de l'emballage sont en voie de disparition. On fait désormais foin de ces poncifs commodes qu'étaient la bande de couleur horizontale, le changement de couleur au centre, le panonceau ovale, le bleu et rouge des articles de quincaillerie, la neutralité des couleurs employées sur les emballages pharmaceutiques. C'étaient là des caractères distinctifs aisément identifiables, qui collaient bien à la conception solide et simpliste des emballages. Le texte apparaissait généralement en lettrage, dans des styles presque exclusivement réservés à l'industrie de l'emballage. Aujourd'hui, les conditionnements risquent de changer non plus progressivement, en respectant la capacité d'accoutumance du consommateur, mais à brûle-pourpoint et même en sens contraire, avec fréquemment pour effet salutaire une brusque flambée des ventes consécutive au changement d'emballage. Les artistes ne s'embarrassent plus de scrupules au sujet de conceptions périmées, ils vont hardiment de l'avant et prennent davantage de risques. La qualité des réalisations s'améliore progressivement. L'identification est obtenue au moyen de procédés plus simples et plus subtils à la fois.

Effets de surprise et humour

La liberté apportée par les possibilités de transformation et de mise à la page a fait découvrir aux emballages le sens de l'humour. Non pas un humour forcé dans le genre des flacons en forme d'animaux, mais la légèreté d'esprit et l'espièglerie qui naissent du jeu avec l'éphémère. L'emballage des collants L'Eggs paré subitement à Pâques des gais coloris des œufs de Pâques (par allusion à «eggs» = œufs) en est un bon exemple. La désinvolture nouvelle qui investit l'emballage trouve également son expression dans une certaine nonchalance formelle. On déserte les systèmes modulaires, les trames graphiques, l'ordonnance régulière à l'horizontale comme à la verticale. Le nom du produit en arrive à être tronqué, ce qui introduit un élément de surprise et provoque l'imagination du consommateur appelé à compléter le nom de la marque. L'énoncé de certaines identités occupe plusieurs faces de l'emballage à la fois, ou bien les marques apparaissent en diagonale. Avec l'avènement de la photocomposition, le lettrage style messageries a fait son temps; on y avait de toute façon eu recours principalement pour pallier les limitations de l'épaulement des caractères métalliques.

La palette des couleurs s'est agrandie. Des couleurs plus variées font leur apparition; on en fait un emploi plus créatif. Les couleurs normalisées que les experts en motivations imposaient jadis aux fabricants comme les seules capables d'emporter une décision d'achat ont fait place à d'autres couleurs et combinaisons de couleurs, qui font vendre tout aussi bien. L'explosion du bizarre et du psychédélique dans la civilisation contemporaine nous a débarrassés de nos œillères.

Qui conçoit ces emballages? Le généraliste passé spécialiste

Si l'on veut réaliser toute l'ampleur des transformations qui affectent le domaine spécialisé de l'emballage, il n'est que de jeter un coup d'œil à la liste des hommes et des femmes qui y sont à l'œuvre. Certains des travaux les plus remarquables de la sélection réunie dans Graphis/Packaging III émanent de designers qui sont en réalité des généralistes — cinéastes, réalisateurs d'expositions, illustrateurs, esthéticiens du livre, peintres, photographes, architectes, esthéticiens industriels. Le meilleur de ce qui se crée dans ce secteur à travers le monde est aujourd'hui l'œuvre d'artistes venus de tous les horizons de pensée et de toutes les disciplines.

Le 2e volume de Graphis/Packaging faisait état des progrès accomplis au cours de la décennie 1960, où les préoccupations majeures étaient axées sur le confort, les gadgets, l'affluence de biens, favorisant l'indolence et la consommation irréfléchie de matières premières assortie d'un certain mépris pour l'écologie. Fidèle à sa mission de livre à faire penser, Graphis/Packaging II posait des questions précisément sur l'écologie et la conservation d'énergie, bien en avance sur le design d'emballages des années 60, d'où cette préoccupation était entièrement absente. A cet égard, les emballages de la première moitié de la décennie 70 ne font état que d'un progrès mesuré.

Petite note sur le gaspillage propre aux emballages

C'est une véritable ironie de l'Histoire qu'au moment même où le gaspillage inconséquent de nos ressources et de l'énergie disponible est sérieusement remis en question, les emballages unitaires continuent sur leur lancée, en visant comme but principal non pas l'économie de matières premières, mais l'économie de temps de travail. En effet, la fragmentation des quantités unitaires dans l'alimentation jusqu'à obtention de portions individuelles, la fabrication d'instruments à jeter non réutilisables et la tendance générale aux emballages unitaires ne se traduisent guère par des économies de matières premières, mais bien par des économies de temps de travail de la part du personnel de vente, des infirmières, des médecins, des techniciens de laboratoire, des garçons de café — sans parler du chômage qu'on impose au lave-vaisselle.

Au début de cet article, j'avançais que l'emballage constitue un reflet fidèle de la société. Ce fait n'apparaît nulle part plus clairement que dans le gaspillage continu des matières premières face à la pénurie du papier, à la crise énergétique et au souci de la préservation des grands équilibres écologiques. L'hyperemballagisme continue de faire loi. Les fabricants acceptent du bout des lèvres les principes du respect de l'environnement, mais nombreux sont ceux qui continuent de gaspiller joyeusement nos ressources en produisant des emballages qui font fi des problèmes de la planète comme s'il n'y avait pas de lendemains à envisager — mais peut-être bien n'y en aura-t-il pas?

KARL FINK, gradué de la Parsons School of Design, a établi en 1951 son propre studio de design — Karl Fink & Associates. Il est co-fondateur, membre, directeur honoraire à vie et ancien président du Package Designers Council. Il a fait partie du corps enseignant du Packaging Institute et de l'administration du Inter-Society Colour Council. A présent il est président de l'American Institute of Graphic Arts (pour la deuxième fois de suite). Il a donné des cours et des conférences sur le design d'emballages et les arts graphiques.

Index to Designers, Artists and Photographers
Verzeichnis der Gestalter, Künstler und Photographen
Index des maquettistes, artistes et photographes

Index to Art Directors
Verzeichnis der künstlerischen Leiter
Index des directeurs artistiques

Index to Agencies and Studios
Verzeichnis der Agenturen und Studios
Index des agences et studios

Index to Clients
Verzeichnis der Auftraggeber
Index des clients

SINGER'S ERBEN AG; SWI. 66, 71
SIPURO AG; SWI. 316, 317
SMIRNOFF. 223
SMITH KLINE & FRENCH LABORATORIES; USA. 627, 629, 633, 671, 680, 701
SPAR; SAF. 4
SPECTRUM COSMETICS, INC.; USA. 523
SPRAY KEMI AB; SWE. 479
SPRENGEL & CO.; GER. 121
SPRING VALLEY PTY LTD.; AUL. 170
SPRINGER, AXEL, VERLAG AG; GER. 679
SQUEEZIT CORP.; USA. 33
S.S.C. & B.; USA. 398
STEINER ARZNEIMITTEL; GER. 645
STEINFELS AG; SWI. 278
STENVAL SA; FRA. 56
STERLING DRUG; USA. 550, 610
STERLING PRODUCTS INTERNATIONAL, INC.; USA. 305, 308
STEWARD WARNER CORP.; USA. 411
SUNSHINE NATURAL PRODUCTS; USA. 544
SUNTORY LTD.; JPN. 165, 166, 172, 200, 208, 213
SUPERMARKETS GENERAL CORP.; USA. 24
SUTTER, A., AG; SWI. 261, 309
SUZUKEN BIKAGAKU LTD.; JPN. 590, 593
SWIFT & CO.; USA. 2, 14
SWISSAIR; SWI. 492
SYNTEX LTD.; CAN. 551
SYSTEMATIC LEARNING CORP.; USA. 437, 438

TAIHO PHARMACEUTICAL CO. LTD.; JPN. 631, 654, 658
TAMAYO, DISTRIBUIDORA; VEN. 236

TARAX PROPRIETARY LTD.; 141, 144
TEBAK AG/CONTINENTAL PNEUS; SWI. 729
TELEGEN; GER. 419
TELEGENE PTY LTD.; AUL. 296
TENSOR CORPORATION; USA. 734
TEXAS PHARMACOL CO.; USA. 662
THERA GMBH. 583
TIEDEMANNS TOBAKKSFABRIKK; NOR. 395
TILE COMPANY OF AMERICA, INC.; USA. 766
TIME-LIFE FILMS; USA. 436
TOGA FOLK ART SHOP; JPN. 494, 495, 497, 498, 500, 501
TOKYO SHIBAURA ELECTRIC CO. LTD.; JPN. 359
TOTES, INC.; USA. 273
TRELAVNEY FOODS; AUL. 84, 87
TREVOR CRADDOCK; AUL. 169
TRISA BÜRSTENFABRIK; SWI. 331, 343
TUBORG BREWERIES; USA. 163, 164
TUPERIN, INDUSTRIAS; SPA. 337
TWO FACES RESTAURANT; AUL. 192

UCO; BEL. 726
UHLMANN-EYRAUD SA, F.; SWI. 594
UNION DE BRASSERIES; FRA. 158
UNIROYAL, INC.; USA. 244, 366, 369
UNITED DISTILLERS PTY LTD.; AUL. 222
UNITED PAPER MILLS LTD.; FIN. 474
UPPER CANADA SOAP & CANDLE MAKERS; CAN. 588
U.S. DEPT. OF AGRICULTURE; USA. 31
U.S. VITAMIN CORP.; USA. 647, 655
USEGO AG; SWI. 42
U.S.P. BENSON; AUL. 725
U.S. SHOE CORP.; USA. 243

VAN SILLEVOLDT; NLD. 16
VERY SPORT SA; SWI. 256
VIGNELLI ASSOCIATES; USA. 355
VILLEROY & BOCH; GER. 353
VINMONOPOLET A/S; NOR. 216
VOLG; SWI. 176
VON HEYDEN GMBH, CHEMISCHE FABRIK; GER. 68

WANDER (AUSTRALIA) PTY LTD.; AUL. 100
WARNER-CHILCOTT LABORATORIES; USA. 682, 723
WATNEY MANN LTD.; GBR. 157
WAYNE POTTERY. 350, 351
WEISFLOG AG, DISTILLERIE; SWI. 220
WESTINGHOUSE ELECTRIC CORP.; USA. 784
WINNER FOOD PRODUCTS LTD.; 32
WINSOR & NEWTON LTD.; GBR. 464–467
WINTHROP LABORATORIES; GBR. 640
WISTY CO.; USA. 134
WORLD OF BEAUTY CLUB; USA. 621
WYNN, S., & CO. PTY LTD.; AUL. 209, 210

XYLON PRODUCTS LTD.; GBR. 334

ZACHARY, J.; USA. 19
ZANE; USA. 480
ZENTRALVERBAND SCHWEIZ. MILCHPRODUZENTEN; SWI. 55
ZIGARETTENFABRIK KRISTINUS; GER. 375, 377, 378, 394
ZIGARETTENGRUPPE BRINKMANN; GER. 397
ZUCCHI, TELERIEITA; ITA. 259
ZYMA SA; SWI. 632, 635

Abbreviations   # Abkürzungen   # Abréviations

Argentinia	ARG	Argentinien	ARG	Afrique du Sud	SAF
Australia	AUL	Australien	AUL	Allemagne	GER
Austria	AUS	Belgien	BEL	Argentine	ARG
Belgium	BEL	Brasilien	BRA	Australie	AUL
Brasil	BRA	Dänemark	DEN	Autriche	AUS
Canada	CAN	Deutschland	GER	Belgique	BEL
Denmark	DEN	Finnland	FIN	Brésil	BRA
Finland	FIN	Frankreich	FRA	Canada	CAN
France	FRA	Grossbritannien	GBR	Danemark	DEN
Great Britain	GBR	Hongkong	HKG	Espagne	SPA
Germany	GER	Indien	IND	Etats-Unis	USA
Hong Kong	HKG	Israel	ISR	Finlande	FIN
India	IND	Italien	ITA	France	FRA
Israel	ISR	Japan	JPN	Grande-Bretagne	GBR
Italy	ITA	Kanada	CAN	Hong Kong	HKG
Japan	JPN	Mexiko	MEX	Inde	IND
Mexico	MEX	Niederlande	NLD	Israël	ISR
Netherlands	NLD	Norwegen	NOR	Italie	ITA
Norway	NOR	Österreich	AUS	Japon	JPN
Peru	PER	Peru	PER	Mexique	MEX
Portugal	POR	Portugal	POR	Norvège	NOR
South Africa	SAF	Schweden	SWE	Pays-Bas	NLD
Spain	SPA	Schweiz	SWI	Pérou	PER
Sweden	SWE	Spanien	SPA	Portugal	POR
Switzerland	SWI	Süd-Afrika	SAF	Suède	SWE
USA	USA	Venezuela	VEN	Suisse	SWI
Venezuela	VEN	Vereinigte Staaten	USA	Venezuela	VEN

Foods
Nahrungsmittel
Produits alimentaires

1

1 Transparent plastic bottle for sunflower oil. The oval form of the bottle offers a surer grip. Colour of oil is golden yellow, top of cap red, stripseal, full-colour label. (GER)
2 Package design for a line of delicatessen products. Typography reflects the stencil imprint characteristic of imported products. Colours associated with wine, cheese, etc. (USA)
3 Three examples from a line of deep-frozen vegetables sold by a supermarket chain. The photos show the contents of the packages in actual size. Silhouetting the vegetables against a white background gives a heightened three-dimensional effect. The M is a trade mark. (SWI)
4 Wrap-around labels for a range of canned soups. Photographic still life reproduced in full colour. Clear differentiation by illustration and text. (SAF)
5, 6, 7 Packaging programme for a line of Japanese food products, created by an American design firm. The trade mark, derived from the initial "a" (for Ajinomoto), provides the graphic theme throughout the range. 5 Bottles for seasonings. 6 Cans containing vegetable oils. 7 Gift boxes, in red to orange hues. (JPN)

1 Transparente Kunststoffflasche für Speiseöl. Ovaler, handlicher Flaschenquerschnitt. Rundum-Etikettierung, Verschlusskapsel rot-weiss mit Aufreiss-Streifen. (GER)
2 Gestaltung einer Serie von Delikatessen. Der einheitliche graphische Stil für die Deklaration der verschiedenen Produkte suggeriert importierte Spezialitäten. (USA)
3 Beispiele aus einem Sortiment von tiefgekühltem Gemüse einer Supermarkt-Handelskette. Die Produktabbildungen zeigen den Inhalt in natürlicher Grösse. Das «M» in der Ecke rechts unten ist das Markenzeichen der Handelskette. (SWI)
4 Einheitliche Gestaltungskonzeption für eine Serie von Suppenkonserven. Eine deutliche Sorten-differenzierung wurde erzielt durch Illustration und Text. (SAF)
5, 6, 7 Prototypen verschiedener Produktsortimente einer japanischen Nahrungsmittelfirma. Die Schutzmarke «a» ist in farblichen Abwandlungen graphisches Grundmotiv für die Gestaltung der Ausstattungen und gleichzeitig Identifikationsmerkmal. 5 Gewürzflaschen, 6 Speiseöl-Behälter, 7 Geschenkkarton, Deckelgestaltung in rot/orangen Tonabstufungen. (JPN)

1 Bouteille plastique transparente pour de l'huile de tournesol. Forme ovale favorisant la prise en main. Huile jaune or, bande de sécurité rouge-blanc, étiquette polychrome. (GER)
2 Design d'une gamme d'articles de traiteur. La typographie évoque l'impression des caisses de produits d'importation. Couleurs associées au vin, au fromage, etc. (USA)
3 Trois exemples d'une gamme de légumes surgelés vendus par une chaîne de supermarchés. Les photos représentent le contenu en grandeur nature. Vus sur un fond blanc, les légumes apparaissent en relief. Le «M» en bas, à droite est la marque déposée de la chaîne en question. (SWI)
4 Etiquettes circulaires pour soupes en boîtes. Les illustrations apparaissent en polychromie. De concert avec le texte, elles assurent une différentiation nette des produits. (SAF)
5, 6, 7 Programme d'emballage pour une ligne de produits alimentaires japonais, créé par un atelier de design américain. La marque déposée, dérivée du «a» (pour Ajinomoto), sert de thème graphique omniprésent. 5 Bouteilles de condiments. 6 Boîtes d'huiles comestibles. 7 Emballages-cadeaux; couvercles en dégradés rouge/orange. (JPN)

2

DESIGNER / GESTALTER / MAQUETTISTE:

1 Nikolaus Müller-Behrendt
2 Eugene J. Grossman
3 Hans Uster (Photo: Achille Weider)
4 Janice Ashby (Photo: Lowe Pretorius)
5–7 Art Goodman/Mamoru Shinmokochi
    (Artist: Mamoru Shinmokochi)

ART DIRECTOR / DIRECTEUR ARTISTIQUE:

2 Eugene J. Grossman
3 Hans Uster
4 Janice Ashby
5–7 Saul Bass/Art Goodman

AGENCY / AGENTUR / AGENCE – STUDIO:

1 Young & Rubicam
2 Anspach Grossman Portugal, Inc.
3 Migros Genossenschaftsbund, Abt. Packungen
4 Janice Ashby Design Studio Pty Ltd.
5–7 Saul Bass & Associates

4

5

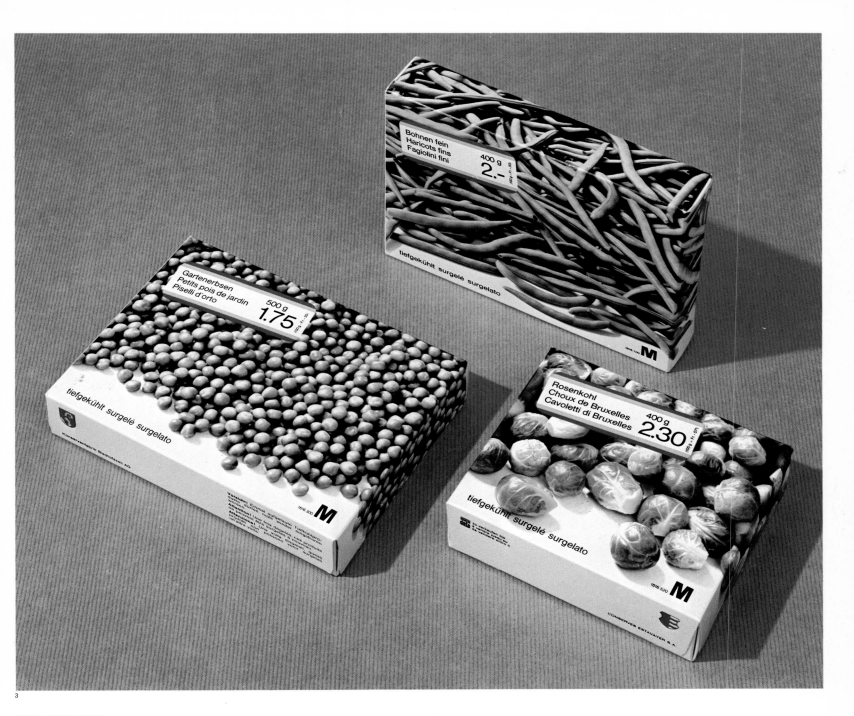

3

CLIENT / AUFTRAGGEBER:

1 Lesieur GmbH
2 Swift & Co.
3 Migros Genossenschaftsbund
4 Spar
5–7 Ajinomoto Co., Inc.

6

7

Foods
Nahrungsmittel
Produits alimentaires

8, 9 Packages for a range of deep-frozen products marketed by a food processing firm. The unifying graphic theme is the three-colour strip. (NLD)
10 Packages for *kuzukiri*, a traditional Japanese food. Wrapper printed in dull red and grey. (JPN)
11 Wrapping and label for chicken. The red and white check "cloth" is actually of paper, held together at the top by a plastic collar. (FRA)
12 Carton (front and back) for a soup mix, specially designed to appeal to children. (USA)
13 Wrap-around labels for a line of canned fruits and vegetables. (USA)
14 Front and back of a prototype package from a re-design programme for a range of over 50 products from a meat processing firm. Lettering black, bar red and orange, photographic illustrations in full colour. (USA)

8, 9 Packungen aus einem Sortiment von Tiefkühlprodukten. Das dreifach gestufte farbige Band ist in seiner charakteristischen Anordnung einheitliche Layoutform der gesamten Serie. (NLD)
10 Ausstattung für ein traditionelles japanisches Nahrungsmittel. Einwickler in zwei Farben, Rot und Grau, bedruckt. (JPN)
11 Rot-weiss kariertes Einwickelpapier mit Textil-Effekt, von einem Plastikring zusammengehalten, als Verpackung für ein ganzes Brathuhn. (FRA)
12 Vorder- und Rückseite einer Packung für Trockensuppen. Die Graphik ist speziell für Kinder konzipiert. (USA)
13 Etikettengestaltung für die Dosen einer Serie von Frucht- und Gemüsekonserven. (USA)
14 Vorder- und Rückseite eines Prototypes für die Neugestaltung einer Serie von über fünfzig Produktausstattungen einer Fleischwaren-Verarbeitungsfirma. Farbige Produktillustrationen, Typographie schwarz, Band rot/orange. (USA)

8, 9 Emballages pour une gamme de produits surgelés mise en vente par une société de produits alimentaires. La bande tricolore disposée de manière caractéristique constitue le sigle d'identité de la gamme. (NLD)
10 Emballages de *kuzukiri*, un plat japonais traditionnel. La bande d'emballage est imprimée en deux couleurs, rouge terne et gris. (JPN)
11 Emballage de poulet, avec étiquette. Papier imitant un tissu à carreaux rouges et blancs. Collerette de fermeture en plastique. (FRA)
12 Carton de soupe en poudre (recto et verso), avec des dessins conçus pour plaire aux enfants. (USA)
13 Exemples d'étiquettes circulaires pour une série de boîtes de fruits et légumes en conserve. (USA)
14 Recto et verso d'un prototype d'emballage pour le remodelage d'une ligne de plus de 50 conditionnements de produits mis en vente par une boucherie en gros. Texte en noir, bande rouge et orange, photos polychromes. (USA)

Foods
Nahrungsmittel
Produits alimentaires

DESIGNER / GESTALTER / MAQUETTISTE:

8, 9 HBM Design (Photo: Toine Nuyten/Foto Unit)
10 Shigeru Komiya/Takeshi Tachi
11 F. Vermeil (Artist: Marie José Mathez)
12 Gianninoto Associates
13 Sheldon Rynser (Artist: Paruiz Sadighian)
14 Eugene J. Grossman (Photo: T. Matsumoto)

ART DIRECTOR / DIRECTEUR ARTISTIQUE:

10 Takeshi Tachi
11 Roger Saingt
12 John Di Gianni
13 Sheldon Rynser
14 Eugene J. Grossman

AGENCY / AGENTUR / AGENCE – STUDIO:

8, 9 HBM Design
10 Honshu Paper Co. Ltd.
11 Depar
12 Gianninoto Associates
13 Goldsholl Associates
14 Anspach Grossman Portugal, Inc.

CLIENT / AUFTRAGGEBER:

8, 9 Groko France
10 Kuzushu
11 Douce-France
12 Thomas J. Lipton, Inc.
13 Charlotte Charles Food
14 Swift & Company

10

11

12

13

14

15

16

17

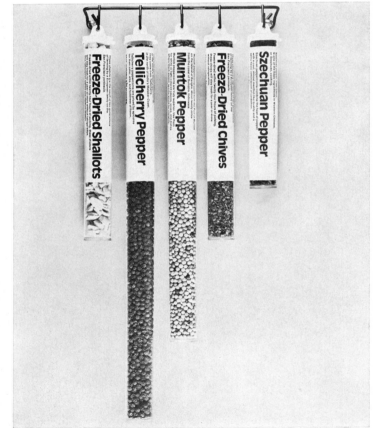

18

15 Folding cartons for frozen seafood. Full-colour photographic illustrations. (GER)
16 Plastic spice shaker bottle shown dismantled and assembled. (NLD)
17 Can for pre-fried chips. The wrap-around illustration shows the wire frying basket with its contents. Full colour. (FRA)
18 Transparent spice containers on a display rack. (USA)
19 Corrugated cardboard box containing an assortment of popcorn sampler bottles. Box graphics maroon and black. Bottle labels maroon, yellow, black and grey. (USA)
20, 21 Die-cut cardboard tray containing a cold drink, hamburger, chips, a biscuit and a surprise package. Fig. 21 shows one of the backdrops with punch-out pictures, games, puzzles, etc., designed to appeal to children. (USA)

15 Gestaltungskonzeption für ein Tiefkühlsortiment. Farbphotos, Schrift schwarz. (GER)
16 Gewürzstreuer aus Kunststoff, ganz und in Einzelteile zerlegt. (NLD)
17 Vorgebackene Pommes frites in einem Fritiersieb sind auf diesem Dosenetikett farbig abgebildet. (FRA)
18 Garnitur transparenter Gewürzbehälter in Röhrenform mit Aufhänger. (USA)
19 Mikrowellkarton für Popcorn-Musterfläschchen. Bedruckung: rotbraun und schwarz. Flaschenetikette: rotbraun, gelb, schwarz und grau. (USA)
20, 21 Gestanztes Serviertablett aus Karton. Es enthält Bechergetränk, Frikadelle, Pommes frites und eine Überraschungstüte. Abb. 21 zeigt ein Gestaltungsthema zur Unterhaltung von Kindern. (USA)

Foods / Nahrungsmittel
Produits alimentaires

DESIGNER / GESTALTER / MAQUETTISTE:

15 Ursula Scherer (Photo: Klaus P. Ohlenforst)
16 Jac. Gorter
17 Roger Saingt (Artist: J. Tournadre/A. Soro)
18 Ira Sturtevant/Meg Crane (Photo: Ivor Parry)
19 Donald K. Skoro
20, 21 Dick Chodkowski

ART DIRECTOR / DIRECTEUR ARTISTIQUE:

15 Ursula Scherer
16 Jac. Gorter
17 Roger Saingt
18 Meg Crane
19 Donald K. Skoro
20, 21 Dick Chodkowski

AGENCY / AGENTUR / AGENCE – STUDIO:

16 Jac. Gorter Design
17 Depar
18 Ponzi & Weill
19 John Howe/Wanigan, Inc.
20, 21 Ogilvy & Mather, Inc.

CLIENT / AUFTRAGGEBER:

15 Dr. Oetker GmbH
16 Van Sillevoldt
17 Bonduelle SA
18 The Flavorbank Co., Inc.
19 J. Zachary
20, 21 Burger Chef Restaurants
         Div. of General Foods Corp.

19

20

21

15 Cartons pliants pour du poisson surgelé. Photos polychromes, lettres noires. (GER)
16 Boîte à épices, en plastique, montrée assemblée et en pièces détachées. (NLD)
17 Boîtes de frites préfrites. L'étiquette circulaire montre le panier-égouttoir de la friteuse avec son contenu. Photo polychrome. (FRA)
18 Boîtes à épices transparentes sous forme de tubes à suspendre. (USA)
19 Boîte de carton ondulé avec un assortiment de flacons d'échantillons de pop-corn. Impression de la boîte brun-rouge et noir. Etiquettes brun-rouge, jaune, noir, gris. (USA)
20, 21 Plateau de carton découpé à l'emporte-pièce et contenant une boisson froide, un hamburger, des frites et une pochette-cadeau. La fig. 21 montre l'une des décorations verticales illustrées de jeux, devinettes et figurines propres à plaire aux enfants. (USA)

22 Paper bag for organically grown rice. The colours, tans, browns and green, suggest pure, wholesome ingredients. (USA)
23 Transparent colour-coded bags for various types of rice. (SWI)
24 Examples from the packaging design programme of a supermarket chain. Uniform graphics identify the various products of the range. (USA)
25–30 Six examples from a packaging re-design programme of a department store chain in which all products have their place in a co-ordinated system. (See also Figs. 111, 112, 248–254.) 25 Plastic bottles for peanut and sunflower oil. 26 Two examples from an extensive range of jams. 27 Tins of beans and peas as examples of the *Gourmet* range (front and back of tin); photographs of the contents in actual size. 28, 29 Transparent bags as used for pasta and peas. 30 Flour bag; graphic elements are used, since the quality of the product cannot be shown by photographs or through cut-out windows. (SWI)
31 Packaging range for government-donated food. Colour coding and illustration are designed to reach semiliterate users. (USA)

22 Papiersack für biologisch angebauten Speise-Reis. Die Farben Beige, Braun und Grün suggerieren ein naturreines Produkt. (USA)
23 Transparente Beutel für ein Reissortiment. (SWI)
24 Beispiele aus dem Packungsgestaltungs-Programm einer Supermarkt-Kette. Konsequente Durchführung des graphischen Grundkonzeptes. (USA)
25–30 Sechs Beispiele aus dem Neugestaltungs-Programm einer Warenhausgruppe, nach dem alle Produkte in koordinierter Aufmachung gestaltet wurden. (Siehe auch Abbildungen 111, 112, 248–254.) 25 Kunststoffflaschen für Erdnuss- und Sonnenblumenöl. 26 Beispiele aus der Serie Konfitüre. 27 Bohnen- und Erbsendosen aus der Produktserie *Gourmet* (Vorder- und Rückseite); Produktabbildungen in natürlicher Grösse. 28, 29 Sichtverpackungen aus der Serie Teigwaren und Hülsenfrüchte. 30 Mehlbeutel; da keine qualitativen Produkteigenschaften direkt erkennbar sind, wurden hier graphische Elemente verwendet. (SWI)
31 Packungsserie für Nahrungsmittel, die von den USA gespendet werden. Farbcodierung und Graphik sind auf leseschwache Verbraucher ausgerichtet. (USA)

22 Sachet de riz de culture biologique. Les couleurs beige, brun et vert évoquent la pureté d'un produit naturel. (USA)
23 Sachets transparents pour des variétés de riz, avec un code-couleur. (SWI)
24 Exemples du programme d'emballages d'une chaîne de supermarchés. Une présentation graphique uniforme sert d'identification aux divers produits. (USA)
25–30 Six exemples d'une conception d'emballages nouvelle réalisée pour une chaîne de grands magasins. Tous les produits s'insèrent dans un système coordonné. (Cf. aussi les fig. 111, 112, 248–254.) 25 Bouteilles plastiques pour de l'huile d'arachide et de tournesol. 26 Deux exemples de bocaux de confiture. 27 Boîtes de haricots et de petits pois de la ligne *Gourmet* (recto et verso); photos grandeur nature. 28, 29 Sachets transparents pour pâtes et légumes secs. 30 Cornet de farine; des éléments graphiques se substituent ici à la visualisation directe ou photographique du produit, qui n'est pas faisable. (SWI)
31 Ligne d'emballages pour des produits alimentaires faisant partie d'un programme d'aide gratuite des Etats-Unis. Le code-couleur employé et la présentation graphique sont étudiés en fonction de consommateurs semi-illettrés. (USA)

Foods
Nahrungsmittel
Produits alimentaires

DESIGNER / GESTALTER / MAQUETTISTE:

22 Fred Ribek/Paul Hawken
23 Migros Genossenschaftsbund, Abt. Packungen
24 Lippincott & Margulies
25–30 E + U Hiestand
31 Marsha Eddins/Jan Proctor

22

23

24

25

26

27

28

29

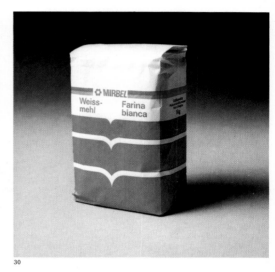

30

ART DIRECTOR / DIRECTEUR ARTISTIQUE:

22 Rod Williams
23 Hans Uster
24 Lippincott & Margulies
25–30 E + U Hiestand
31 David Sutton

AGENCY / AGENTUR / AGENCE – STUDIO:

22 Williams & Associates
23 Migros Genossenschaftsbund, Abt. Packungen
24 Lippincott & Margulies
25–30 E + U Hiestand/H. M. Eggmann

CLIENT / AUFTRAGGEBER:

22 Erewhon Trading Co.
23 Migros Genossenschaftsbund
24 Supermarkets General Corp.
25–30 Maus Frères SA
31 U.S. Dept. of Agriculture

31

32

32 Tins for vegetable oil made from corn. Front and back. (JPN)
33 Display box with transparent windows revealing the contents, two plastic dispensers for catsup and mustard. (USA)
34 Design of glass jar, metal lid and labels for a family range of preserved vegetables and fruits. (USA)
35 Re-usable plastic dispenser for flour. White container, label red, maroon and yellow. (FRA)
36 Plastic salt dispenser. The lable can be removed and the container used as a combined salt cellar and pourer. (USA)
37 Metal can for peanut oil. Symbol in red. (HKG)
38 Cotton sacks containing peppercorns and rock salt, sold by a chain of home furnishing stores. (GBR)

32 Dosen für Speiseöl aus Mais. Vorder- und Rückseite. (JPN)
33 Ausstell-Schachtel mit Sichtfenstern für Ketchup- und Senfspender in Fruchtform aus weichem Kunststoff. (USA)
34 Gestaltung von Glasbehältern, Deckel und Etiketten für ein Sortiment von Essiggemüsen und -früchten. (USA)
35 Wiederverwendbare Kunststoff-Streudose für Mehl. Behälter weiss, Etikett rot, rotbraun und gelb. (FRA)
36 Salzbehälter aus Kunststoff. Nach Entfernung des Etiketts als Tisch-Salzstreuer verwendbar. (USA)
37 Metalldose für Erdnussöl. Symbol in Rot. (HKG)
38 Baumwollene Säcke für Pfefferkörner und Salz aus einem Sortiment einer Kette von Wohnbedarfsgeschäften. (GBR)

32 Boîtes d'huile comestible à base de maïs (recto, verso). (JPN)
33 Boîte-présentoir vitrée montrant un moutardier et un distributeur de ketchup fructiformes en plastique mou. (USA)
34 Etude de bocal avec couvercle métallique et étiquettes, pour une gamme de conserves de fruits et de légumes. (USA)
35 Boîte à farine réutilisable indéfiniment, en plastique. Récipient blanc, étiquette rouge, brun-rouge et jaune. (FRA)
36 Salière en matière plastique. Une fois l'étiquette enlevée, elle s'utilise comme salière de table. (USA)
37 Bidon d'huile d'arachide. Symbole en rouge. (HKG)
38 Sacs de coton contenant du poivre en grains et du sel gemme, mis en vente par une chaîne de magasins d'ameublement. (GBR)

33

34

ART DIRECTOR / DIRECTEUR ARTISTIQUE:

32 Alan Zie Yongder
33 Herb Lubalin
34 John Di Gianni
36 Jerome Gould

35

36

37

38

DESIGNER / GESTALTER / MAQUETTISTE:	AGENCY / AGENTUR / AGENCE – STUDIO:	CLIENT / AUFTRAGGEBER:
32 Alan Zie Yongder	32 LTZ Ltd.	32 Winner Food Products Ltd.
33 Alan Peckolick	33 Lubalin Smith Carnase	33 Squeezit Corp.
34 Gianninoto Associates	34 Gianninoto Associates	34 Beatrice Foods Co.
35 Paul Barzilay	35 Agence Dela Vasselais	35 Farines Nationales
36 Jerome Gould	36 Gould & Associates	36 Morton Salt Co.
37 Henry Steiner	37 Graphic Communications Ltd.	37 Amoy Canning Co. (Hong Kong) Ltd.
38 Conran Associates	38 Conran Associates	38 Habitat Designs Ltd.

39

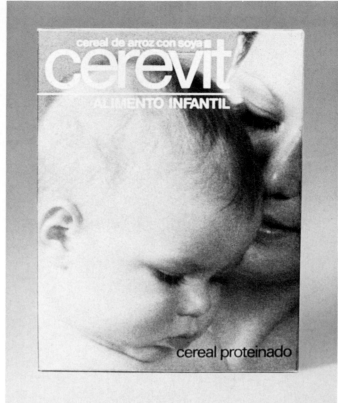

40

41

42

39 Package for baby food. Photograph reproduced in full colour. (CAN)
40 Folding box for baby cereal. Photo printed in red-brown hues. (MEX)
41 Package for a ready-mixed omelette flour. Photographic illustration is printed in full colour. The dominant colour is golden yellow. (SWI)
42 Cardboard package for rice imported from the USA. Background colour yellow; the red, white and blue stripe design symbolizes the US flag. (SWI)
43 Design for the label of canned soup marketed by a restaurant. (AUL)
44 Folding carton for onion rings. Photo in brown and yellow shades. (USA)
45 Label design for a tin of dog food. Lettering black, bottom bar red on white background, vignette with dogs in full colour. (USA)
46 Box for a dry dog food. Lettering black. Head of puppy reproduced in full colour on white background. (AUL)
47 Tear-open cartons for ice milk. The photographs, reproduced in full colour, refer to the flavours. Sides of boxes in primary colours. (USA)

39 Packung für ein Kindernahrungsmittel. Photographie vierfarbig. (CAN)
40 Faltschachtel für Kindernährmittel. Photo in rot-braunen Tönen gedruckt. (MEX)
41 Faltschachtel für fixfertiges Omeletten-Mehl. Die photographische Illustration ist vierfarbig reproduziert. Goldgelbe Farben dominieren. (SWI)
42 Kartonpackung für Reis aus den USA. Grundfarbe gelb. Das rot-blau-weisse Streifenmotiv erinnert an die amerikanische Flagge. (SWI)
43 Etikett für Suppenkonserven, die von einem Restaurant verkauft werden. (AUL)

44 Faltkarton für Snacks mit Zwiebelgeschmack. Braun- und Gelbtöne. (USA)
45 Etikettgestaltung für eine Hundefutter-Konserve. Farbige Illustration, schwarze Typographie. (USA)
46 Faltschachtel für Trocken-Hundefutter. Beschriftung schwarz, Kopf des Hundes vierfarbig reproduziert, weisser Grund. (AUL)
47 Aufreiss-Schachteln für Eiscreme. Die photographischen Sujets, vierfarbig reproduziert, beziehen sich auf die Aromen. Seiten in Primärfarben. (USA)

39 Emballage pour un aliment de bébé. Photo polychrome. (CAN)
40 Boîte pliante pour un aliment pour bébés. Photo: tons brun rougeâtre. (MEX)
41 Emballage pour une farine à crêpes prête à l'emploi. La photo est polychrome. Le ton prédominant est le jaune or. (SWI)
42 Emballage de carton pour du riz importé des E.-U. Fond jaune; les bandes rouges, blanches, bleues évoquent les couleurs du drapeau américain. (SWI)
43 Etiquette d'une soupe en boîte vendue par un restaurant. (AUL)
44 Carton pliant pour un mélange d'apéritif à goût d'oignon. Bruns et jaunes. (USA)
45 Etiquette pour une boîte de viande pour chiens. Lettres noires, bande inférieure rouge sur blanc, illustration polychrome. (USA)
46 Boîte pliante pour un aliment sec pour chiens. Typo noire, tête du chien polychrome sur fond blanc. (AUL)
47 Cartons avec bandes d'arrachage pour de la crème glacée. Les photos polychromes se rapportent aux différents parfums. Couleurs primaires sur les côtés. (USA)

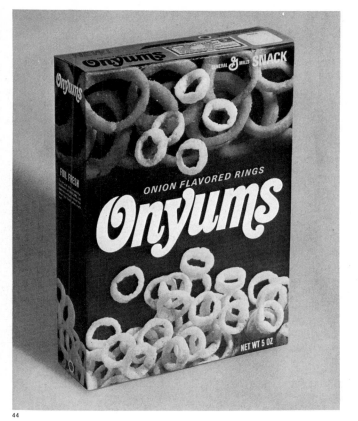

DESIGNER / GESTALTER / MAQUETTISTE:

39 Raymond Lee
40 G. Edwards
   (Photo: Enrique Bostelmann)
41 Armin Müller (Photo: Armin Müller)
42 Jacqueline Bühler
43 Les Mason (Artist: Malcolm Smith)
44 Dickens Design Group
   (Photo: Allen Snook)
45 Herb Lubalin
46 Les Mason (Photo: Kevin Gleeson)
47 Howard C. Grant/Richard Ritter/
   Dante E. Evangelista

ART DIRECTOR / DIRECTEUR ARTISTIQUE:

44 Robert Sidney Dickens
47 Jerry Siano

AGENCY / AGENTUR / AGENCE – STUDIO:

39 Raymond Lee & Associates
40 Lab. Diseño Carton y Papel
   de Mexico SA
41 Atelier Armin Müller
42 Atelier Fritz Bühler AG
43 Studio Les Mason
45 Lubalin Smith Carnase
46 Hayes Cowcher-Dailey Pty Ltd.
47 Ayer Design

CLIENT / AUFTRAGGEBER:

39 Mead Johnson
40 Industrial de Alimentos SA
41 Migros Genossenschaftsbund
42 Usego AG
43 Riverboat Investments
44 General Mills
45 Gaines, Inc.
46 KMM Pty Ltd.
47 Sealtest Foods

43

44

45

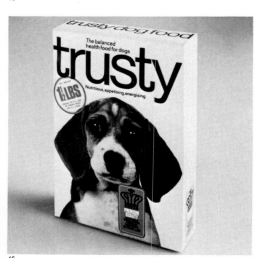

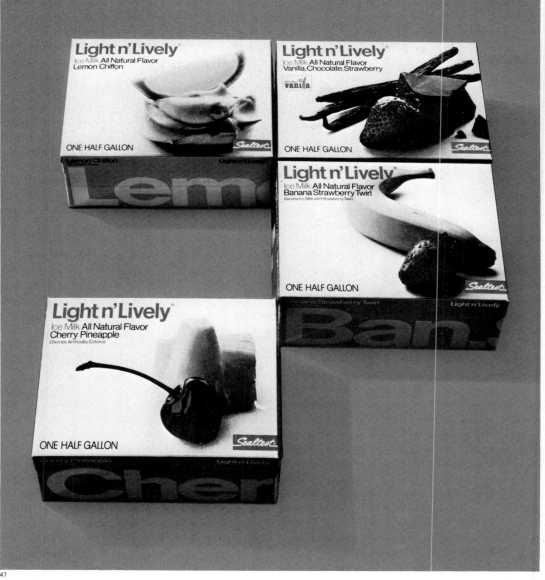

46

47

45

48

49

50

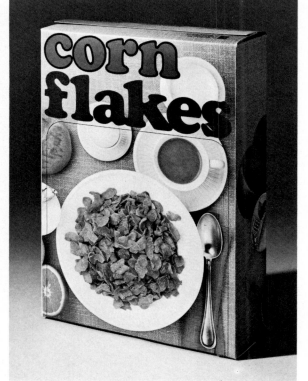

51

DESIGNER / GESTALTER / MAQUETTISTE:

48 Jean Larcher
49 Lis Knudsen
50 Peter Dixon/Mike Cheveralls
    (Artist: Sid Day)
51 Migros Genossenschaftsbund, Abt.
    Packungen
52, 53 Castle
54 Eugene J. Grossman
    (Artist: Ken Cooke)
55 Urs Roos

ART DIRECTOR / DIRECTEUR ARTISTIQUE:

49 Peter Weyrich
50 Peter Dixon
51 Hans Uster
54 Eugene J. Grossman
55 Erich Hartmann

AGENCY AGENTUR / AGENCE – STUDIO:

49 Plan Design A/S
50 Sainsbury's Design Studio
51 Migros Genossenschaftsbund,
    Abt. Packungen
52, 53 Castle Chappell & Partners
54 Anspach Grossman Portugal, Inc.
55 Gisler & Gisler

CLIENT / AUFTRAGGEBER:

48 Lactel
49 Mejeriselskabet Denmark
50 J. Sainsbury Ltd.
51 Migros Genossenschaftsbund
52, 53 Castle Chappell & Partners
54 The Quaker Oats Co.
55 Zentralverband
    Schweiz. Milchproduzenten

Foods
Nahrungsmittel
Produits alimentaires

48 Milk carton. Lettering and arches blue, dot red on white. (FRA)
49 Carton for fruit yoghurt. Printed in red and magenta. (DEN)
50 Folding box for cereal. (GBR)
51 Cereal box. The photographic illustration, printed in full colour, extends over three sides. Lettering red and blue. (SWI)
52, 53 Tissue paper wrappers with imprint (52) for apples given as Christmas presents by a firm of advertising consultants. (GBR)
54 Box for a high-protein cereal. (USA)
55 Cardboard packages for a range of Swiss cheeses. (SWI)

48 Milchkarton. Schrift und Bogen blau, Punkt rot auf Weiss. (FRA)
49 Karton für Fruchtjoghurt. In zwei Rottönen gedruckt. (DEN)
50 Faltschachtel für Maisflocken. (GBR)
51 Maisflocken-Packung. Die vierfarbig gedruckte, photographische Illustration reicht über drei Seiten. Schrift blau und rot. (SWI)
52, 53 Einwickelpapier mit Aufdruck für Äpfel, die von einer Werbeagentur als Weihnachtsgeschenk an Kunden verschickt wurden. (GBR)
54 Schachtel für eine Protein-Frühstücksnahrung. (USA)
55 Kartonschachteln für ein Sortiment Schweizer Käse. (SWI)

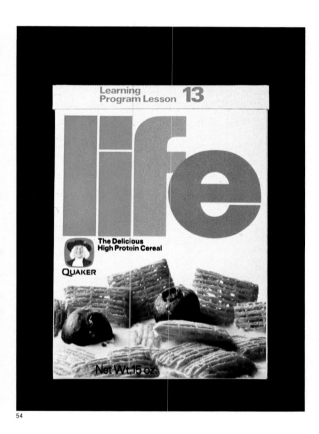

48 Brique de lait. Texte et arcs bleus, point rouge sur blanc. (FRA)
49 Carton de yogourts aux fruits. Impression rouge et magenta. (DEN)
50 Boîte pliante pour des flocons de maïs. (GBR)
51 Boîte de flocons de maïs. La photo qui la décore sur trois faces est imprimée en polychromie. Typo rouge et bleue. (SWI)
52, 53 Cadeau de Noël d'une agence publicitaire pour sa clientèle: chaque pomme est enveloppée d'un papier fin au nom de l'agence. (GBR)
54 Boîte réalisée pour un déjeuner de flocons aux protéines. (USA)
55 Boîtes en carton pour une gamme de fromages suisses. (SWI)

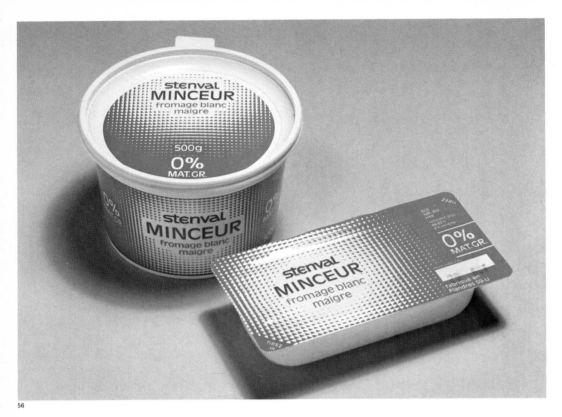

56

DESIGNER / GESTALTER / MAQUETTISTE:

56 Horst Mewes
57 Bruno Oldani
58 Joe Selame/Logan Smith
59 Shigeru Akizuki
60 Harry Murphy/Doug Akagi/Victor Larger
61 Henning Lykstoft
62 G. Edwards

ART DIRECTOR / DIRECTEUR ARTISTIQUE:

56 Anke-Maria Weber
57 Bruno Oldani
58 Joe Selame
61 Peter Weyrich
62 G. Edwards

AGENCY / AGENTUR / AGENCE – STUDIO:

56 Institut für Packungsgestaltung
57 Bruno Oldani
58 Selame Design Associates
59 Akizuki Design Office
60 Harry Murphy & Friends
61 Plan Design A/S
62 Lab. Diseño Carton y Papel de Mexico SA

CLIENT / AUFTRAGGEBER:

56 Stenval SA
57 Lillehammer Bryggeri
58 Prince Macaroni Manufacturing Co.
59 Fujiya Confectionery Co. Ltd.
60 Le Fromage
61 Mejeriselskabet Denmark
62 Nacma SA

57

56 Plastic containers for low-calorie cottage cheese. (FRA)
57 Plastic jars containing 1 kg of fruit jams. Clear differentiation of contents. (NOR)
58 Folding box for egg noodles. The "yolk" of the egg suggests a window revealing the contents. (USA)
59 Foil bag for ice sherbet. Blue, red and black on silver. (JPN)
60 Carry cartons for cheese products. (USA)
61 Plastic cups for yoghurt with fruit flavours. (DEN)
62 Hexagonal cardboard box for pasta products. (MEX)

56 Tiefgezogene Kunststoffbehälter für ein Sortiment fettloser Frischkäse. (FRA)
57 Gestaltungskonzept mit deutlicher Sortendifferenzierung für ein Fruchtkonfitüren-Sortiment. Die Kunststoffbecher beinhalten jeweils 1 kg. (NOR)
58 Faltschachtel für Eiernudeln. Das kreisförmige Eidotter wirkt wie ein Sichtfenster. (USA)
59 Beutel aus Aluminiumfolie für Sorbet-Eis. Blau, rot und schwarz auf Silbergrund. (JPN)
60 Faltschachtel als Tragkarton für Käsprodukte. (USA)
61 Kunststoffbecher für Yoghurt mit Frucht-Aromen. (DEN)
62 Sechseckige Faltschachtel für Teigwaren. (MEX)

56 Récipients de plastique moulé par compression, pour du fromage blanc maigre. (FRA)
57 Pots de confitures d'un kilo, en matière plastique. Les conditionnements sont nettement différenciés d'après le contenu. (NOR)
58 Boîte pliante pour des pâtes aux œufs. Le contenu apparaît derrière la fenêtre délimitée par le jaune d'œuf circulaire. (USA)
59 Sachet en feuille d'aluminium pour un sorbet glacé. Bleu, rouge, noir sur argent. (JPN)
60 Cartons portatifs pour fromages. (USA)
61 Gobelets de yogourt aux fruits, en plastique. (DEN)
62 Boîte de section hexagonale pour des pâtes alimentaires. (MEX)

58

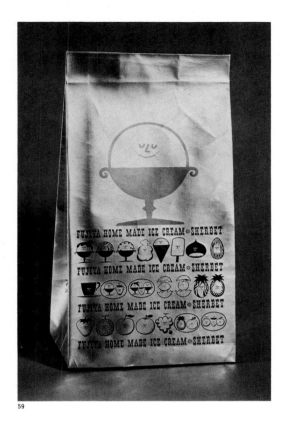

59

60

61

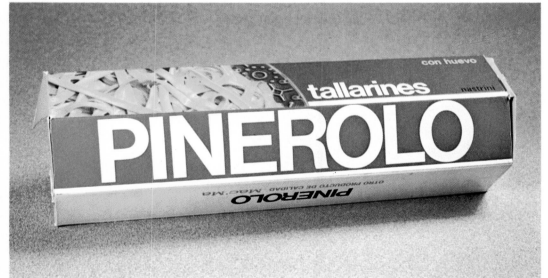

62

Foods
Nahrungsmittel
Produits alimentaires

63

64

65

Foods
Nahrungsmittel
Produits alimentaires

67

63, 64 Two cardboard folding boxes from a line of deep-frozen food products. The dotted band with the logotype is the unifying graphic theme throughout the range. Colour photographs illustrate the contents at about actual size. (SWI)
65 Can styling for tomato purée. The design is printed on the can. (JPN)
66 Folding box for rusks. Full-colour photographic illustration. (SWI)
67 Pre-perforated tear-open package for a series of cracker products. Photos of contents in full colour. (GER)
68 Cardboard box for sweetening tablets, inserted in a transparent plastic slide box, to become a tablet dispenser after punching out the pre-cut hole. (GER)
69 One of a series of pie boxes. Colours vary according to contents. (USA)

63, 64 Faltschachteln für ein Sortiment von Tiefkühlprodukten. Das punktierte Band mit dem Namenszug dient als verbindendes graphisches Element. (SWI)
65 Dosengestaltung für Tomatenpurée. Graphik auf die Dose aufgedruckt. (JPN)
66 Faltschachtel für Zwieback. Vierfarbige, photographische Illustration. (SWI)
67 Vorgestanzte Aufreisspackungen für eine Serie von Backprodukten. Photos des Inhalts vierfarbig gedruckt. (GER)
68 Faltschachtel für Süssstoff-Tabletten. Durch Einschieben in einen Kunststoffschieber wird die Verpackung zu einem Tablettenspender, nachdem die vorgestanzte Öffnung durchstossen wurde. (GER)
69 Aus einer Serie von Kuchenschachteln. Farben variieren je nach Inhalt. (USA)

63, 64 Cartons pliants pour une gamme de produits surgelés. La bande en pointillé avec le logo du fabricant est l'élément graphique unifiant la gamme. Des photos couleur approximativement grandeur nature illustrent le contenu. (SWI)
65 Etude de boîte de concentré de tomates. Impression à même la boîte. (JPN)
66 Boîte pliante pour biscottes. Photo polychrome. (SWI)
67 Emballage à bande d'arrachage préperforée pour une série de biscuits. Photo polychrome du contenu. (GER)
68 Boîte pliante pour un édulcorant, glissant dans un casier en plastique pourvu d'un orifice de distribution préestampé, à percer du pouce. (GER)
69 Exemple d'une série de cartons à gâteaux; couleurs en fonction du contenu. (USA)

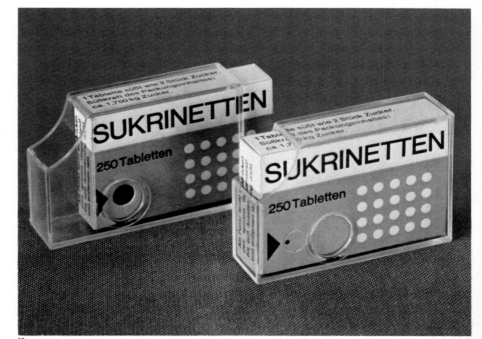

68

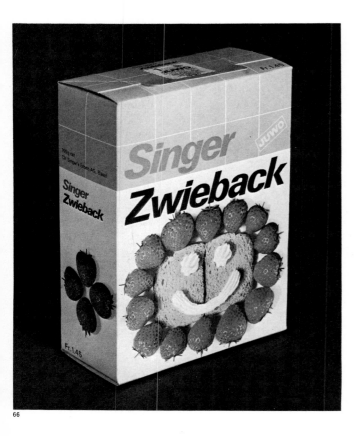

66

69

70

DESIGNER / GESTALTER / MAQUETTISTE:

70 Schakhine Guila (Photo: Miki Koren/Photo «Jaacobs»)
71 Armin Müller (Photo: Armin Müller)
72 Keith Bright/Patrick Soo Hoo (Artist: Robert Maile/
    (Photo: Roger Marshutz)
73 Lyndon Whaite
74 Armin Müller
75 Eugene J. Grossman (Photo: T. Matsumoto)
76 Armin Müller (Photo: Max Buchmann)
77 Yasuo Tanaka/Nobuo Kizuka
78 Gerhard Bergmayer (Photo: Humes & Himmel)

ART DIRECTOR / DIRECTEUR ARTISTIQUE:

70 Schakhine Guila
71, 74, 76 Armin Müller
72 Keith Bright
75 Eugene J. Grossman
77 Yasuo Tanaka
78 Klaus P. Assmann

AGENCY / AGENTUR / AGENCE – STUDIO:

71, 74, 76 Atelier Armin Müller
72 Keith Bright & Associates
73 Emery, Fowler-Brown, Sadgrove & Whaite Pty Ltd.
75 Anspach Grossman Portugal, Inc.
78 Parkring Werbegesellschaft mbH

CLIENT / AUFTRAGGEBER:

70 Elite
71 Ch. Singer's Erben AG
72 Pacific United Services
73 H. Adams Manufacturing Pty Ltd.
74 Schnebli AG
75 Morton Frozen Foods
76 Roland Murten AG
77 Nada Coop Bakery
78 Ed. Haas

71

70 Folding boxes for cream-filled and rolled wafers. Contents illustrated in natural colours. Lettering red and brown. (ISR)
71 Set-up box for a sweetmat speciality from Basle. Printed in full colour. (SWI)
72 Set-up boxes for a range of chocolate candies. Illustrations of contents in full colour. Cartouche in green, blue and ochre. Sides of boxes green. (USA)
73 Carton for a Christmas cake. Polychrome printing. (AUL)
74 Folding boxes for biscuits. Contents shown in natural colours. The colours of the stripes are green, light green and white on one box, red, orange and white on the other. (SWI)
75 Zip-open box for frozen doughnuts. Full-colour printing. Part of a packaging system for supermarket distribution. (USA)
76 Folding box for almond biscuits. Three-colour printing. (SWI)
77 Carrier box for biscuits. Polychrome printing. (JPN)
78 Packaging series for cake mixes. Full colour. (AUS)

70 Faltschachteln für gefüllte und gerollte Waffeln. Inhalt in natürlichen Farben illustriert, Schrift rot und braun. (ISR)
71 Faltschachtel für Leckerli, eine Basler Spezialität. Vierfarbig gedruckt. (SWI)
72 Kartonschachteln für eine Serie von Schokoladekonfekt. Inhalt ist vierfarbig abgebildet. Kartuschen-Ornament in Grün, Blau und Ocker. Seitenwände grün. (USA)
73 Packung für einen Weihnachtskuchen. Mehrfarbig. (AUL)
74 Faltschachteln für Biscuits. Inhalt ist vierfarbig abgebildet. Die Farben der Streifen sind Grün, Hellgrün und Weiss auf der einen Schachtel, Rot, Orange und Weiss auf der anderen. (SWI)
75 Aufreisspackung für tiefgekühlte Backwaren. Mehrfarbig. Aus einem Packungssystem für den Supermarkt-Vertrieb. (USA)
76 Faltschachtel für Mandelgebäck. Dreifarbendruck. (SWI)
77 Tragpackung für Biscuits. Mehrfarbendruck. (JPN)
78 Packungsserie für vorgemischte Backzutaten. (AUS)

70 Boîtes pliantes pour gaufrettes roulées à la crème. L'illustration reproduit les contenus dans les couleurs naturelles. Texte rouge et brun. (ISR)
71 Boîte rigide pour une spécialité de biscuits bâlois. Impression polychrome. (SWI)
72 Boîtes de carton pour une gamme de bonbons au chocolat. Illustrations polychromes. La cartouche est imprimée en vert, bleu et ocre. Faces latérales vertes. (USA)
73 Carton pour un gâteau de Noël. En polychromie. (AUL)
74 Boîtes pliantes pour biscuits. Le contenu est illustré en polychromie. Les bandes sont respectivement vert, vert clair, blanc et rouge, orange, blanc. (SWI)
75 Emballage à bande d'arrachage pour pets-de-nonne surgelés. Impression polychrome. Elément du système de conditionnement d'une gamme d'articles de supermarchés. (USA)
76 Boîte pliante pour des biscuits aux amandes. Trichromie. (SWI)
77 Carton portatif pour biscuits. En polychromie. (JPN)
78 Série d'emballages pour pâtes à gâteaux. Polychromie. (AUS)

72

73

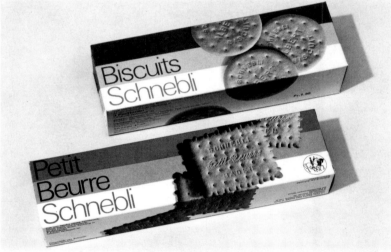

74

75

76

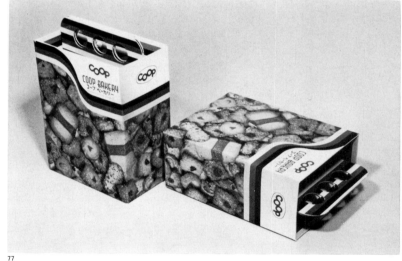

77

78

79

80

81

82

83

DESIGNER / GESTALTER / MAQUETTISTE:

79 Joe Selame (Photo: Jack O'Mahony Studio)
80 David Talmadge
81 Guglielmo Balucani
82 Don Weller
83 Doug Kato (Artist: Bob Densham)
84 Lyndon Whaite/Brian Sadgrove
85 Gonzalez Eusevi/Walter Köhler (Photo: Jorge Dahl)
86 Lothar Böhm
87 Lyndon Whaite

ART DIRECTOR / DIRECTEUR ARTISTIQUE:

79 Selame Design
81 Guglielmo Balucani
82 Dick Drayton
83 Tom Robbins
85 Gonzalez Eusevi/Walter Köhler

AGENCY / AGENTUR / AGENCE – STUDIO:

79 Selame Design Associates
80 THM Design Consultants Ltd.
81 Servizi Creativi IBP
82 Weller Institute
83 Southern California Carton Co.
84, 87 Emery, Fowler-Brown, Sadgrove & Whaite
85 Grant Advertising
86 Pack'age Promotion

CLIENT / AUFTRAGGEBER:

79 Concord Foods, Inc.
80 Nuttall Riley Co. Ltd.
81 IBP Industrie Buitoni Perugina
82, 83 Blum's Candies
84, 87 Trelavney Foods
85 Bonafide
86 Brokufa GmbH

84

85

79 Package for ingredients for preparing candy apples. Full colour. (USA)
80 Folding box for chocolate-covered brazil nuts. (GBR)
81 Packaging system for chocolate Easter eggs. The contents are enveloped in brightly coloured paper which is die-cut and glued to open up into a honeycomb pattern in egg form. The ribbons are either in matching or contrasting colours. (ITA)
82 Metal can containing fruit cake. Graphics in vivid colours. (USA)
83 Carrier carton representing an old-fashioned San Francisco street car, containing sugar candies. Colours are bright red, pink, ochre and black. (USA)
84, 87 Printed tin for biscuits and cloth bag containing a plum pudding. From a packaging range for speciality confections. (AUL)
85 Cardboard box for liqueur-filled chocolates. Full-colour printing. (ARG)
86 Printed acetate wrapper for sliced bread. (GER)

79 Verpackung für Zutaten zur Bereitung von gezuckerten «Liebesäpfeln». Vierfarbig. (USA)
80 Faltschachtel für Paranüsse mit Schokoladeüberzug. (GBR)
81 Packungssystem für Schokolade-Ostereier. Der Inhalt ist von einer farbenfrohen gestanzten und geklebten Papierhülle umgeben, die sich wabenartig zu einer Eiform öffnet. Die Bänder sind entweder in harmonierenden oder in kontrastierenden Farben gehalten. (ITA)
82 Metalldose für Fruchtkuchen. Graphik in lebhaften Farben. (USA)
83 Tragkarton in der Form eines alten Strassenbahnwagens aus San Francisco. Die Farben sind Grellrot, Rosa, Ocker und Schwarz. (USA)
84, 87 Bedruckte Blechdose für Gebäck und aus Tuch zusammengeknoteter Sack für Plumpudding. Aus einer Packungsreihe für Spezialitäten-Konfekt. (AUL)
85 Kartonschachtel für Liqueur-Pralinen. Mehrfarbige Illustration. (ARG)
86 Bedruckter Cellophanbeutel für in Scheiben geschnittenes Brot. (GER)

79 Emballage renfermant les ingrédients nécessaires pour la préparation de pommes confites. En polychromie. (USA)
80 Boîte pliante pour châtaignes du Brésil chocolatées. (GBR)
81 Ligne d'emballages pour œufs de Pâques en chocolat. Le papier aux couleurs vives est découpé à l'emporte-pièce et collé de manière à produire un relief en nid d'abeilles prenant la forme d'un œuf. Pour les rubans, on a employé des couleurs soit assorties, soit contrastantes. (ITA)
82 Boîte plate en métal pour un gâteau aux fruits. Présentation graphique aux couleurs vives. (USA)
83 Bonbonnière portative en carton sous forme d'un tramway de San Francisco de la Belle Epoque. Rouge vif, rose, ocre, noir. (USA)
84, 87 Boîte métallique à biscuits, avec impression à même le fer-blanc, et sachet textile contenant du plum-pudding. Exemples tirés d'une ligne d'emballages d'articles de confiserie fine. (AUL)
85 Boîte en carton pour des bonbons à la liqueur. Illustration polychrome. (ARG)
86 Sachet cellophane imprimé pour du pain en tranches. (GER)

86

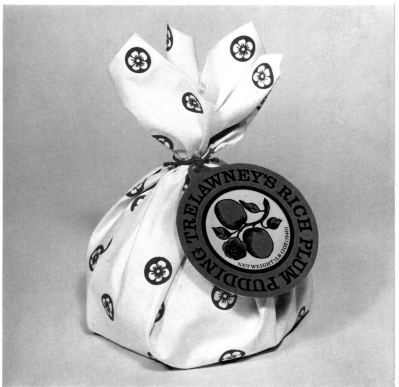

87

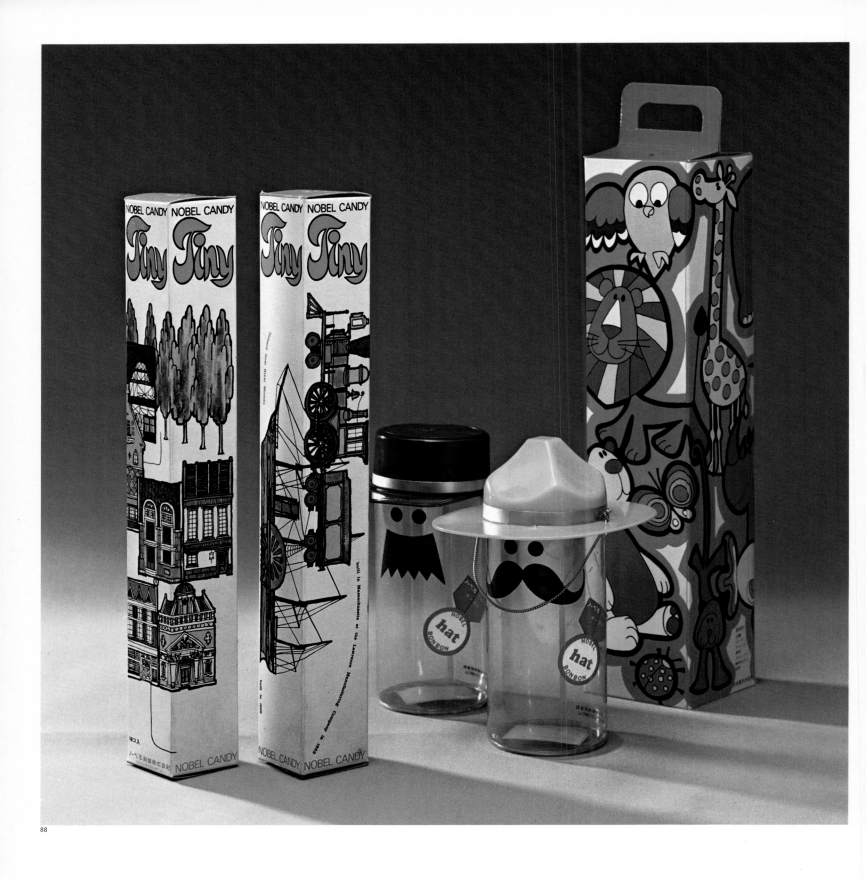

88

DESIGNER / GESTALTER / MAQUETTISTE:

88, 90 Hayao Kikuchi
89 Georges Lemoine
91 Gianni Marazzi
92 Erich Augstein

ART DIRECTOR / DIRECTEUR ARTISTIQUE:

88, 90 Hayao Kikuchi
89 Jacques Lavaux
91 Gianni Marazzi

CLIENT / AUFTRAGGEBER:

88, 90 Nobel Confectionery Co. Ltd.
89 Prisunic
91 Motta Panettoni S. p. A.
92 Born KG

Foods
Nahrungsmittel
Produits alimentaires

89

90

91

92

88 Folding boxes, carrier carton and transparent jars with plastic lids in the form of policemen's hats, from a line of gaily embellished candy packages. (JPN)
89 Design for a Christmas candy gift box for children, sold by a department store. The colourful mosaic is made entirely of wooden beads. (FRA)
90 Cardboard box and tin for candy. The outline drawing on the box is repeated on the tin, but with bright colours added. (JPN)
91 Christmas gift carton in white and two reds for confectionery. (ITA)
92 Folding box for dietary chocolate nuts. Four-colour printing. (GER)

88 Faltschachteln, Tragkarton und transparente Dosen mit Kunststoffdeckeln in Form von Polizistenhüten. Aus einer Serie farbenfroher Pralinenpackungen. (JPN)
89 Gestaltung einer Weihnachts-Schokoladepackung für Kinder aus einem Warenhaus-Sortiment. Das farbige Mosaik besteht aus Holzperlen. (FRA)
90 Kartonschachtel und Blechdose für Pralinen. Die Kontourzeichnung auf der Schachtel ist auf der Dose wiederholt, aber farbig ausgefüllt. (JPN)
91 Weihnachts-Geschenkpackung für Konfekt. Weiss und zwei Rottöne. (ITA)
92 Faltschachtel für Diät-Schokoladenüsse. Vierfarbig gedruckt. (GER)

88 Boîtes pliantes, carton portatif et verres transparents à couvercle plastique en forme de chapeau de policier. Ligne d'emballages de bonbons haute en couleur. (JPN)
89 Conception d'un emballage de Noël pour des chocolats pour enfants vendus dans un grand magasin. La mosaïque haute en couleur est entièrement en perles de bois. (FRA)
90 Bonbonnières en carton et en métal. Le motif du carton se retrouve sur la boîte ronde, mais en couleurs vives. (JPN)
91 Emballage-cadeau de confiserie pour Noël. Blanc et deux rouges. (ITA)
92 Boîte pliante pour des noisettes chocolatées de régime. Impression en 4 couleurs. (GER)

AGENCY / AGENTUR / AGENCE – STUDIO:

91 Studio G.M.D.
92 Erich Augstein

93

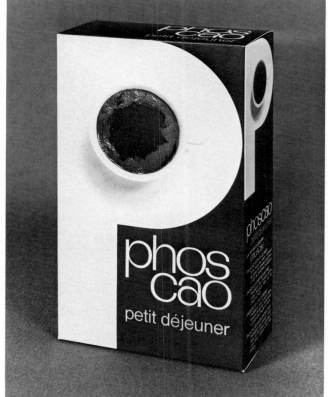

96

94

95

97

ART DIRECTOR / DIRECTEUR ARTISTIQUE:

95 Vincenzo Selmi
96 Francis Maurus
97 H. Uster
99 Roger Mayer
100 Cato Hibberd Hawksby Pty Ltd.
101 C. E. I.-Loewy
102 Pierre Rousselet

Foods
Nahrungsmittel
Produits alimentaires

98

99

100

101

102

93 Corrugated cardboard carrier pack for a fortifying instant drink. Lettering brown, ovals red to yellow, lid yellow. (SWI)
94 Salt and pepper dispenser boxes. White type on brightly coloured backgrounds. Used in cafeterias and lunchrooms. (USA)
95 Folding box for tea bags. Yellow, green and black. (SWI)
96 Box for a cocoa powder with phosphates. Brown, white. (FRA)
97 Can with plastic lid for an instant cocoa drink. Lettering red, blue, brown and black on beige. (SWI)
98 Can with plastic cover for an instant cocoa drink. (SWI)
99 Jar and label for freeze-dried instant coffee. (SWI)
100 Label design for a vitamin supplement drink. Lettering white, dots yellow, red to orange on black. (AUL)
101 Glass jar with plastic cover for a soluble chicory. Cover white, lettering white on red. (FRA)
102 Glass jar with plastic cover for instant coffee. Cover red, lettering white and red on black. (BRA)

93 Tragpackung aus Wellkarton für ein lösliches Nährmittel. Schrift braun, Ovale rot bis gelb, Deckel gelb. (SWI)
94 Salz- und Pfefferspender für Cafeterias und Snackrestaurants. Weisse Schrift auf farbigem Grund. (USA)
95 Schachtel für Teebeutel. Gelb, grün und schwarz. (SWI)
96 Schachtel für Kakaopulver mit Phosphaten. Braun, weiss. (FRA)
97 Dose mit Plastikdeckel für ein Kakaogetränk. Schrift rot, blau, braun und schwarz auf Beige. (SWI)
98 Dose mit Plastikdeckel für ein Kakaogetränk. (SWI)
99 Glas und Etikett für gefriergetrockneten Kaffee. (SWI)
100 Etikettgestaltung für ein Vitamin-Nährmittel. Schrift weiss, Punkte gelb, rot bis orange auf Schwarz. (AUL)
101 Glas mit Plastikdeckel für lösliches Zichorienpulver. Deckel weiss, Schrift weiss auf Rot. (FRA)
102 Glas mit Plastikdeckel für löslichen Kaffee. Deckel rot, Schrift weiss und rot auf Schwarz. (BRA)

93 Carton portatif ondulé pour une boisson fortifiante instantanée. Texte brun, ovales rouges à jaunes, couvercle jaune. (SWI)
94 Salière et poivrière pour cafétérias et snacks. Typo en blanc sur fond de couleur vive. (USA)
95 Boîte pliante pour sachets de thé. Jaune, vert, noir. (SWI)
96 Boîte pour un déjeuner phosphaté au cacao. Brun, blanc. (FRA)
97 Boîte à couvercle plastique, pour une boisson instantanée au cacao. Lettres blanc, bleu, brun, noir sur beige. (SWI)
98 Boîte à couvercle plastique pour une boisson au cacao. (SWI)
99 Verre et étiquette pour du café soluble lyophilisé. (SWI)
100 Conception d'étiquette pour une boisson fortifiante vitaminée. Texte blanc, points jaunes et rouges à oranges. (AUL)
101 Bocal en verre, à couvercle plastique blanc, pour de la chicorée soluble. Texte blanc sur rouge. (FRA)
102 Verre à couvercle plastique rouge pour du café soluble. Texte blanc et rouge sur noir. (BRA)

103

DESIGNER / GESTALTER / MAQUETTISTE:

103 H. Eichenberger
104 H. Eichenberger (Photo: Attilo Schuppisser)
105, 106, 108, 109 Gianni Marazzi
107 Marcello Minale/Brian Tattersfield
110 Mamoru Shiumokochi/Saul Bass & Assoc.
111, 112 E + U Hiestand

ART DIRECTOR / DIRECTEUR ARTISTIQUE:

103, 104 H. Eichenberger
105, 106, 108, 109 Gianni Marazzi
107 Marcello Minale/Brian Tattersfield
110 Art Goodman
111, 112 E + U Hiestand

AGENCY / AGENTUR / AGENCE – STUDIO:

103, 104 H. R. Abächerli
105, 106, 108, 109 Studio G. M. D.
107 Minale Tattersfield Provinciali Ltd.
110 Saul Bass & Assoc.
111, 112 E + U Hiestand/H. M. Eggmann

CLIENT / AUFTRAGGEBER:

103, 104 Coop Schweiz
105, 106, 108, 109 Motta Panettoni S. p. A.
107 Harrods Ltd.
110 Lawry's Foods, Inc.
111, 112 Maus Frères SA

104

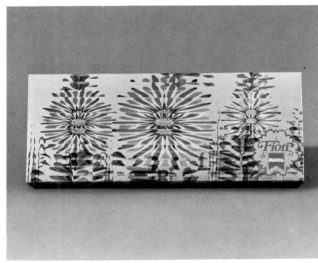

105

106

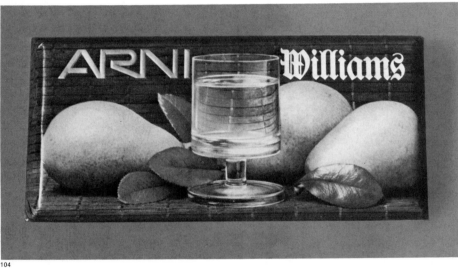

103, 104 Three examples from a line of chocolate bar wrappers. 103, top: Black, red and gold on white. Bottom and 104: Full-colour photos. (SWI)
105 From a range of colourful chocolate boxes with flower motifs. (ITA)
106 Display boxes for chocolates, colour coded in bright hues. (ITA)
107 Folding box for icing sugar. (GBR)
108 Gift boxes for chocolates for St. Valentine's Day. (ITA)
109 Box for iced chestnuts. The contents are shown in full colour in a setting of natural chestnut leaves and burrs. (ITA)
110 Front and back of a plastic bag for a snack food. Printed in red, green, brown and black. (USA)
111, 112 Chocolate bar wrappers. From a department-store family range. (SWI)

103, 104 Drei Beispiele aus einer Serie von Schokoladepackungen. 103, oben: Schwarz, Rot, Gold auf Weiss, Unten und 104: Farbaufnahmen. (SWI)
105 Aus einer Serie farbiger Pralinenschachteln mit Blumenmotiven. (ITA)
106 Ausstellschachteln für Schokolade. In lebhaften Farben gedruckt. (ITA)
107 Faltschachtel für Puderzucker. (GBR)
108 Geschenkpackungen für Schokolade für den St.-Valentins-Tag. (ITA)
109 Faltschachtel für kandierte Kastanien. Der Inhalt, umgeben von natürlichen Kastanienblättern und Hülsen, ist vierfarbig reproduziert. (ITA)
110 Vorder- und Rückseite eines Kunststoff-Beutels für getrocknete Apfelschnitze. Rot, grün, braun und schwarz bedruckt. (USA)
111, 112 Schokoladetafel-Einwickler. Beispiele aus einem Warenhaus-Packungssystem. (SWI)

103, 104 Trois exemples de conditionnement d'une gamme de tablettes de chocolat. 103, en haut: noir, rouge, or sur blanc. 103, en bas, et 104 en polychromie. (SWI)
105 Série de boîtes de chocolats aux gais coloris et motifs floraux. (ITA)
106 Boîtes présentoirs pour chocolats, codées en couleurs vives. (ITA)
107 Boîte pliante pour du sucre en poudre. (GBR)
108 Emballages-cadeaux de la St-Valentin pour des chocolats. (ITA)
109 Boîte de marrons glacés. Le contenu est reproduit en polychromie dans un décor de feuilles de châtaignier et de cupules épineuses. (ITA)
110 Recto et verso d'un sachet plastique pour tranches de pommes séchées. Impression en rouge, vert, brun et noir. (USA)
111, 112 Emballages de tablettes de chocolat pour un grand magasin. (SWI)

107

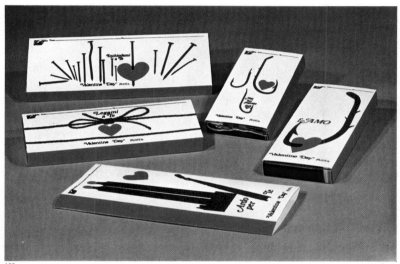

108

109

110

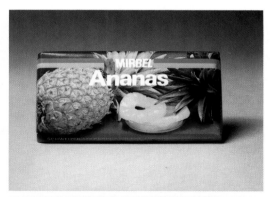

111, 112

113

114 , 115

DESIGNER / GESTALTER / MAQUETTISTE:

113 Yoshinori Ito/Atsuko Yamanaka
114–117 José Baquès/Martin Ballada
118, 119 Victoria Cero (Artist: Paul Davis)
120 Merrick Gagliani/Nancy Neidhammer
121 Jeissing Beiersdorf

ART DIRECTOR / DIRECTEUR ARTISTIQUE:

113 Yoshinori Ito
114–117 José Baquès
118, 119 Victoria Cero
120 Merrick Gagliani
121 Jeissing Beiersdorf

AGENCY / AGENTUR / AGENCE – STUDIO:

114–117 Estudio Baquès
118, 119 Young & Rubicam, Inc.
120 The Cadwell Davis Co.
121 Jeissing Beiersdorf

CLIENT / AUFTRAGGEBER:

114–117 Simel Vich
118–120 Chipurnoi, Inc.
121 Sprengel & Co.

116

117

118, 119

113 Prototype mock-up for a cardboard gift package for cakes and confectionery. (JPN)
114–117 Examples from a series of gaily coloured bonbon tins. Designs are based on the Zodiac. (SPA)
118, 119 Complete illustration and actual appearance of the wrapper for a roll of liquorice dragées. The wrapper is printed in full colour. (USA)
120 Display box and tin with traditional design for a syrup. Polychrome printing. (GBR)
121 Set-up gift box for chocolate candy. Embossed gold foil on black ground. (GER)

113 Prototyp-Entwurf für eine Karton-Geschenkschachtel für Kuchen und Konfekt. (JPN)
114–117 Beispiele aus einer Serie farbenfroher Bonbons-Blechdosen. Die Motive sind graphische Interpretationen der Zeichen des Tierkreises. (SPA)
118, 119 Ganze Illustration und vollständige Packung für eine Rolle Lakritzenbonbons. Mehrfarbig. (USA)
120 Ausstellschachtel und Dose mit traditioneller Gestaltung für einen Melassesirup. Mehrfarbig. (GBR)
121 Geschenkpackung für Pralinen. Goldfolienprägung auf schwarzem Grund. (GER)

113 Maquette d'un prototype de boîte-cadeau en carton pour pâtisserie et confiserie. (JPN)
114–117 Exemples d'une série de bonbonnières en fer-blanc aux couleurs gaies. Motifs empruntés au zodiaque. (SPA)
118, 119 Illustration polychrome complète et la forme qu'elle prend dans l'emballage d'un rouleau de bonbons à la réglisse. Le papier est imprimé en polychromie. (USA)
120 Boîte-présentoir et boîte métallique à la décoration traditionnelle pour un sirop de mélasse. Polychrome. (GBR)
121 Boîte de carton rigide pour chocolats. Feuille dorée gaufrée dans la masse, sur fond noir. (GER)

120

121

122

Foods
Nahrungsmittel
Produits alimentaires

123

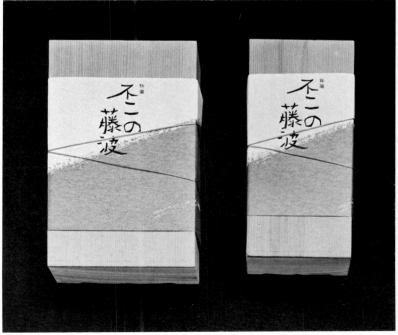

124

125

The last two double pages of this section have been set aside for the presentation of a sampling of typical Japanese food packages, most of them incorporating traditional design features. We wish to express our gratitude to the Japan Package Design Association for the help given in collecting this material.
122 Traditional Japanese confectionery packages. Lettering white on blue, wrapper printed black and red, tied with red and white cord.
123 Package of corrugated cardboard for plum candy, a traditional local sweetmeat.
124 Wooden boxes with a paper wrapper tied with string, containing kelp. Printed gold and black.
125 Cardboard folding boxes for green tea.
126 Cardboard and paper package for rice crackers. Yellow and brown ''poetry'' paper wrapper, gold cord.

Auf den letzten zwei Doppelseiten dieses Sektors sind einige Beispiele typisch japanischer Packungen für Nahrungsmittel gezeigt, wovon sich die meisten an traditionelle Vorbilder halten. Wir sind der Japan Package Design Association zu Dank verpflichtet für die uns beim Sammeln des Materials geleistete Hilfe.
122 Traditionelle japanische Konfekt-Packung. Schrift weiss auf Blau, Umschlagpapier schwarz und rot bedruckt, rot-weisse Kordel.
123 Packung aus Wellkarton für Bonbons aus Pflaumen, eine traditionelle Spezialität.
124 Holzschachteln mit verschnürtem Einwickler, für Seetang. Gold und schwarz bedruckt.
125 Faltschachtel für grünen Tee.
126 Packung aus Karton und Papier für Reisbiskuits. «Poesie»-Papiereinwickler mit Goldkordel.

Les deux dernières doubles pages de la présente section ont été réservées pour la présentation d'exemples typiques d'emballages japonais pour produits alimentaires, la plupart inspirés de modèles traditionnels. Nous remercions la Japan Package Design Association de son assistance lors de la collecte des matériaux réunis ici.
122 Emballage japonais traditionnel de confiserie. Texte blanc sur bleu, papier imprimé en noir et rouge, cordelette rouge et blanc.
123 Sachet de carton micro-ondulé pour des bonbons à base de prunes, une friandise traditionnelle.
124 Boîtes de varech, en bois, enveloppées de papier et ficelées. Impression noir et or.
125 Boîtes pliantes en carton pour du thé vert.
126 Emballage de carton et papier pour des biscuits au riz. Papier «de poésie» jaune et brun. L'emballage est retenu par une cordelette or.

126

DESIGNER / GESTALTER / MAQUETTISTE:

122 Katsu Kimura
123 Ryoichi Yamamoto
124 Takeshi Ohtaka
125 Eiko Sugimura
126 Kenji Maezawa/Takao Miura/Kenni Mura

ART DIRECTOR / DIRECTEUR ARTISTIQUE:

122 Katsu Kimura
123 Ryoichi Yamamoto
124 Takeshi Ohtaka
125 Toshio Sugimura
126 Kenji Maezawa

AGENCY / AGENTUR / AGENCE – STUDIO:

122 Packaging Direction Co. Ltd.

CLIENT / AUFTRAGGEBER:

122 Roba Confectionery
123 Ryurindo Confectionery Co.
124 Fuji Food Co. Ltd.
125 Chikumeido
126 Kakiyama Meika Co. Ltd.

127

DESIGNER / GESTALTER / MAQUETTISTE:

127 Yoshimasa Kawakami/Akemi Kashima
128 Yoshiaki Kubota
129 Shigeru Akizuki
130 Kokichi Shirakawa
131 Shozo Kakutani
132 Shigeo Okamoto/Shunyo Yamauchi (Artist: Shunyo Yamauchi)

ART DIRECTOR / DIRECTEUR ARTISTIQUE:

127 Yoshimasa Kawakami
128 Soyama Haruo
130 Kokichi Shirakawa
131 Shozo Kakutani
132 Shigeo Okamoto

AGENCY / AGENTUR / AGENCE – STUDIO:

127 Honshu Paper Co. Ltd.
128 Kubota Design
130 Shirakawa Design Office Co.
131 Kakutani Design Office

CLIENT / AUFTRAGGEBER:

127 Hyobando Co. Ltd.
128 Harada Seicha Co. Ltd.
130 Hoshigen Confectionery Co.
131 Hareruya Confectionery Co.
132 France-ya Confectionery

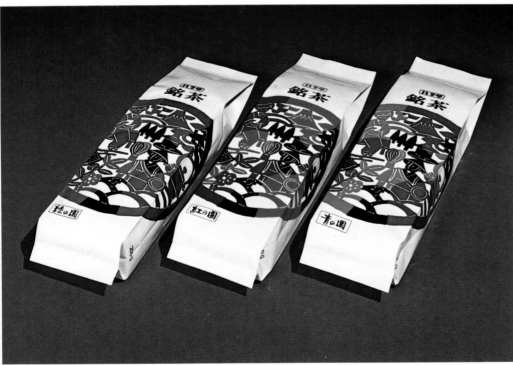

128

127–132 See note on the previous page concerning the illustrations on the last two double pages of this section.
127 Cardboard boxes from a range of packages for rice crackers.
128 Paper bags with patterns in a woodcut technique, containing different blends of tea.
129 Cylindrical carton for bottles of seasoning. Project prepared for an exhibition.
130 Packs of rolled sweet jelly beans in a wooden gift box.
131 Traditional bamboo basket and wrapper for rice cake.
132 Cardboard slide box containing chocolate candy. Stripe design in gold, dark brown and purple. Lettering dark brown on purple ground.

Foods
Nahrungsmittel
Produits alimentaires

129

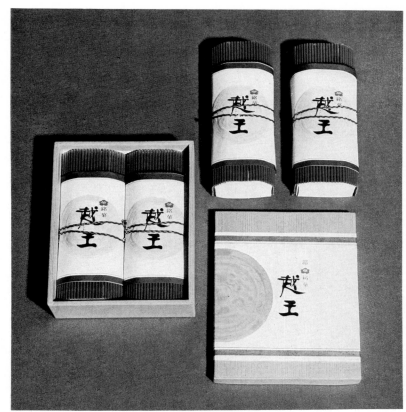

130

131

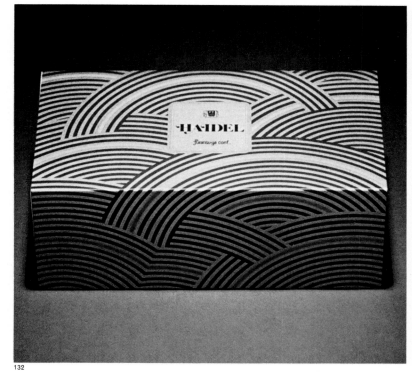

132

127–132 Siehe Mitteilung auf Seite 65 in bezug auf die auf den letzten zwei Doppelseiten dieses Sektors gezeigten Packungen.
127 Karton-Faltschachteln aus einer Packungsreihe für Reisbiskuits.
128 Papierbeutel mit Motiv in Holzschnitt-Technik für drei verschiedene Teesorten.
129 Zylindrischer Karton für Gewürzflaschen. Entwurf für eine Ausstellung.
130 Packungen für süsse Gummibonbons in einer Geschenkschachtel aus Holz.
131 Traditioneller Bambuskorb mit Papiereinwickler für Reiskuchen.
132 Schieberschachtel aus Karton für Pralinen. Streifenmuster in Gold, Dunkelbraun und Violett, Schrift dunkelbraun auf violettem Grund.

127–132 Voir la notice de la page précédente relative aux illustrations des deux dernières doubles pages de la présente section.
127 Boîtes pliantes en carton figurant dans une ligne de conditionnements de biscuits au riz.
128 Sachets en papier illustrés de motifs de gravures sur bois, avec diverses sortes de thé.
129 Etui cylindrique en carton pour des flacons de condiments. Etude pour une exposition.
130 Emballages de bonbons à la gomme en rouleaux présentés dans une boîte-cadeau en bois.
131 Emballage traditionnel de gâteau au riz: panier de bambou enveloppé de papier.
132 Boîte coulissante en carton pour des bonbons au chocolat. Rayures or, brun foncé et pourpre, texte brun foncé sur fond pourpré.

Beverages
Getränke
Boissons

2

133

DESIGNER / GESTALTER / MAQUETTISTE:

133 Morton Goldsholl
134 Vance Johnson
135–137 Bruno Oldani
138 Cato Hibberd Hawksby Pty Ltd.
139 Jerome Gould

ART DIRECTOR / DIRECTEUR ARTISTIQUE:

133 Morton Goldsholl
134 Vance Johnson
135–137 Bruno Oldani
138 Cato Hibberd Hawksby Pty Ltd.
139 Jerome Gould

AGENCY / AGENTUR / AGENCE – STUDIO:

133 Goldsholl Associates
134 John Rockwell & Assoc.
135–137 Bruno Oldani
138 Masius Wynne Williams D'Arcy MacManus (Aust.)
139 Gould & Assoc., Inc.

CLIENT / AUFTRAGGEBER:

133 The Seven-up Company
134 Wisty Co.
135 Holmen Braenderi
136, 137 Lillehammer Bryggeri
138 Cadbury Schweppes Pty Ltd.
139 Pepsi Cola Co.

134

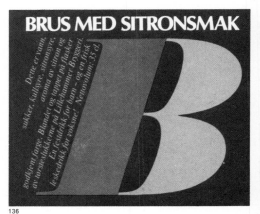

136

133 Design concept carried through on can, bottle and carrier carton for a soft drink. (USA)
134 Carrier carton and bottle design for a soft drink. (USA)
135 Label designs for a range of soft drinks used as cocktail mixers. Very bright colours are used for the various focal ornaments as well as for the backgrounds. (NOR)
136, 137 Bottle labels for a range of mineral waters. The large letters represent the initials of the various contents. Fig. 136 shows the entire label. (NOR)
138 Labels and collars for a line of fruit-flavoured soft drinks. Colours harmonize with contents. (AUL)
139 Re-styling of the can design for the regular and the dietary variant of a cola soft drink. (USA)

133 Packungsausstattung für Büchse, Flasche und Tragkarton eines alkoholfreien Getränkes. (USA)
134 Tragkarton- und Flaschengestaltung für ein alkoholfreies Fruchtsaft-Getränk. (USA)
135 Etikettgestaltung für eine Serie alkoholfreier Getränke, die auch zum Mixen von Cocktails verwendet werden. Starke Farben für Grund sowie für Ornamente. (NOR)
136, 137 Flaschenetiketten für eine Reihe von Mineralwassern. Die grossen Buchstaben stellen die Initialen des jeweiligen Inhalts dar. 136 Ganzes Etikett. (NOR)
138 Flaschenausstattung für Getränke mit Fruchtaromen. Die Etikettfarben harmonieren mit dem Inhalt. (AUL)
139 Neugestaltung der Büchsen für ein Kolagetränk und seine Diät-Variante. (USA)

133 Conception unitaire du conditionnement appliquée à une boîte, une bouteille et un carton portatif pour une boisson sans alcool. (USA)
134 Carton portatif et bouteille pour une limonade. (USA)
135 Etiquettes pour une gamme de boissons sans alcool également utilisées pour mixer des cocktails. Les motifs décoratifs et le fond sont imprimés en couleurs brillantes. (NOR)
136, 137 Etiquettes de bouteilles pour une série d'eaux minérales. Les lettres géantes sont les initiales des noms des boissons en question. 136 Etiquette complète. (NOR)
138 Etiquettes et collerettes d'une gamme de boissons sans alcool à goût fruité. Couleurs accordées au contenu. (AUL)
139 Nouvelle conception de boîtes pour une boisson au cola et sa variante diététique. (USA)

135

137

138

139

140

141

142

DESIGNER / GESTALTER / MAQUETTISTE:

140 Manfred Dietze/Werner Würdinger
141, 144 Les Mason (Artist: Bill Kwan)
142 Beni Schalcher
143 Eurographic Ltd.
145 Eric Small/Herman L. Vanderberg
146 Willy Althaus
147 Dieter Cordes/Ulrich Jennessen (Photo: Rolf Dieter Best)

140 Bottle and label styling for fruit juices. (GER)
141 Can, bottle and label design for an orange drink. (AUL)
142 Label design for a black-currant drink. Lettering and design in shades of purple. (SWI)
143 Cans and carrier pack for beer. Lettering yellow and white on blue, ship black. (GBR)
144 Can design for a lemon drink. (AUL)
145 Bottle design for a cola drink. The lettering is printed directly on the bottle. (USA)
146 Bottle and label for an orange drink. (SWI)
147 Folding box for an instant orange drink. Lettering black, photo reproduced in full colour. (GER)

140 Flaschen-Ausstattung für Fruchtsäfte. (GER)
141 Flaschen- und Büchsenausstattung für ein Getränk. (AUL)
142 Etikettgestaltung für ein Getränk aus schwarzen Johannisbeeren. Graphik in Violett-Tönen. (SWI)
143 Büchsen und Tragpackung für Bier. Schrift gelb und weiss auf Blau. Segelschiff schwarz. (GBR)
144 Büchsengestaltung für ein Zitronengetränk. (AUL)
145 Flaschengestaltung für ein Kolagetränk. Die Schrift ist direkt auf die Flasche aufgedruckt. (USA)
146 Flasche und Etikett für ein Orangengetränk. (SWI)
147 Faltschachtel für ein lösliches Orangengetränk. Schrift schwarz, Photo vierfarbig reproduziert. (GER)

140 Présentation de bouteilles et étiquettes de jus de fruits. (GER)
141 Boîte, bouteille, étiquettes pour une orangeade. (AUL)
142 Etiquette pour une boisson à base de cassis. Lettres et dessin en tons pourprés. (SWI)
143 Boîte et carton six-packs de bière. Texte jaune et blanc sur bleu, navire noir. (GBR)
144 Etude de boîte pour une citronnade. (AUL)
145 Conception de bouteille pour une boisson au cola. Impression du texte à même la bouteille. (USA)
146 Bouteille et étiquette pour une orangeade. (SWI)
147 Brique de carton pour une orangeade instantanée en poudre. Caractères noirs, photo polychrome. (GER)

143

144

ART DIRECTOR / DIRECTEUR ARTISTIQUE:

140 Werner Würdinger
141, 144 Les Mason
142 Pierre Jeanmonod
143 Eurographic Ltd.
145 Herman L. Vanderberg
146 Willy Althaus
147 Dieter Cordes

AGENCY / AGENTUR / AGENCE – STUDIO:

140 Werbeagentur Gottschling
141, 144 Masius Wynne Williams D'Arcy MacManus Pty Ltd.
142 Roth & Sauter SA
143 Eurographic Ltd.
145 The Marschalk Co.
146 Jean P. Wälchli
147 Institut für Packungsgestaltung

CLIENT / AUFTRAGGEBER:

140 Robbe & Berking
141, 144 Tarax Proprietary Ltd.
142 Hertig Vins
143 Hull Brewery Co. Ltd.
145 Coca Cola Co.
146 Mars, Rheinfelder Mineralquellen AG
147 S. A. Bacona

145

146

147

148

149

150

151

DESIGNER / GESTALTER / MAQUETTISTE:

148 Edgar Wyard
149 Jerome Gould
150 F. Steiner
151 Morgan Ziller
152 Nikolaus Müller-Behrendt
153 Paul Buelman
154, 155 Bruno Oldani
156 Gen Naito
157 Siebert/Head Ltd.
158 C. E. I.-Loewy

ART DIRECTOR / DIRECTEUR ARTISTIQUE:

150 Max Rindlisbacher
152 Hans Demuth
153 Paul Buelman
154, 155 Bruno Oldani
156 Gen Naito
157 Ed Siebert/Tony Watts
158 C. E. I.-Loewy

AGENCY / AGENTUR / AGENCE – STUDIO:

148 THM Design Consultants Ltd.
149 Gould & Assoc., Inc.
150 Gisler & Gisler
151 Bloom Agency
152 Marktwerbung H. J. Wagner GmbH & Co.
153 Buelman & Klaesi Pty Ltd.
154, 155 Bruno Oldani
157 Siebert/Head Ltd.
158 C. E. I.-Loewy

CLIENT / AUFTRAGGEBER:

148 Schweppes (Home) Ltd.
149 Associated Products & Distribution Pty Ltd.
150 Bier-Interessengemeinschaft Lubi AG
151 Jackson Brewing Co.
152 Iserlohner Brauerei AG
153 Brauerei Feldschlösschen AG
154, 155 Lillehammer Bryggeri
156 Kirin Beer Co. Ltd.
157 Watney Mann Ltd.
158 Union de Brasseries

152

148 Labels for a line of soft drinks. (GBR)
149 Bottle styling for lemonade. Lettering printed directly on the bottle. (USA)
150 Bottle and label for a premium beer. (SWI)
151 Bottle and can for beer. Ground colour silver, stripes black, orange and yellow. (USA)
152 Bottle styling for premium beer. Labels white, gold and black, lettering black and gold. (GER)
153 One of a series of beer labels. Lettering blue on white. Trade mark red and yellow. (SWI)
154, 155 Beer bottle with die-cut label (155). Anchor in bright colours, lettering black. (NOR)
156 Can styling for lager beer. Gold, red and white, black lettering. (JPN)
157 Beer can. Lettering red and gold on white. (GBR)
158 Styling for beer bottle and glass. Label black and gold, brand name white. (FRA)

Beverages
Getränke
Boissons

155

153

154

156

157

158

159

Beverages
Getränke
Boissons

160

161

162

CLIENT / AUFTRAGGEBER:

159 Brauerei Riegele
160 Sais AG
161 Brauerei Rob. Leicht AG
162 Arthur Guinness Son & Co. Ltd.
163, 164 Tuborg Breweries

163

164

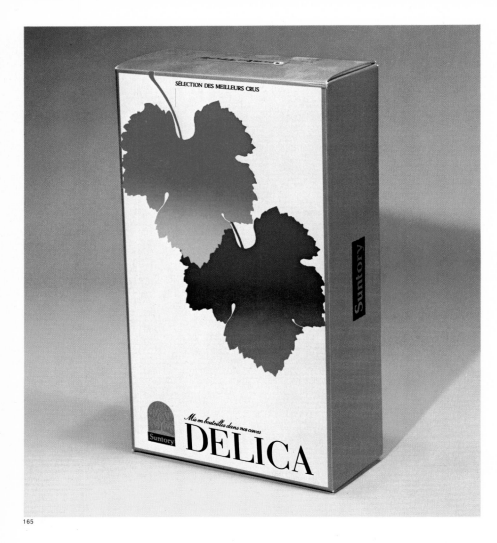

165

166

167

168

169

Beverages
Getränke
Boissons

170

171

DESIGNER / GESTALTER / MAQUETTISTE:

165, 166, 172 Shigeshi Omori
167, 168 Ernest Witzig
169 Les Mason
170 Fred Huber
171 G. Rampazzo

ART DIRECTOR / DIRECTEUR ARTISTIQUE:

165, 166, 172 Shigeshi Omori
167, 168 Michel Logoz
169 Les Mason
170 Jonathan Milne
171 G. Rampazzo

AGENCY / AGENTUR / AGENCE – STUDIO:

167, 168 Roth & Sauter SA
169 Hayes Advertising
170 Taylor O'Brian Advertising
171 Studio Erre

CLIENT / AUFTRAGGEBER:

165, 166, 172 Suntory Ltd.
167 Hammel SA
168 Orsat SA
169 Trevor Craddock
170 Spring Valley Pty Ltd.
171 Friuldistillati S. p. A.

165 Cardboard gift package for two bottles of wine. (JPN)
166 Bottle and label styling for a rosé wine. (JPN)
167 Labelling for a bottle of rosé wine. Ground colour of label and collar is beige, name and emblem printed in gold and orange-brown. (SWI)
168 Label design for a bottle of white wine. Labels white, lettering and ornamentation printed in gold, black, brown and beige. (SWI)
169 Bottle styling for a red wine. (AUL)
170 Bottle styling for cider. Black and silver, red apple, green bottle. (AUL)
171 Bottle and label design for a twenty-year-old Sicilian wine. The die-cut label has the shape of the island of Sicily. Bottle brown, label gold-coloured. (ITA)
172 Cartons for wine bottles. Printed in brown, yellow, beige and black. (JPN)

165 Geschenkschachtel aus Karton für zwei Flaschen Wein. (JPN)
166 Flaschen- und Etikettgestaltung für einen Roséwein. (JPN)
167 Etikettierung für eine Roséweinflasche. Grundfarbe des Etiketts und des Kragens ist beige, Name und Schutzmarke in Rotorange und Gold. (SWI)
168 Etikettgestaltung für eine Flasche Weisswein. Etikette weiss. Beschriftung und Ornamentierung in Gold, Schwarz, Braun und Beige. (SWI)
169 Flaschenausstattung für einen Rotwein. (AUL)
170 Flaschenausstattung für Apfelsaft. Schwarz und Silber, Apfel rot, Flasche grün. (AUL)
171 Flaschenausstattung für einen 20jährigen sizilianischen Wein. Das gestanzte Etikett hat die Form der Insel Sizilien. Flasche braun, Etikett in Gold. (ITA)
172 Weinflaschen-Packungen. Braun, gelb, beige und schwarz bedruckt. (JPN)

165 Carton-cadeau renfermant deux bouteilles de vin. (JPN)
166 Conception de bouteille et d'étiquette pour un rosé. (JPN)
167 Etiquette conçue pour une bouteille de rosé. Le nom et l'emblème sont imprimés en or et orange-brun sur fond beige, tant sur l'étiquette que sur la collerette. (SWI)
168 Conception d'étiquette pour une bouteille de vin blanc. Etiquettes blanches, typo et motifs décoratifs en or, noir, brun et beige. (SWI)
169 Etude de bouteille pour un vin rouge. (AUL)
170 Etude de bouteille pour du cidre. Noir, argent, pomme rouge, bouteille verte. (AUL)
171 Conception de l'étiquette (or) et de la bouteille (brune) pour un vin de Sicile de vingt ans d'âge. L'étiquette découpée à l'emporte-pièce affecte la forme de l'île. (ITA)
172 Cartons de bouteilles de vin. Impression en brun, jaune, beige et noir. (JPN)

172

173

174

175

176

Beverages
Getränke
Boissons

DESIGNER / GESTALTER / MAQUETTISTE:

173, 176, 183, 184 Emanuel Bosshart
174, 175, 179, 180 Ernest Witzig
177 Danny Bhang/Jerome Gould
178 Peter Dixon
181 Charles Goslin
182, 185 Ivan Chermayeff

ART DIRECTOR / DIRECTEUR ARTISTIQUE:

173–175, 180, 183, 184 Michel Logoz
176, 179 Peter Strickler
177 Jerome Gould
178 Peter Dixon
181 Charles Goslin

AGENCY / AGENTUR / AGENCE – STUDIO:

173–176, 179, 180, 183, 184 Roth & Sauter SA
177 Gould & Associates, Inc.
178 Sainsbury's Design Studio
181 Barnett/Goslin/Barnett
182, 185 Chermayeff & Geismar Associates

CLIENT / AUFTRAGGEBER:

173, 175, 183, 184 Coop Schweiz
174 Obrist SA
176 Volg
177 Paul Masson Vineyards
178 J. Sainsbury Ltd.
179 Schuler & Cie SA
180 Henri Badoux
181 Crescenzo Winery
182, 185 S. E. A. R. SA

177

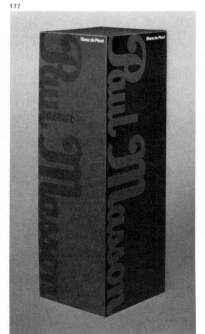

178

179

180

181

173 Labelling for a bottle of red wine. Red, white and gold on black. (SWI)
174 Bottle label for a Spanish wine bottled in Switzerland. Portrait in grey tones on brown ground. (SWI)
175 Bottle styling for a Provence wine bottled in Switzerland. (SWI)
176 Labelling for a Swiss wine. A historical figure from the region is used for the illustration. (SWI)
177 Carton for a bottle of white wine. In glossy and dull blacks. (USA)
178 Labelling for a bottle of Spanish sherry sold in England. (GBR)
179 Label for a Swiss rosé wine. Gold birds, name and rose in light red, black lettering, pale yellow label. (SWI)
180 Bottle styling for a Swiss red wine. Labels and cap gold on black. (SWI)
181 Label design for a line of American wines. Label colours vary. (USA)
182, 185 Bottle and label for a red Rhone wine sold in America. (USA)
183, 184 Bottle and label for an Italian wine marketed in Switzerland. Red, orange, yellow and gold on black. (SWI)

173 Flaschen-Etikettierung für einen Rotwein aus dem Wallis. Beschriftung in Rot, Weiss und Gold auf schwarzem Grund. (SWI)
174 Flaschen-Etikett für einen in der Schweiz abgefüllten spanischen Wein. Portrait in Grautönen auf braunem Grund. (SWI)
175 Etikettierung für einen in der Schweiz abgefüllten Provencewein. (SWI)
176 Flaschenausstattung für einen Schweizer Wein. Eine Figur aus der Lokalgeschichte dieses Weinbaugebietes dient als Illustration. (SWI)
177 Packung für eine Weissweinflasche. In Matt- und Glanzschwarz. (USA)
178 Flaschenetikettierung für spanischen Sherry, in England verkauft. (GBR)
179 Etikett für eine Flasche Schweizer Roséwein. Vögel in Gold, Name und Rose in Hellrot, schwarze Schrift, hellgelbes Etikett. (SWI)
180 Flaschengestaltung für einen Rotwein aus der Schweiz. Etikett und Verschluss in Gold auf Schwarz. (SWI)
181 Etikettgestaltung für eine Serie amerikanischer Weine. Die Grundfarbe der Etiketten variiert je nach Sorte. (USA)
182, 185 Flasche und Etikett für einen in Amerika vertriebenen Wein. (USA)
183, 184 Flasche und Etikett für einen in der Schweiz verkauften italienischen Wein. Rot, Orange, Gelb und Gold auf Schwarz. (SWI)

173 Etiquette pour un vin rouge du Valais. Rouge, blanc, or sur noir. (SWI)
174 Etiquette de bouteille pour un vin espagnol embouteillé en Suisse. Portrait imprimé en tons gris sur fond brun. (SWI)
175 Etude de bouteille pour un vin de Provence embouteillé en Suisse. (SWI)
176 Etiquette conçue pour un vin suisse. Un personnage historique de la région vinicole en question sert d'élément accrocheur. (SWI)
177 Carton pour une bouteille de vin blanc. Noirs mats et brillants. (USA)
178 Etiquette pour un xérès espagnol vendu en Grande-Bretagne. (GBR)
179 Etiquette conçue pour un rosé suisse. Motif d'oiseaux en or, nom et rose en rouge clair, texte noir, étiquette jaune clair. (SWI)
180 Bouteille pour un vin rouge suisse. Etiquette et capsule or sur noir. (SWI)
181 Etiquette-type, à code-couleur, pour une gamme de vins américains. (USA)
182, 185 Bouteille et étiquette pour un rouge français vendu aux USA. (USA)
183, 184 Etude de bouteille et d'étiquette pour un vin italien distribué en Suisse. Rouge, orange, jaune et or sur noir. (SWI)

184

182

183

185

Beverages
Getränke
Boissons

DESIGNER / GESTALTER / MAQUETTISTE:

186 Claude Dietrich
187 Jacques Perrenoud
188, 189 Les Mason/Sandie Clarke
190, 191 Malcolm Smith
192 Les Mason
    (Artist: Les Mason/Sylvia Hennessey)
193 Malcolm Smith/Les Mason
194, 195 Ernest Smith
196 John Blackburn

ART DIRECTOR / DIRECTEUR ARTISTIQUE:

186 Claude Dietrich
187 Pierre Jeanmonod
188, 189, 192, 193 Les Mason
190, 191 Malcolm Smith
194, 195 Michel Logoz

AGENCY / AGENTUR / AGENCE – STUDIO:

187, 194, 195 Roth & Sauter SA
188–193 Les Mason Graphic Design

CLIENT / AUFTRAGGEBER:

186 Diner's Club
187 La Cave Vevey-Montreux
188, 189 Riverboat Investments
190, 191 Cumberland Hotels
192 Two Faces Restaurant
193 Eagle Hotel
194 Orsat SA
195 Merkur AG
196 Cockburn Smithes & Co. Ltd.

186

187

186 Labelling for a bottle of Peruvian wine specially bottled for use in Diner's Club restaurants. (PER)
187 Bottle styling for a Swiss white wine. The illustration of the quaffing scene is done in the manner of a mediaeval illumination, in full colour. (SWI)
188, 189 House labels for Australian wines specially bottled for a restaurant installed aboard a paddle steamer. Gold foil capping. (AUL)
190 Bottle label for an Australian wine from the cellars of a hotel. (AUL)
191 Labelling for Australian wine privately bottled for a hotel. (AUL)
192 Two variants of the bottle styling for an Australian white wine specially bottled for a restaurant. Black and white and black and gold. (AUL)
193 Bottle styling for an Australian wine privately bottled for a hotel. Lettering black on white ground, seal red. (AUL)
194 Styling for a bottle of clear distilled spirit made from wine. (SWI)
195 Bottle styling for a Swiss white wine. Labels gold on brown. (SWI)
196 Styling for a bottle of port wine in traditional shape. Lettering is applied by means of silk-screen fired-in ceramic printing. Embossed seal. (GBR)

186 Etikettierung für eine Flasche peruanischen Weins, der speziell für den Ausschank in Diner's Club Restaurants abgefüllt wird. (PER)
187 Flaschenausstattung .für einen Schweizer Weisswein. Die farbige Illustration der Trinkszene imitiert den Stil mittelalterlicher Illuminationen. (SWI)
188, 189 Haus-Flaschenetiketten für speziell abgefüllte australische Weine für ein Restaurant, das sich auf einem Raddampfer befindet. Goldfolienverschluss. (AUL)
190 Flaschenetikett für einen australischen Wein aus dem Keller eines Hotels. (AUL)
191 Etikettierung für einen speziell für ein Hotel abgefüllten Wein. (AUL)
192 Zwei Variationen der Flaschenausstattung für einen speziell für ein Restaurant abgefüllten Weisswein. Weiss auf Schwarz und Schwarz auf Gold. (AUL)
193 Flaschenausstattung für einen speziell für ein Hotel abgefüllten Wein. Schrift weiss auf Schwarz, rotes Siegel. (AUL)
194 Flaschenausstattung für einen klaren Branntwein. (SWI)
195 Flaschenausstattung für einen Weisswein. Etikett Gold auf Braun. (SWI)
196 Ausstattung für eine Portweinflasche in traditioneller Form. Beschriftung in Siebdruck mit keramischer Farbe angebracht und eingebrannt. (GBR)

186 Etiquette pour une bouteille de vin péruvien embouteillée à l'usage exclusif des restaurants affiliés au Diner's Club. (PER)
187 Conception de bouteille pour un vin blanc suisse. L'illustration polychrome (scène de taverne) est exécutée dans le style d'une enluminure du Moyen Age. (SWI)
188, 189 Etiquettes maison pour des vins australiens embouteillés à l'usage exclusif d'un restaurant installé à bord d'un bateau à aubes. Capsule dorée. (AUL)
190 Etiquette de bouteille pour un vin australien embouteillé pour un hôtel. (AUL)
191 Conception d'étiquette pour un vin australien embouteillé pour un hôtel. (AUL)
192 Deux variantes du style de bouteille conçu pour un vin blanc australien embouteillé pour un restaurant. Noir sur blanc et noir sur or. (AUL)
193 Etude de bouteille pour un vin australien embouteillé pour un hôtel. Lettres noires sur fond blanc, sceau rouge. (AUL)
194 Etude de bouteille pour une eau-de-vie claire. (SWI)
195 Conception de bouteille pour un vin blanc suisse. Etiquette or sur brun. (SWI)
196 Conception de bouteille traditionnelle pour un porto. Le texte est imprimé en sérigraphie, en couleurs céramiques recuites. Sceau en relief. (GBR)

192

188

189

190

191

193

194

195

196

197

197 Gift carton for a sweet wine and a whisky. Wine-red and pink. (JPN)
198 Cardboard box for sample bottles of four different champagnes. The die-cut windows expose the differently coloured labels. (USA)
199 Folding boxes for California champagnes. Emblem and lettering printed red on white and black on brown board. (USA)
200 Gift carton and bottle for a dessert wine. Illustrations and label in subdued colours. Bright red dot on bottle collar. (JPN)
201 Gift carton and bottle for champagne. Black, gold and red. (GER)
202 Carrier carton for Madeira wine bottles. Full colour. (POR)
203 Gift carton for a cherry wine imported from Denmark. Brand name black, figure in full colour on white ground. (USA)
204 Carrier bag for wine bottle. Red, orange, white on metallic stock. (USA)

197 Geschenkschachtel für süssen Wein und Whisky. Weinrot und rosa. (JPN)
198 Kartonschachtel für Champagner-Musterfläschchen. Die gestanzten Fenster machen die verschiedenfarbige Etikette sichtbar. (USA)
199 Faltschachteln für kalifornischen Champagner. Schutzmarke und Beschriftung rot auf Weiss und schwarz auf Braun. (USA)
200 Geschenkkarton und Flasche für einen Dessertwein. Illustration und Etikett in verhaltenen Farben. Roter Punkt auf Flaschenkragen. (JPN)
201 Geschenkschachtel und Flasche für Sekt. Schwarz, Gold und Rot. (GER)
202 Tragschachtel für Madeirawein-Flaschen. Vierfarbig gedruckt. (POR)
203 Geschenkschachtel für einen aus Dänemark importierten Kirschenwein. Markenname schwarz, Figur vierfarbig auf weissem Grund. (USA)
204 Tragtasche für Weinflaschen. Rot, Orange, Weiss auf Metallfolie. (USA)

197 Carton-cadeau (vin sucré et whisky). Rouge vineux et rose. (JPN)
198 Boîte en carton pour flacons-échantillons de quatre champagnes différents, dont les étiquettes au code-couleur sont visibles. (USA)
199 Cartons pliants pour du champagne de Californie. Marque déposée et texte imprimés en rouge sur blanc et noir sur brun. (USA)
200 Carton-cadeau et bouteille réalisés pour un vin de dessert. Illustration et étiquette en tons mats. Point rouge vif sur la collerette. (JPN)
201 Carton-cadeau et bouteille de champagne. Noir, or, rouge. (GER)
202 Carton portatif pour des bouteilles de madère. En polychromie. (POR)
203 Carton-cadeau pour un vin aux cerises importé du Danemark. Marque déposée en noir, personnage polychrome sur fond blanc. (USA)
204 Sac en feuille métallique rouge, orange, blanc pour bouteilles de vin. (USA)

DESIGNER / GESTALTER / MAQUETTISTE:

197 Shigeru Akizuki
198, 199 Graeme Thomson
200 Kanji Sasaki
201 Dieter Brunnet
202 Bruno Oldani
203 Sidney Rothberg
204 Primo Angeli (Artist: Primo Angeli)

198

199

200

201

ART DIRECTOR / DIRECTEUR ARTISTIQUE:

197 Shigeru Akizuki
198, 199 David Reid
200 Kanji Sasaki
201 Dieter Brunnet
202 Bruno Oldani
203 Frederick Siebel
204 Primo Angeli/David Reid

AGENCY / AGENTUR / AGENCE – STUDIO:

197 Akizuki Design Office
201 Werbeabteilung Henkell
202 Bruno Oldani
203 Sidney Rothberg Associates
204 Primo Angeli Graphics

CLIENT / AUFTRAGGEBER:

197 Godo Shusei Co.
198, 199, 204 Paul Masson Vineyards
200 Suntory Ltd.
201 Henkell & Co.
202 Leacock & Co.
203 General Wine & Spirits

202

203

204

205

206

207

208

209

210

205 Carrier carton for a bottle of pear brandy. Polychrome. (SWI)
206 Folding box for a bottle of choice cognac. (FRA)
207 Bottle styling for a brand of vodka. Red and white on black. (USA)
208 Bottle styling for white and red wines. Label lettering in black and gold on white ground. (JPN)
209 Labelling for a bottle of old rum. Bottle brown. Upper label gold with black and red lettering, oval label gold and white on black. (AUL)
210 Brandy bottle. Lettering gold on black label. (AUL)
211 Bottle styling for white and gold tequila, an imported Mexican brandy. Labels in colour with embossed gold embellishments. (USA)
212 Bottle styling for a clear grain spirit. (NLD)

205 Tragkarton für eine Flasche Birnenbranntwein. Mehrfarbig. (SWI)
206 Faltschachtel für einen französischen Cognac. (FRA)
207 Flaschengestaltung für eine Wodkamarke. Rot-weiss auf Schwarz. (USA)
208 Flaschenausstattung für Weiss- und Rotwein. Beschriftung der Etikette in Schwarz und Gold auf weissem Grund. (JPN)
209 Etikettierung für eine Rumflasche. Glas braun, oberes Etikett in Gold mit schwarzer und roter Schrift. Oval in Gold und Weiss auf Schwarz. (AUL)
210 Brandy-Flasche. Beschriftung in Gold auf schwarzem Etikett. (AUL)
211 Flaschenausstattung für zwei Sorten Tequila, ein aus Mexiko importierter Branntwein. Etiketten mehrfarbig, mit geprägter Goldverzierung. (USA)
212 Flaschenausstattung für einen Kornbranntwein. (NLD)

205 Carton portatif pour une bouteille d'eau-de-vie de poires. (SWI)
206 Boîte pliante pour un grand cognac français. (FRA)
207 Bouteille étudiée pour une marque de vodka. Rouge, blanc sur noir. (USA)
208 Etudes de bouteilles pour des vins blancs et rouges. Texte de l'étiquette noir et or sur fond blanc. (JPN)
209 Etiquette pour une bouteille de vieux rhum. Bouteille brune; étiquette supérieure or, lettres noires et rouges; étiquette ovale or et blanc sur noir. (AUL)
210 Bouteille de brandy. Ecriture or sur étiquette noire. (AUL)
211 Bouteille conçue pour deux variétés de tequila (alcool d'agave importé du Mexique), blanche et or. Etiquettes en couleurs, décoration or gaufrée. (USA)
212 Etude de bouteille pour une eau-de-vie de grain claire. (NLD)

211

212

DESIGNER / GESTALTER / MAQUETTISTE:

205 Michel Logoz
206 Knud Rasmussen
207 Jerry Berman/Linda Armistead
208 Shigeshi Omori
209, 210 Les Mason/Bill Kwan/Sandie Clarke
211 Gianninoto Assoc., Inc. (Artist: Art Accardy)
212 Boudwijn Ietswaard

ART DIRECTOR / DIRECTEUR ARTISTIQUE:

206 Palle Kaas
207 Jerry Berman
208 Shigeshi Omori
209, 210 Les Mason
211 John Di Gianni
212 Carli Van Emde Boas

AGENCY / AGENTUR / AGENCE–STUDIO:

205 Klausfelder SA
206 Kaas & Martaeng I/S
207 Jerry Berman & Associates
209, 210 Les Mason Graphic Design
211 Gianninoto Assoc., Inc.
212 Prad BV

CLIENT / AUFTRAGGEBER:

205 Orsat SA
206 A. de Luze & Fils
207 House of Sobel
208 Suntory Ltd.
209, 210 S. Wynn & Co. Pty Ltd.
211 Bacardi Corp.
212 Koninklijke Distillerderij Erven Lucas Bols

DESIGNER / GESTALTER / MAQUETTISTE:
213 Michio Yamato
214 Helmut Hoffmann (Photo: Klaus P. Ohlenforst)
215 Tom Curtos
216 Bruno Oldani
217, 218 Atelier Clormann (Photo: Werner A. Kilian)
219 Alan Zie Yongder
220 Atelier W. Schefer

ART DIRECTOR / DIRECTEUR ARTISTIQUE:
213 Michio Yamato
215 Tom Curtos/George Lois
216 Bruno Oldani
217, 218 Atelier Clormann
219 Alan Zie Yongder

AGENCY / AGENTUR / AGENCE – STUDIO:
214 Team Werbeagentur GmbH & Co.
215 Lois/Chajet Design Group, Inc.
216 Bruno Oldani
217, 218 Werbeabteilung Henkell
219 LTZ Ltd.
220 Werbeagentur Teamag

CLIENT / AUFTRAGGEBER:
213 Suntory Ltd.
214 H. C. König
215 Buckingham Corp.
216 A/S Vinmonopolet
217, 218 Henkell & Co.
219 Nash & Dymock Ltd.
220 Distillerie Weisflog AG

213

213 Gift packages for Japanese whisky. (JPN)
214 Presentation box for a vodka, containing ingredients for making Bloody Mary's. (GER)
215 Gift box for whisky. The graphics of the bottle label were enlarged and used as the design elements of the box. Lettering black on yellow, white ship. (USA)
216 Label for a brandy bottle. Lettering and ornament white and gold on blue. (NOR)
217, 218 Gift box containing a bottle of whisky, an ice carafe, poker cards, dice and dice cup. Lettering black on white, photographic illustration in full colour. (GER)
219 Cardboard box with hinged lid, containing a bottle of whisky and a can of a soft drink. Lettering black on pale gold foil. (HKG)
220 Gift box containing a bottle of bitter and a set of four glasses. Graphics in red, gold and white on black ground. (SWI)

214

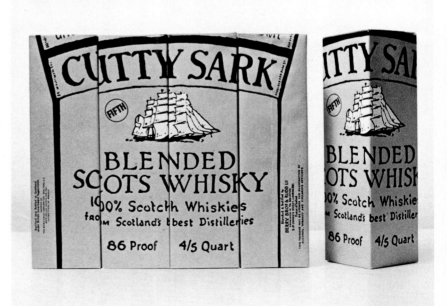

215

216

217, 218

213 Geschenkschachteln für einen japanischen Whisky. (JPN)
214 Geschenkpackung für Wodka, mit den Zutaten für einen «Bloody Mary». (GER)
215 Geschenkkarton für Whisky. Die Graphik des Flaschenetiketts, vergrössert, dient als Gestaltungselement für die Schachtel. Schrift schwarz auf Gelb, Segelschiff weiss. (USA)
216 Etikett für Brandy-Flasche. Schrift und Ornament in Weiss und Gold auf Blau. (NOR)
217, 218 Geschenkschachtel enthaltend eine Flasche Whisky, Eis-Karaffe, Poker-Kartenspiel, Würfel und Würfelbecher. Schrift schwarz auf Weiss, Illustration mehrfarbig. (GER)
219 Kartonschachtel mit aufklappbarem Deckel für eine Flasche Whisky und eine Büchse Tafelwasser. Schrift schwarz auf Goldfolie. (HKG)
220 Geschenkschachtel für eine Flasche Bitter und vier Trinkgläser. Graphik in Rot, Gold und Weiss auf schwarzem Grund. (SWI)

213 Boîtes-cadeaux pour du whisky japonais. (JPN)
214 Boîte-cadeau pour de la vodka, avec les ingrédients pour mixer des «Bloody Mary». (GER)
215 Boîte-cadeau pour du whisky. La composition de l'étiquette a été agrandie pour servir de décoration à l'emballage. Lettres noires sur jaune, clipper blanc. (USA)
216 Etiquette pour une bouteille de brandy. Lettres et motif blanc et or sur bleu. (NOR)
217, 218 Boîte-cadeau contenant une bouteille de whisky, un cruchon à glace, un jeu de poker (cartes, dés, cornet à dés). Lettres noir sur blanc, photo polychrome. (GER)
219 Boîte en carton avec couvercle rabattable, contenant un flacon de whisky et une boîte de boisson gazeuse. Texte noir sur feuille or pâle. (HKG)
220 Boîte-cadeau contenant une bouteille de bitter et quatre verres. Composition en rouge, or et blanc sur fond noir. (SWI)

219

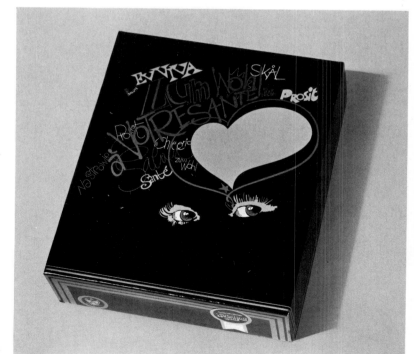

220

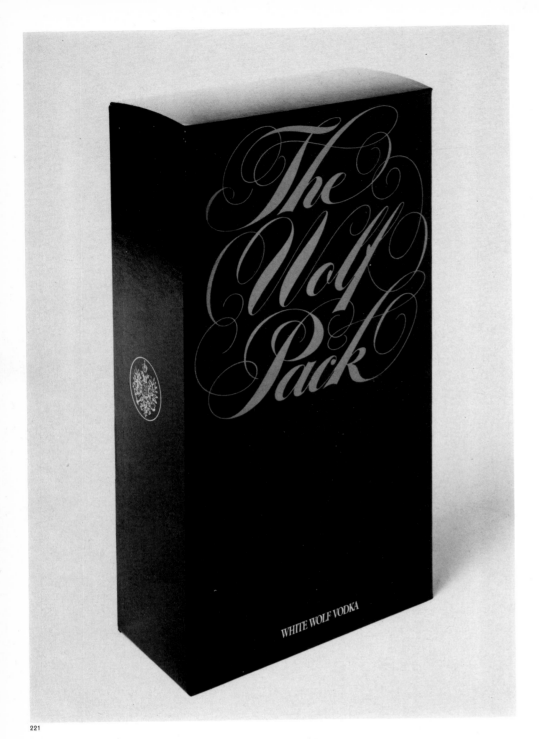

221

222

DESIGNER / GESTALTER / MAQUETTISTE:

221 Jerry Berman/Gene Icardi (Artist: Richard Leech)
222 Cato Hibberd Hawksby Pty Ltd.
223 Linda Hinrichs
224, 225 Matti Viherjuuri/Tapio Wirkkala
226 Studio Goossens
227 Jay Doblin/Stephen Dunne/Phil Seefeld
228 Wolfgang Gesing

ART DIRECTOR / DIRECTEUR ARTISTIQUE:

221 Jerry Berman/Gene Icardi
222 Cato Hibberd Hawksby Pty Ltd.
223 Terry Stokes
224, 225 Tapio Wirkkala
226 Francis Maurus
227 William N. Lucas/Joseph T. Simmons
228 Wolfgang Gesing

AGENCY / AGENTUR / AGENCE – STUDIO:

221 Berman, Icardi, Inc.
222 George Patterson Pty Ltd.
223 Product Development Workshop
226 Goossens SA
227 Unimark International
228 Special Design

CLIENT / AUFTRAGGEBER:

221 House of Sobel
222 United Distillers Pty Ltd.
223 Smirnoff
224, 225 Alko Oy
226 Armagnac Saint Vivant
227 Brown-Forman Distillers Corp.
228 H.C. König

221 Gift box design for vodka. Red lettering on black. (USA)
222 Three examples from a series of cans for mixed drinks, such as rum and cola, brandy and dry ginger, etc. Each can has a different colour scheme: the rum can is printed dark green with copper, gold and red in the oval. The ouzo can is black with copper, blue and red. The brandy can is brown with orange, yellow and black. (AUL)
223 Decanter bottle for a martini vodka. Lettering black, printed directly on the glass. Gold cap. (USA)
224, 225 Sculptured bottle for Finnish vodka. Fig. 225 shows a bottle with glass in a styrofoam case. (FIN)
226 Carton for a bottle of armagnac. Bottle shapes orange, lettering and castle in gold and white on black. (FRA)
227 Gift carton for whisky. A facsimile of the bottle label is attached on a removable transparent band. (USA)
228 Bottle styling for vodka. (GER)

221 Geschenkschachtel für Wodka. Schrift rot auf Schwarz. (USA)
222 Drei Beispiele aus einer Serie von Büchsen für gemischte Drinks, wie Rum und Cola, Brandy und Ingwer, etc. Alle Büchsen sind verschieden in den Farben. Die Rumbüchse hat einen dunkelgrünen Grund, mit Kupfer, Gold und Rot für das Oval. Die Ouzobüchse ist schwarz mit Kupfer, Blau und Rot. Die Brandybüchse ist braun mit Orange, Gelb und Schwarz. (AUL)
223 Wodkaflasche für Tafelgebrauch. Beschriftung schwarz, direkt auf Glas gedruckt. Verschluss in Gold. (USA)
224, 225 Strukturierte Flasche für finnischen Wodka. Abb. 225 zeigt eine Flasche mit Trinkglas in Schaumstoffschachtel. (FIN)
226 Schachtel für eine Flasche Armagnac. Flaschenformen orange, Schrift und Burg in Gold und Weiss auf Schwarz. (FRA)
227 Geschenkschachtel für Whisky. Ein Faksimile des Flaschenetiketts ist auf abnehmbarem Cellophanband gedruckt. (USA)
228 Flaschenausstattung für Wodka. (GER)

221 Boîte-cadeau pour de la vodka. Texte rouge sur noir. (USA)
222 Trois exemples de boîtes utilisées pour des mélanges de boissons tels que rhum et coca cola, brandy et dry ginger, etc. Chaque boîte affecte des couleurs différentes: celle de rhum est en vert sombre et cuivre, avec du rouge et de l'or pour l'ovale; celle d'ouzo est noir et cuivre, bleu et rouge; celle de brandy est brun et orange, jaune et noir. (AUL)
223 Bouteille-carafe pour une vodka-Martini. Texte noir imprimé à même le verre. Capsule dorée. (USA)
224, 225 Bouteille à surface structurée pour une vodka finlandaise. 225 Bouteille et verre dans emballage de styrofoam. (FIN)
226 Carton conçu pour un armagnac. Dessins de bouteilles orange, texte et château blanc et or sur noir. (FRA)
227 Boîte-cadeau pour un whisky. Un fac-similé de l'étiquette de la bouteille figure sur une bande transparente amovible. (USA)
228 Etude de bouteille pour une marque de vodka. (GER)

223

224

225

226

227

228

DESIGNER / GESTALTER / MAQUETTISTE:

229 Tom Cain
230 Malcolm Feinstein
231 Paul Gee
232 Raymond Loewy
233 Umeji Ueda
234 Hans Kleefeld
235 Irv Koons
236 Jesus Emilio Franco
237 George Rumsey/Roger Lundquist
238 Susumu Masunaka/Masaaki Hirai

229 Gift cartons for bourbon whisky. Colourful graphics to suggest its Kentucky origin. (USA)
230 Gift carton for whisky. White, black, orange and purple. (USA)
231 Gift carton for vodka. Blue, green, embossed gold. (USA)
232 Polychrome embossed foil gift carton for a whisky decanter. Commercial copy on removable transparent band. (USA)
233 Bottle styling for *sake:* Black, red, gold on white. (JPN)
234 Bottle and carton for Irish whisky. (CAN)
235 Ceramic gift decanter in the shape of an antique vessel, for a liqueur from Israel. Bluish-green colour. (USA)
236 Carrier carton for whisky. Black and white. (VEN)
237 Holiday gift carton for whisky. The top of the box is in the form of a knitted cap with a real pompon attached. (USA)
238 Carrier carton for a bottle of *sake.* (JPN)

229 Geschenkpackungen für Bourbon Whisky. Die farbige Gestaltung suggeriert den Kentucky-Ursprung. (USA)
230 Whisky-Geschenkkarton. Weiss, schwarz, orange, violett. (USA)
231 Geschenkkarton für Wodka. Blau, grün, Goldprägung. (USA)
232 Geschenkkarton für Whisky. Mehrfarbendruck auf Metallfolie. Beschriftung auf abnehmbarem Cellophanband. (USA)
233 Flaschenausstattung für Sake. Schwarz, Rot und Gold. (JPN)
234 Flasche und Packung für irischen Whisky. (CAN)
235 Keramische Geschenkkanne in Form einer antiken Karaffe, für einen Likör aus Israel. Farbe bläulich-grün. (USA)
236 Tragkarton für Whisky. Schwarzweiss. (VEN)
237 Weihnachts-Geschenkkarton für Whisky. Der Verschluss ist in Form einer Wollkappe mit angehefteter Quaste. (USA)
238 Tragkarton für eine Sake-Flasche. (JPN)

229 Emballages-cadeaux en carton pour du bourbon. Les motifs décoratifs évoquent l'origine de ce whisky (Kentucky). (USA)
230 Carton-cadeau pour un whisky. (USA)
231 Carton-cadeau pour une vodka. Bleu, vert, gaufrage or. (USA)
232 Carton-cadeau pour un flacon de whisky. Impression gaufrée polychrome sur feuille métallique. Texte sur bande amovible. (USA)
233 Etude de bouteille pour du saké. Noir, rouge, or. (JPN)
234 Bouteille et emballage pour un whisky irlandais. (CAN)
235 Bouteille de liqueur sous forme d'une carafe antique en céramique, pour un produit israélien. Vert bleuâtre. (USA)
236 Carton portatif pour un whisky. Noir et blanc. (VEN)
237 Emballage de Noël pour un whisky. Le haut du carton affecte la forme d'un bonnet de ski coiffé d'un vrai pompon. (USA)
238 Carton portatif pour une bouteille de saké. (JPN)

230

231

232

233

234

235

236

237

238

Textiles
Clothing and Accessories

Textilien
Kleidung und Zubehör

Textiles
Habillement et accessoires

3

DESIGNER / GESTALTER / MAQUETTISTE:

239 Douglas Boyd (Artist: Gordon Tani)
240 Hal Frazier/Paul Hauge
241 Seiji Murakami
242 Chris Groeneveld
243 Stan Brod
244 Robert A. Gale

ART DIRECTOR / DIRECTEUR ARTISTIQUE:

239 Douglas Boyd
240 Hal Frazier/Paul Hauge
241 Seiji Murakami
243 Beverly Erbacher
244 Robert A. Gale

AGENCY / AGENTUR / AGENCE – STUDIO:

239 Douglas Boyd Design
240 Newmarket Design Assoc.
241 Group "Hold Up"
243 Lipson-Jacob Associates

CLIENT / AUFTRAGGEBER:

239 Robinson's
240 Mike Bain Men's Store
242 Marsi's
243 U.S. Shoe Corp.
244 Uniroyal, Inc.

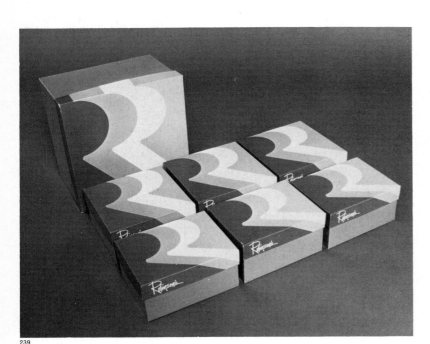

239

240

239 Set-up boxes for a chain of department stores. Two blues and white. (USA)
240 Carrier cartons for a men's clothier. The design is based on an old fabric pattern. Brown and red tones predominate. (USA)
241 Package design for men's crocodile-skin belts. (JPN)
242 Gift packages for a women's apparel shop. (USA)
243 Set-up box for women's shoes. Lettering and box dark blue, lid mustard and orange. (USA)
244 Folding box for rubber boots. (USA)

239 Stülpschachteln für eine Kette von Warenhäusern. Zwei Blautöne und Weiss. (USA)
240 Kartontragtaschen für ein Herrenmodegeschäft. Das Motiv basiert auf einem alten Stoffmuster. Braun- und Rottöne dominieren. (USA)
241 Schachteln für Herrengürtel aus Krokodilleder. (JPN)
242 Geschenk-Verpackungen eines Damenmodegeschäfts. (USA)
243 Stülpschachtel für Damenschuhe. Schrift und unterer Teil der Schachtel dunkelblau, Deckel senffarbig und orange. (USA)
244 Faltschachtel für Gummistiefel. (USA)

239 Boîtes à couvercle pour une chaîne de grands magasins. Deux bleus, un blanc. (USA)
240 Cartons portatifs pour un magasin de modes masculines. Composition imitant un tissu du bon vieux temps. Prédominance de tons bruns et rouges. (USA)
241 Conception d'emballage pour des ceintures en croco pour hommes. (JPN)
242 Emballages-cadeaux pour une boutique de modes féminines. (USA)
243 Boîte à couvercle pour des chaussures de dames. Texte et partie inférieure de la boîte en bleu foncé, couvercle moutarde et orange. (USA)
244 Boîte pliante pour des bottes en caoutchouc. (USA)

Textiles, Clothing and Accessories
Textilien, Kleidung und Zubehör
Textiles, habillement et accessoires

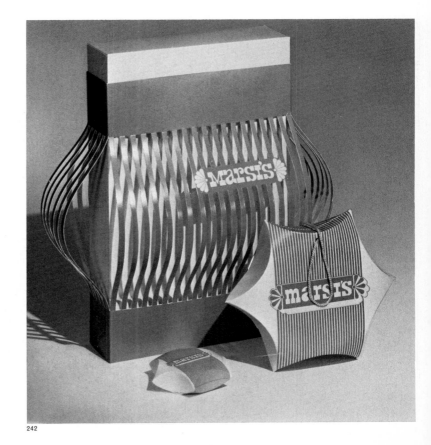

242

241

243

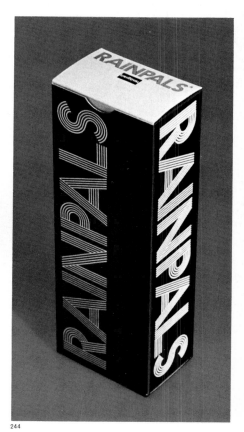

244

Textiles, Clothing and Accessories
Textilien, Kleidung und Zubehör
Textiles, habillement et accessoires

DESIGNER / GESTALTER / MAQUETTISTE:

245 Rinaldo Cutini
246 R. A. Astley/S. Crossley
247 Werbeagentur Hans Dubach
248–254 E + U Hiestand

ART DIRECTOR / DIRECTEUR ARTISTIQUE:

245 Rinaldo Cutini
248–254 E + U Hiestand

AGENCY / AGENTUR / AGENCE – STUDIO:

247 Werbeagentur Hans Dubach
248–254 E + U Hiestand/H. M. Eggmann

CLIENT / AUFTRAGGEBER:

245 Datti
246 Dorma Sheets
247 Schweizer Decken- und Tuchfabrik
248–254 Maus Frères SA

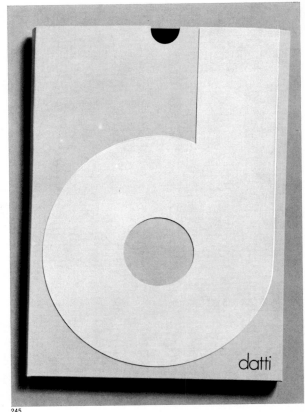

245

248–253

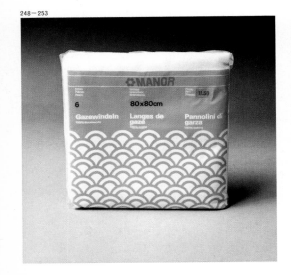

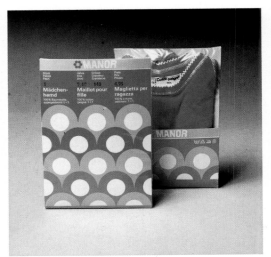

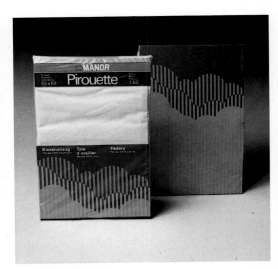

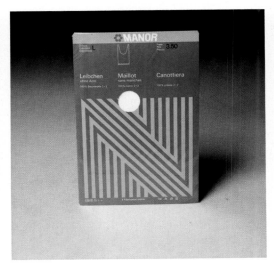

246

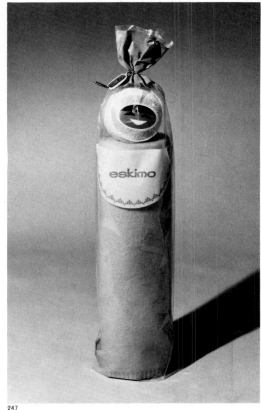

247

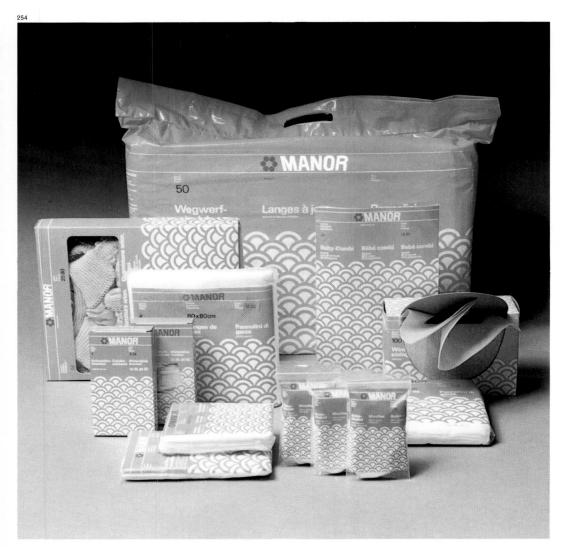

254

245 Cardboard box with blind-embossed initial, for a men's apparel store. (ITA)
246 Range of gift packages for towels. Clear cellulose acetate and cardboard combination. (GBR)
247 Polyethylene bag, printed in two colours, containing a baby blanket and a ball, made up as the head of an Eskimo. (SWI)
248–254 Examples from a co-ordinated packaging programme of a department-store chain. (See also Figs. 25–30.) (SWI)

245 Kartonschachtel mit blindgeprägtem Initial, für ein Herrenbekleidungsgeschäft. (ITA)
246 Serie von Geschenkpackungen für Frottiertücher. Kombination von transparentem Acetat mit Karton. (GBR)
247 Zweifarbig bedruckter Polyäthylenbeutel für eine Baby-Wolldecke, mit Ball als Eskimokopf. (SWI)
248–254 Beispiele aus einem koordinierten Packungsprogramm einer Warenhausgruppe. (Siehe auch Abb. 25–30.) (SWI)

245 Boîte en carton avec initiale gaufrée à sec, pour un magasin de modes masculines. (ITA)
246 Gamme d'emballages-cadeaux pour serviettes-éponges. Carton et acétate de cellulose transparent. (GBR)
247 Sachet en polyéthylène, impression en deux couleurs, pour couverture de bébé, avec ballon (tête d'Esquimau). (SWI)
248–254 Exemples d'un programme d'emballages coordonné pour une chaîne de grands magasins. (Cf. les fig. 25–30.) (SWI)

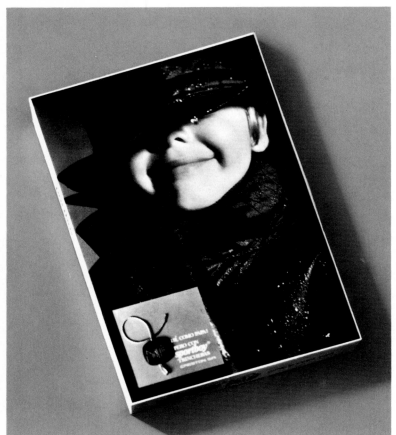

255

257

256

258

CLIENT / AUFTRAGGEBER:

255 Creston SA
256 Very Sport SA
257 Joseph Magnin & Co.
258 Knoll International
259 Telerie Zucchi
260 Eurocologne Parfums SA

DESIGNER / GESTALTER / MAQUETTISTE:

255 Ramon Roda/Jordi Sebastian (Photo: J.A. Alonso)
256 Collis Clements
257 Marlon Chapman
258 Massimo Vignelli
259 Silvio Coppola
260 Richard Tobler

ART DIRECTOR / DIRECTEUR ARTISTIQUE:

255 Ramon Roda
256 Collis Clements
257 Marlon Chapman
258 Massimo Vignelli
259 Silvio Coppola
260 Leonard Diepenbrock

AGENCY / AGENTUR / AGENCE – STUDIO:

255 Art/3
256 Clarke/Clements/Hughes
258 Vignelli Associates
259 Studio Coppola
260 Meiendorfer Unternehmensberatung

100

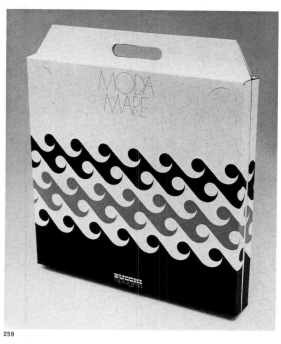

259

255 Set-up box for a brand of children's rainwear. Full-colour reproduction of photographic illustration. (SPA)
256 Examples from a range of labels and packaging for skiing apparel and accessories. The brand insignia VS is used as the unifying graphic element. (SWI)
257 Examples from an extensive range of folding boxes and other packaging materials used by a chain of fashion stores. (USA)
258 Boxes containing samples of a textile collection for interior decorators. (USA)
259 Carrier carton for beachwear sold by a fashion store. (ITA)
260 Boutique gift packages consisting of double-decker plexiglass tubes containing a bottle of eau de cologne and a belt, a scarf or a doll. (FRA)

255 Stülpschachtel für die Produkte einer Herstellerfirma von Regenbekleidung für Kinder. Farbphotographische Illustration. (SPA)
256 Beispiele aus einer Serie von Etiketten und Packungen für Skibekleidung und -ausrüstungen. Das Firmenzeichen VS dient als verbindendes graphisches Element. (SWI)
257 Beispiele aus dem umfangreichen Sortiment von Faltschachteln und anderem Verpackungsmaterial einer Kette von Modegeschäften. (USA)
258 Schachteln für Stoffmuster aus einer Kollektion für Innenarchitekten. (USA)
259 Tragkarton für Strandmodeartikel einer Bekleidungsfirma. (ITA)
260 Boutique-Geschenkpackungen bestehend aus einem zylindrischen Doppeldecker-Behälter aus Plexiglas, der eine Flasche Kölnischwasser und einen zweiten Artikel enthält. (FRA)

255 Boîte rigide pour une marque d'imperméables pour enfants. L'illustration photographique est reproduite en polychromie. (SPA)
256 Exemples d'étiquettes et d'emballages pour des vêtements et accessoires de ski. Le sigle VS est utilisé comme repère graphique aux fins d'identification de la série. (SWI)
257 Exemples tirés d'une gamme étendue de boîtes pliantes et autres éléments d'emballages conçus pour une chaîne de magasins de modes. (USA)
258 Boîtes d'échantillons textiles pour ensembliers décorateurs. (USA)
259 Carton portatif pour les articles d'un magasin de modes de plage. (ITA)
260 Emballages-cadeaux pour une boutique. Il s'agit d'un tube en plexiglas compartimenté, qui renferme une eau de Cologne ainsi qu'une ceinture, un foulard ou une poupée. (FRA)

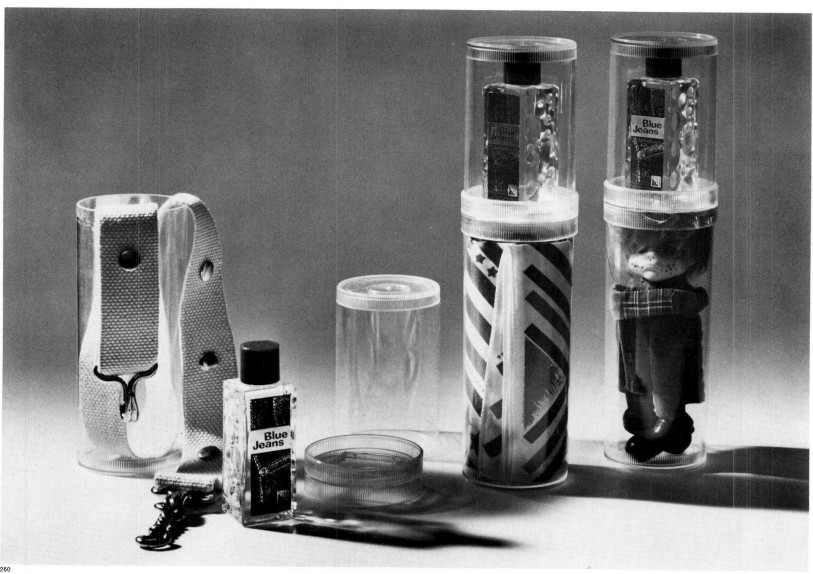

260

DESIGNER / GESTALTER / MAQUETTISTE:

261 Paul Maurer (Artist: Jean-Louis Bertrand)
262 Ruedi Rüegg (Photo: H. P. Mühlemann)
263 Georg Staehelin (Photo: Claudia Schneider)
264 Constance von Collande (Artist: Constance von Collande)
265 R. Roda/Soro (Photo: Jeroni)
266 Salvatore Adduci

ART DIRECTOR / DIRECTEUR ARTISTIQUE:

261 André Heidelberger
262 Ruedi Rüegg
263 Georg Staehelin
264 Constance von Collande
265 R. Roda

AGENCY / AGENTUR / AGENCE – STUDIO:

261 Wiener, Deville & Wälchli
262 MB + Co.
263 Pentragram Design SA
264 Elizabeth Arden Creative Packaging Dept.
265 Industrias Graficas Pauta

CLIENT / AUFTRAGGEBER:

261 A. Sutter AG
262 Benedict Mäser
263 BP Schweiz
264 Elizabeth Arden, Inc.
265 Marie Claire

261

263

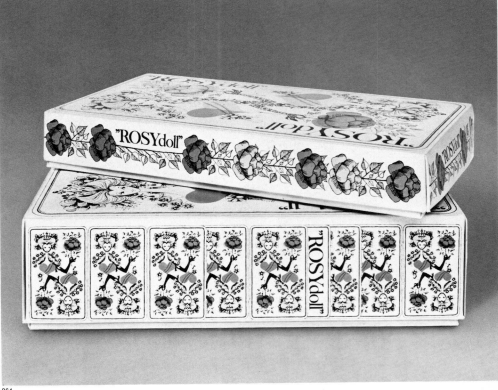

264

262

261 Folding box used as a display prop in stores. Illustration in full colour. Top of box green, stripe yellow and green. (SWI)
262 Printed plastic pouch for pantyhose. (AUS)
263 Folding boxes for pantyhose. (SWI)
264 Lidded boxes for lingerie. Pink and black. (USA)
265 Folding box for pantyhose. Photo in duotone, vignettes in full colour, sides of box black. (SPA)
266 Folding box for a lady's slip. Black and white, with die-cut window in heart shape to reveal the colour of the contents. (SPA)

261 Faltschachtel zum Gebrauch als Schaufensterblickfang. Illustration vierfarbig, Oberseite grün. (SWI)
262 Bedruckter Kunststoffbeutel für Strumpfhosen. (AUS)
263 Faltschachteln für Strumpfhosen. (SWI)
264 Stülpschachteln für Damenwäsche. Rosa und schwarz. (USA)
265 Faltschachtel für Strumpfhosen. Photo in Doppelton, Vignetten vierfarbig, Schachtelseiten schwarz. (SPA)
266 Faltschachtel für Damenwäsche. Schwarzweiss, mit ausgestanzter Herzform zur Sichtbarmachung der Farbe des Inhalts. (SPA)

261 Boîte pliante utilisée pour accrocher l'attention des lécheurs de vitrines. Illustration polychrome. Dessus vert, bande jaune et verte. (SWI)
262 Pochette plastique pour collants, avec impression. (AUS)
263 Boîtes pliantes pour collants. (SWI)
264 Boîtes à couvercle pour de la lingerie fine. Rose et noir. (USA)
265 Boîte pliante pour des collants. Photo en double ton, vignettes polychromes, côtés de la boîte en noir. (SPA)
266 Boîte pliante pour un slip de dame. Noir et blanc, avec fenêtre en forme de cœur pour le repérage de la couleur du contenu. (SPA)

266

265

DESIGNER / GESTALTER / MAQUETTISTE:

267, 268 Roger Ferriter
269 Rodd V. Bixler (Photo: Seymour Mednick)
270 Androus Noyes/Gary Procano
271 Les Mason (Artist: Les Mason/Bill Kwan)
272 Heinz R. Grunwald
273 Larry Profancik/Frank Ross
       (Artist: P.W., Inc. Joyce Morgan Studio)
274 Bruno Kessler (Photo: Thomas Cugini)
275 Louis Nelson/Wayne Creekmore/
       David Hulbert

ART DIRECTOR / DIRECTEUR ARTISTIQUE:

267, 268 Roger Ferriter
269 Larry Alten
270 Ken Macay
271 Noel Delbridge
272 Heinz R. Grunwald
273 Larry Profancik/Frank Ross
274 Cesare Chiogna

AGENCY / AGENTUR / AGENCE – STUDIO:

267, 268 Lubalin Smith Carnase
269 Alten, Cohen & Naish, Inc.
270 DeMartin, Marona, Cranstoun, Downes
271 Les Mason Graphic Design/
       Masius Wynne Williams Pty Ltd.
272 Neish, Tutt, Grunwald Pty Ltd.
273 P.W., Inc. Swearingen Graphics Div.
274 Bruno Kessler
275 Robert P. Gersin Assoc., Inc.

CLIENT / AUFTRAGGEBER:

267, 268, 270 L'Eggs Products, Inc.
269 Stetson Hats, Inc.
271 Julius Marlow Shoes
272 Candy Footwear Pty Ltd.
273 Totes, Inc.
274 Neue Warenhaus AG
275 Head Ski & Sportswear, Inc.

267

268

270

273

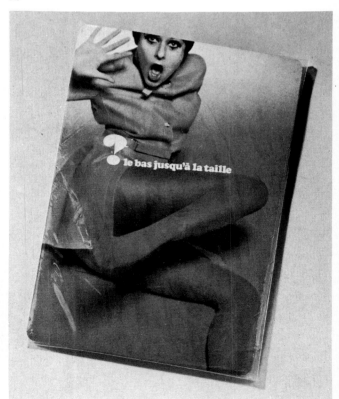

274

269

267 Packaging concept for a line of stockings and pantyhose. The brand name *L'eggs* is a play on the word "legs". The package consists of a cylindrical cardboard part, printed in one colour, seated on a white plastic base, and an eggshaped container in white plastic. The colours vary throughout the range. (USA)
268 Store display table for the line of packages described in Fig. 267. (USA)
269 Lidded cardboard box for a brand of men's hats. An association with the American West is created by the use of an illustration in bright colours showing a glowing branding iron as used on Texan ranches. (USA)
270 Package for the same hosiery brand as in Fig. 267. The graphic motif is an enlargement of the logotype. (USA)
271 Design of a lidded set-up box for an exclusive brand of men's shoes. Printed in black and white, black lid. (AUL)
272 Cardboard box for ladies' shoes. Black and silver. (AUL)
273 Translucent plastic package for a folding umbrella. (USA)
274 Package for pantyhose — "the stocking up to the waist". Yellowish shades. (SWI)
275 Transparent plastic cases for sports apparel and accessories. (USA)

267 Verpackungskonzept für ein Sortiment von Damenstrümpfen und -strumpfhosen. Die Packung besteht aus einem einfarbig bedruckten zylindrischen Unterteil und einem weissen Kunststoffbehälter in Eiform. Die Farben variieren nach Inhalt. (USA)
268 Ausstellständer für die in Abb. 267 beschriebenen Packungen. (USA)
269 Stülpdeckelschachtel für einen Herrenhut. Die in leuchtenden Farben gedruckte Illustration eines von Viehzüchtern verwendeten, glühenden Brenneisens stellt eine Gedankenassoziation her mit dem amerikanischen Westen. (USA)
270 Packungsvariante für dieselbe Strumpfwarenmarke wie in Abb. 267. Der Schriftzug, überdimensioniert und angeschnitten, dient als graphisches Motiv. (USA)
271 Gestaltung einer Stülpdeckelschachtel für eine exklusive Herrenschuhmarke. Schwarzweiss gedruckt, Deckel schwarz. (AUL)
272 Kartonschachtel für Damenschuhe. Schwarz und Silber. (AUL)
273 Durchsichtige Kunststoffpackung für einen zusammenfaltbaren Regenschirm. (USA)
274 Packung für Strumpfhosen — «der Strumpf bis zur Taille». In Gelbtönen. (SWI)
275 Transparente Plastikhüllen für Sportbekleidung und -artikel. (USA)

271

272

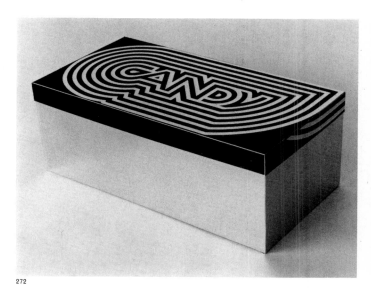

267 Conception d'emballage pour un assortiment de bas pour dames et collants. La marque *l'eggs* est un jeu de mots sur «legs» (jambes) et «eggs» (œufs). L'emballage se compose d'un cylindre en carton à décoration monochrome emboîté sur une base en plastique blanc, et d'une boîte ovoïde en plastique blanc. Les couleurs varient en fonction du contenu. (USA)
268 Table-présentoir pour magasins, recevant les articles décrits à la fig. 267. (USA)
269 Boîte à couvercle, en carton, pour un chapeau d'homme. Le motif associe la marque à l'Ouest américain en utilisant une illustration aux couleurs éclatantes montrant un fer à marquer chauffé au rouge vif, tel qu'en utilisent les cowboys au Texas. (USA)
270 Emballage pour la marque de bonneterie présentée à la fig. 267. Le motif est constitué par une version surdimensionnée et tronquée du logo. (USA)
271 Conception d'une boîte rigide pour une marque exclusive de chaussures pour messieurs. Impression noir et blanc, couvercle noir. (AUL)
272 Boîte en carton pour des chaussures de dames. Noir et argent. (AUL)
273 Emballage plastique transparent pour un tom-pouce. (USA)
274 Emballage de collants — «le bas jusqu'à la taille». Tons jaunâtres. (SWI)
275 Cartouche plastique transparente pour des vêtements et accessoires de sports. (USA)

275

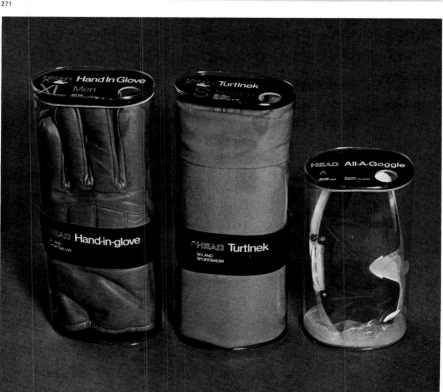

Textiles, Clothing and Accessories
Textilien, Kleidung und Zubehör
Textiles, habillement et accessoires

Household, Hardware
Miscellaneous

Haushalt, Werkzeug
Verschiedenes

Articles ménagères
outillages, divers

4

DESIGNER / GESTALTER / MAQUETTISTE:
276 Mitsuo Mihira
277 Bob Broadley
278 Michael Freisager
(Photo: Jürgen Tapprich)
279 Terry Baker
280 Linda Hinrichs
(Artist: Guy Billout)
281 Les Mason
282, 283 Gene Szafran

ART DIRECTOR / DIRECTEUR ARTISTIQUE:
276 Yasui Kumai
277 Oliver Waley
279 Terry Baker
280 Jay Dederick
281 Les Mason
282, 283 W. M. Stark

AGENCY / AGENTUR / AGENCE – STUDIO:
276 Shiseido Creative Room
277 London Design Unit
278 Werbeabteilung F. Steinfels AG
280 J. Walter Thompson Co.
282, 283 Artists Associates

CLIENT / AUFTRAGGEBER:
276 Shiseido Co. Ltd.
277 Bowater-Scott (U.K.) Ltd.
278 Steinfels AG
279, 281 Bowater-Scott Australia Ltd.
280 Scott Paper Co.
282, 283 Kimberley-Clark Corp.

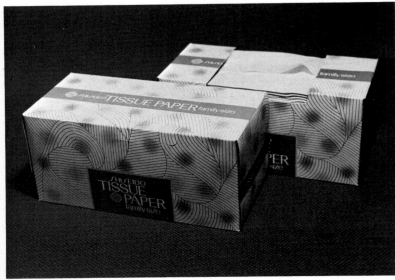 

276

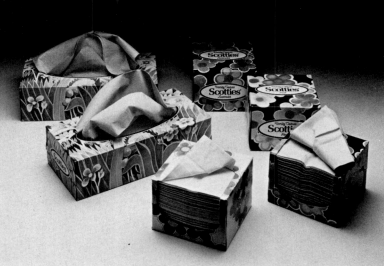

277

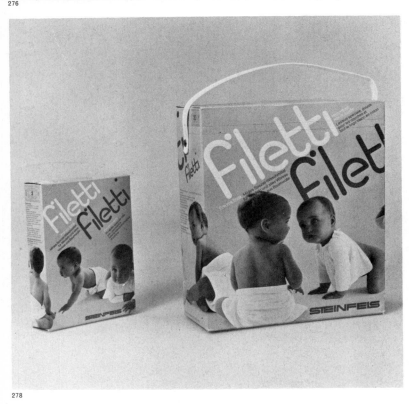

278

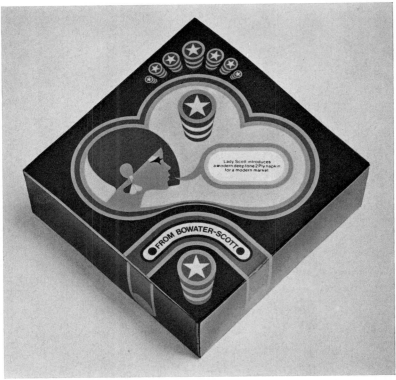

279

276 Boxes for paper tissues. Panels and pattern brownish grey, dots in pastel colours. (JPN)
277 Dispenser boxes for paper tissues. Colourful graphics. (GBR)
278 Box and carrier pack for a mild detergent for napkins and bed linen. (SWI)
279 Folding box for paper table napkins. (AUL)
280 Clear plastic wrapper for a roll of recycled paper towels. The printed scene hints at the environmental benefits of paper recycling. (USA)
281 Dispenser boxes in various colour combinations for facial paper tissues. (AUL)
282, 283 Side and top of paper tissue box, simulating an early American carved wooden box. The side (Fig. 282) gives information on American folk art, such as wood carving. Produced on the occasion of the American Bicentennial celebrations. (USA)

276 Schachteln für Haushaltstücher, Muster braungrau, Punkte in Pastellfarben. (JPN)
277 Spenderschachteln für Papiertüchlein. Farbenfrohe Gestaltung. (GBR)
278 Packung und Tragkarton für ein mildes Spezial-Waschmittel für Windeln und Weisswaren. (SWI)
279 Faltschachtel für Papierservietten. (AUL)
280 Durchsichtige Plastikhülle für eine Rolle Handtücher aus wiedergewonnenem Papier. Der Aufdruck weist auf die Umweltschutzaspekte von solchem Papier hin. (USA)
281 Spenderschachteln in verschiedenen Farbkombinationen für Papier-Gesichtstücher. (AUL)
282, 283 Ober- und Unterseite einer Schachtel für Papiertüchlein. Die Aufmachung imitiert eine frühamerikanische geschnitzte Holzschachtel. Die Rückseite informiert über amerikanische Volkskunst, z. B. Holzschnitzerei. Zum Anlass der 200-Jahr-Feier der USA. (USA)

280

281

282

283

276 Boîtes de serviettes en papier pour le ménage. Décor gris-brun, points au pastel. (JPN)
277 Boîtes de serviettes en papier servant aussi de distributeurs. Décor aux couleurs vives. (GBR)
278 Boîte et carton portatif pour une lessive douce pour langes et literie. (SWI)
279 Boîte pliante pour serviettes de table en papier. (AUL)
280 Emballage plastique transparent pour un rouleau de serviettes en papier recyclé, dont les effets bénéfiques pour l'environnement sont démontrés par l'illustration. (USA)
281 Boîtes de serviettes à démaquiller servant aussi de distributeurs. Diverses couleurs. (AUL)
282, 283 Dessus et dessous d'une boîte de serviettes en papier imitant une boîte en bois sculptée main des débuts des USA. Le dessous (282) renseigne sur divers aspects de l'art populaire américain (sculpture sur bois, etc.). Pour le Bicentenaire des Etats-Unis. (USA)

284

284 Sprinkler can for a disinfectant detergent powder. (CAN)
285 Red polyethylene bottle for a rinse conditioner. (DEN)
286 Folding box with pre-perforated dispensing slot for the removal of the contents – twenty dispensers for five razor blades each. (IND)
287 Cardboard box containing a water softening powder for use in washing machines. (ITA)
288, 289 Design for a cardboard folding box containing two bars of laundry soap. Blue tones on white. Fig. 289 shows the graphic pattern obtained when the boxes are stacked. (AUL)
290 Box for a synthetic fabric detergent. Pink rose, lettering white, "y" blue. (SWI)
291 Detergent carton. Full-colour photograph of flower. Brand name red. (USA)
292 Cardboard folding box with pouring spout for a laundry detergent. Lettering and surrounding circles in bright reds, blues and greens. (JPN)

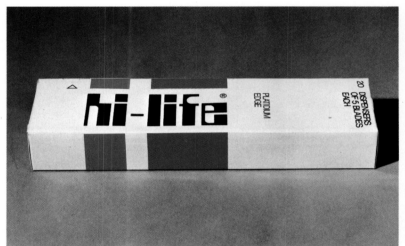

286

285

287

284 Streudose für ein desinfizierendes Reinigungsmittel. (CAN)
285 Rote Polyäthylen-Flasche für ein Spülmittel. (DEN)
286 Faltschachtel mit vorperforiertem Öffnungsschlitz zur Entnahme des Inhalts – zwanzig Spenderbehälter für je fünf Rasierklingen. (IND)
287 Kartonschachtel für ein Entkalkungsmittel zum Gebrauch in Waschmaschinen. (ITA)
288, 289 Gestaltung einer Schachtel für zwei Stücke Waschseife. Blautöne auf Weiss. Abb. 289 zeigt das graphische Muster, das sich durch Aufeinanderstellen der Schachteln ergibt. (AUL)
290 Packung für Waschmittel für synthetische Stoffe. Rose rosa, Schrift weiss, «y» blau. (SWI)
291 Waschpulverpackung. Blume vierfarbig reproduziert, Markenname rot. (USA)
292 Karton-Faltschachtel mit eingebautem Ausgussschnabel für ein Waschmittel. Schrift und umgebende Kreise in lebhaftem Rot, Blau und Grün. (JP)

284 Boîte saupoudreuse pour un détersif désinfectant en poudre. (CAN)
285 Flacon en polyéthylène rouge pour un produit de rinçage. (DEN)
286 Boîte pliante pourvue d'une fente préperforée permettant de retirer le contenu – vingt distributeurs de lames de rasoirs contenant cinq lames chacun. (IND)
287 Boîte en carton, pour un produit adoucissant l'eau utilisé dans les machines à laver. (ITA)
288, 289 Conception d'une boîte pliante en carton conditionnant deux savons à lessive. Tons bleus sur blanc. La fig. 289 montre le motif graphique obtenu en empilant les boîtes. (AUL)
290 Boîte pour une lessive pour tissus synthétiques. Rose rose, lettres blanches, «y» bleu. (SWI)
291 Emballage carton pour une lessive. Fleur polychrome. Nom de la marque en rouge. (USA)
292 Boîte pliante en carton avec bec verseur pour une lessive. Texte et cercles concentriques en couleurs vives – rouge, bleu, vert. (JP)

290

289

DESIGNER / GESTALTER / MAQUETTISTE:
284 Pierre Kohler
285 Ørn Vidarsson
286 Yeshwant Chaudhary
287 Dante Vernice
288, 289 Les Mason
290 Migros, Abt. Verpackung
291 Paula Halpern
292 Yukio Konda/Masayoshi Nakajo

ART DIRECTOR / DIRECTEUR ARTISTIQUE:
284 Hans Kleefeld
285 Ørn Vidarsson
286 Yeshwant Chaudhary
287 Dante Vernice
288, 289 Les Mason
290 Hans Uster
291 Frank Diassi
292 Hideo Amano

AGENCY / AGENTUR / AGENCE – STUDIO:
284 Gottschalk & Ash Ltd.
285 Plan Design A/S
286 Communica/Corporate Communications
287 Studio Vernice
288, 289 Hayes Advertising Pty Ltd.
290 Migros, Abt. Verpackung
291 Robert P. Gersin Assoc., Inc.

CLIENT / AUFTRAGGEBER:
284 Canada Packers Ltd.
285 Oliemøllen A/S
286 Centron Industrial Alliance Ltd.
287 CIS
288, 289 Preservene Pty Ltd.
290 Migros Genossenschaftsbund
291 Darrill Industries, Inc.
292 Kao Soap Co. Ltd.

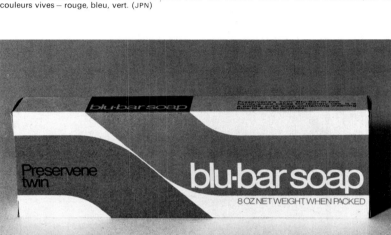
288

291

292

DESIGNER / GESTALTER / MAQUETTISTE:

293 Paul S. Hastings
294 Hidetoshi Akazawa
295, 296 Les Mason
297 August Maurer
298 Bruno K. Wiese
300 Studio Kreuser

ART DIRECTOR / DIRECTEUR ARTISTIQUE:

293 John S. Blyth/Paul S. Hastings
294 Yasuo Tanaka
295, 296 Les Mason
297 August Maurer
298 Bruno K. Wiese
300 Studio Kreuser

AGENCY / AGENTUR / AGENCE – STUDIO:

293 Peterson & Blyth Assoc., Inc.
295, 296 Hayes Advertising Pty Ltd.
297 Ciba-Geigy Zentrale Werbung
298 Studio für Visual Design
300 Studio Kreuser

CLIENT / AUFTRAGGEBER:

293 Calgon Corp.
294 Daiichi Soap Co. Ltd.
295 Preservene Pty Ltd.
296 Telegene Pty Ltd.
297 Ciba-Geigy AG/Metrofa International
298 Henkel Werke
300 Dr. Farner

293

294

295

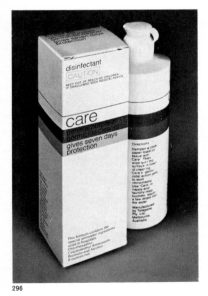

296

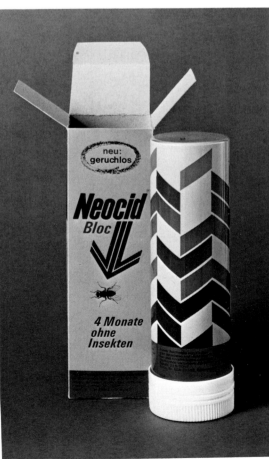

297

298

Household, Hardware
Haushalt, Werkzeug
Articles ménagers, outillages

299

300

293 Spray can for an anti-static fabric softener. (USA)
294 Folding box for a detergent. (JPN)
295 Package for a soap powder. (AUL)
296 Styling of the folding box and the plastic bottle of a germicide household cleaner. (AUL)
297 Folding box and metal container for an insecticide stick. Box yellow, lettering dark blue and red. Chevrons on tube red, maroon, orange and brown, red stripe at bottom of box and tube. (SWI)
298 Styling of a plastic bottle for a dish-washing detergent. Red bottle with white cap. (GER)
299 Various plastic bottles from a show of well-designed bottles at The Design Centre in London. (GBR)
300 Package for a laundry detergent. Lettering red, design in bright colours on silver. (ITA)

293 Sprühdose für ein antistatisches Textilbehandlungsmittel. (USA)
294 Faltkarton für ein Waschmittel. (JPN)
295 Typographisch gestaltete Packung für ein Seifenpulver. (AUL)
296 Packungsausstattung von Faltschachtel und Kunststoff-Flasche für ein keimtötendes Haushalt-Reinigungsmittel. (AUL)
297 Faltschachtel und Metallbehälter für ein Insektenvertilgungsmittel. Die Grundfarbe der Schachtel ist gelb, Schrift dunkelblau und rot. Das Muster auf der Metallröhre ist rot, braunrot, orange und braun. Roter Abschlussstreifen auf Röhre und Schachtel. (SWI)
298 Formgebung einer Plastikflasche für ein Geschirrspülmittel. Flasche zinnoberrot, Schraubverschluss weiss. (GER)
299 Verschiedene Kunststoff-Flaschen aus einer Ausstellung gut gestalteter Flaschen im Design Centre, London. (GBR)
300 Packung für Waschmittel. Schrift rot, Graphik mehrfarbig. (ITA)

293 Bombe aérosol pour un adoucisseur de tissus antistatique. (USA)
294 Boîte pliante pour une lessive. (JPN)
295 Emballage de conception typo pour une poudre de savon. (AUL)
296 Etude d'une boîte pliante et d'un flacon plastique pour un produit de nettoyage bactéricide. (AUL)
297 Boîte pliante et conditionnement métallique pour un insecticide. Boîte jaune, typo bleu foncé et rouge. Chevrons rouge, brun-rouge, orange et brun, bande rouge au bas de la boîte et du cylindre. (SWI)
298 Etude d'une bouteille plastique pour un produit à laver la vaisselle. Bouteille vermillon, couvercle à vis blanc. (GER)
299 Diverses conceptions de bouteilles en plastique réunies à l'occasion d'une exposition de bouteilles au Design Centre londonien. (GBR)
300 Emballage de lessive. Lettres rouges, composition en couleurs vives sur fond argent. (ITA)

DESIGNER / GESTALTER / MAQUETTISTE:

301 Peter J. Dixon
302 Ford, Byrne & Assoc.
303 Albin Kirchhofer
304 K. Vogelbach
305 Edward C. Kozlowski/Sandy Foose
    (Artist: Jack Campbell)
306 Patrick Ventujol
307 Bruce Beck
308 Stephen Goss/Edward C. Kozlowski

ART DIRECTOR / DIRECTEUR ARTISTIQUE:

301 Peter J. Dixon
302 Ford, Byrne & Assoc.
303 Albin Kirchhofer
305, 308 Edward C. Kozlowski/
    Herbert R. Nubel
306 Patrick Ventujol
307 Bruce Beck

AGENCY / AGENTUR / AGENCE – STUDIO:

301 Sainsbury's Design Studio
302 Ford, Byrne & Assoc.
303 Kirchhofer Werbeagentur
304 Werbeagentur Paul Ruetz
305, 308 Edward C. Kozlowski Design, Inc.
306 M & P
307 The Design Partnership, Inc.

CLIENT / AUFTRAGGEBER:

301 J. Sainsbury Ltd.
302 Pennwalt Corp.
303 Po. Ho-Co AG
304 Neue Warenhaus AG
305, 308 Sterling Products International, Inc.
306 Sani Flor
307 S. C. Johnson & Son

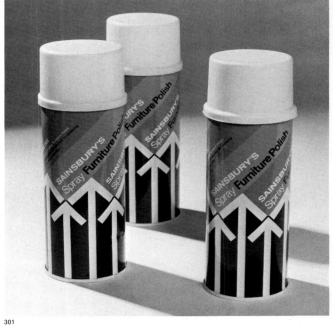

301

302

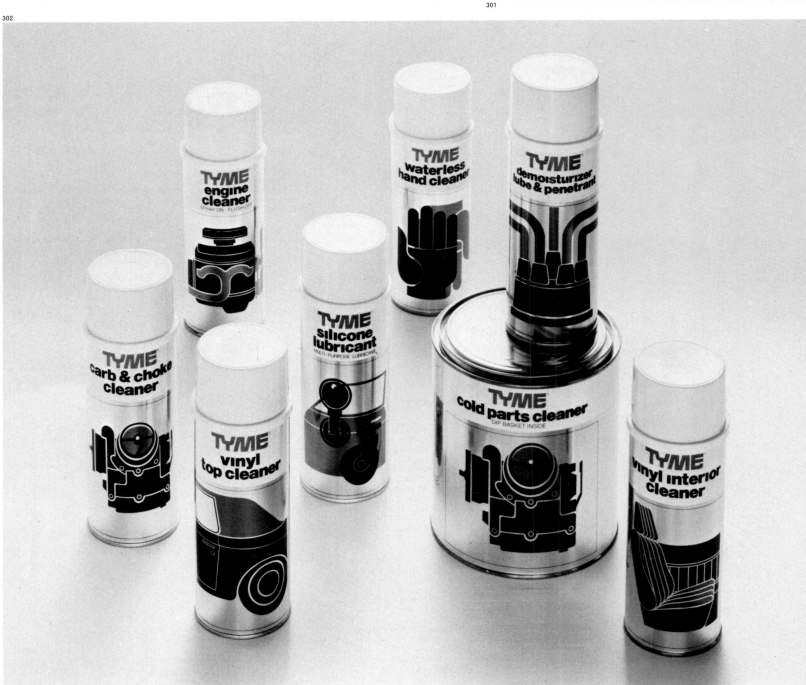

303

304

305

306

307

308

301 Design of spray can containing furniture polish. (GBR)
302 Group of spray cans and lidded metal can from a total packaging design programme for a line of automotive products. (USA)
303 Spray can for a scented air freshener. Ground colour of wrap-around label blue-green, brand name orange, arrow white. (SWI)
304 Series of spray cans for an air freshener in various scents. The chevron-like stripes are in tones of green, blue, orange and violet on white, each scent having a different colour. (SWI)
305 Can and label styling for an air freshener spray. (USA)
306 Can for a room deodorizing spray. Ground colour of label is green, "balloons" yellow, cap white. (FRA)
307 Spray can for a flying insect killer. Brand name yellow on black, arrow white, cap yellow and orange. (USA)
308 Plastic bottle for a laundry disinfectant. From a packaging design programme adapted for Latin-American countries. (USA)

301 Gestaltung von Sprühdosen für Möbelpolitur. (GBR)
302 Gruppe von Sprüh- und Metalldeckeldosen aus einem umfassenden Packungsgestaltungs-Programm für einen Hersteller von Produkten für die Automobilbranche. (USA)
303 Sprühdose für ein parfümiertes Luftverbesserungsmittel. Grundfarbe blaugrün, Markenname orange, Pfeil weiss. (SWI)
304 Serie von Sprühdosen für einen parfümierten Luftverbesserer. Die Streifen sind je nach Duftnote in grünen, blauen, orangen oder violetten Farbtönen auf weissem Grund. (SWI)
305 Dosen- und Etikettgestaltung für einen Luftverbesserer. (USA)
306 Sprühdose für ein desodorierendes Mittel für die Zimmerluft. Grundfarbe des Etiketts ist grün, «Blasen» gelb, Deckel weiss. (FRA)
307 Sprühdose für ein Mittel zur Vertilgung von fliegenden Insekten. Markenname gelb auf Schwarz, Pfeil weiss, Deckel gelb/orange. (USA)
308 Kunststoff-Flasche für ein desinfizierendes Waschmittel. Aus einem für südamerikanische Länder adaptierten Packungsprogramm. (USA)

301 Conception de bombes aérosol pour du vernis pour meubles. (GBR)
302 Ensemble de bombes aérosol et boîte métallique à couvercle figurant dans un programme global d'emballages pour un fabricant de produits de nettoyage pour l'auto. (USA)
303 Bombe aérosol pour un désodorisant de l'air ambiant parfumé à diverses essences. Etiquette circulaire bleu-vert, nom de la marque orange, flèche blanche. (SWI)
304 Gamme de bombes aérosols pour un désodorisant de l'air ambiant. Les chevrons sont de couleur différente suivant les parfums — vert, bleu, orange, violet — sur fond blanc. (SWI)
305 Bombe aérosol et étiquette pour un désodorisant de l'air ambiant. (USA)
306 Bombe de désodorisant. Bulles jaunes sur blanc, couvercle blanc. (FRA)
307 Bombe aérosol contre les insectes volants. Nom de la marque jaune sur noir, éclair blanc, couvercle jaune et orange. (USA)
308 Flacon plastique pour une lessive désinfectante. Elément d'un programme d'emballages conçu en fonction des marchés sud-américains. (USA)

Household, Hardware, Miscellaneous
Haushalt, Werkzeug, Verschiedenes
Articles ménagers, outillages, divers

309 Three variants from a line of cans for shoe care sprays. Humorous illustrations on white ground. Full colour. (GBR)
310 Pack for pelleted seeds with dispenser feature to facilitate sowing. Full colour. (GBR)
311 Cardboard box and its contents – a plastic bottle for a liquid weed killer and its applicator. (GBR)
312 Can for leather impregnating spray. Label brown, yellow, red and black. White cap. (SWI)
313 Package for lawn seed. Two greens, white and black. (USA)
314 Sprinkler containers for various types of fertilizer. The pattern is green and white. (GER)
315 Spray cans for insecticides. Left: white can, red cap, fly in full colour. Right: white can, colour stripes from yellow to red. Orange cap. (SPA / FRA)
316, 317 Components and entire applicator package for a drain cleaner. Pressure on top punctures the bottom of the can and releases its contents. Fig. 316: Cross-sectional diagram. (SWI)

309 Drei Varianten aus einer Serie von Sprühdosen für Schuhpflegemittel. Humoristische Illustrationen auf Weiss. (SWI)
310 Packung für pillierte Samen mit Spender-Ausguss zur Erleichterung des Säens. Mehrfarbig. (GBR)
311 Kartonschachtel und Inhalt – eine Kunststoff-Flasche für flüssigen Unkrautvertilger mit Sprühvorrichtung. (GBR)
312 Sprühdose für Lederimprägnierungsmittel. Etikett braun, gelb, rot und schwarz. Weisser Verschluss. (SWI)
313 Rasensamenpackung. Zwei Grüntöne, weiss, schwarz. (USA)
314 Streudosen für verschiedene Arten von Düngern. Die Farben des Musters sind Grün und Weiss. (GER)
315 Sprühdosen für Insektizide. Links: Weisse Dose, roter Verschluss, Fliege mehrfarbig. Rechts: Weisse Dose, Farbstreifen von Gelb bis Rot, Verschluss orange. (SPA / FRA)
316, 317 Einzelteile und ganze Applikator-Packung für einen Ablaufreiniger. Durch einen Schlag auf die Dose wird deren Boden durchstossen und der Inhalt ausgeleert. 316: Querschnitt. (SWI)

309 Trois variantes d'une gamme de sprays à chaussures. Dessins d'humour sur fond blanc. (SWI)
310 Sachet de graines avec orifice de distribution facilitant les semailles. En polychromie. (GBR)
311 Boîte en carton et son contenu: un désherbant liquide en bouteille plastique avec dispositif de vaporisation. (GBR)
312 Bombe aérosol pour l'imperméabilisation du cuir. Etiquette brun, jaune, rouge et noir. Couvercle blanc. (SWI)
313 Emballage de semences de gazon. Vert, blanc, noir. (USA)
314 Boîtes saupoudreuses pour divers engrais. Le motif employé est exécuté en vert et en blanc. (GER)
315 Bombes d'insecticides. A gauche: bombe blanche, couvercle rouge, mouche polychrome. A droite: bombe blanche, bandes couleur allant du jaune au rouge, couvercle orange. (SPA / FRA)
316, 317 Composants et conditionnement complet d'un débouche-tout comprenant un dispositif d'application. En appuyant fortement sur le couvercle, on libère le contenu. Coupe en 316. (SWI)

309

310

311
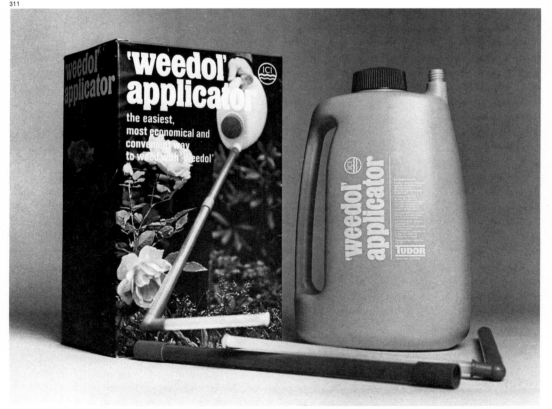

312

313

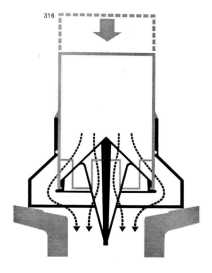

316

314

317

315

DESIGNER / GESTALTER / MAQUETTISTE:

309 Paul Maurer (Artist: René Fehr)
310 A. Robinson
311 George Smith
312 Migros Genossenschaftsbund,
    Abt. Verpackung
313 R. G. Smith/C. C. Woodring
314 Heinz Kroehl/Peter Offenberg
316, 317 Hans Beat Grimm

ART DIRECTOR / DIRECTEUR ARTISTIQUE:

309 André Heidelberger
311 George Smith
312 H. Uster
313 Harry Beatty
314 Heinz Kroehl/Peter Offenberg
316, 317 W. Nydegger

AGENCY / AGENTUR / AGENCE – STUDIO:

309 Wiener, Deville & Wälchli
311 Design Research Unit
312 Migros Genossenschaftsbund,
    Abt. Verpackung
314 Kroehl Design Gruppe
316, 317 Werbeagentur Hans Beat Grimm AG

CLIENT / AUFTRAGGEBER:

309 Sutter AG
310 Hurst Gunson Cooper Taber Ltd.
311 Plant Protection Ltd.
312 Migros Genossenschaftsbund
313 J. C. Penney Co.
314 Heims Baumschule & Landschaftsbau
315 Productos Bufalo/Shell Chimie
316, 317 Sipuro AG

Household, Hardware, Miscellaneous
Haushalt, Werkzeug, Verschiedenes
Articles ménagers, outillages, divers

318

318 Corrugated cardboard boxes containing meat-wrapping tissues. (SWI)
319 Plastic bottle of soft low-density polyethylene, with built-in bellows for a dusting powder against insects and fungi. (SWI)
320 Envelopes for flower and vegetable seeds. Printed in full colour. (GBR)
321 Boxes, spray and sprinkler cans for garden chemicals. (FRA)
322 Plastic carrier sacks for a range of garden fertilizers. The background colour photographs are printed in gravure. (GBR)

318 Wellpappeschachteln für Fleischwickler-Papiere. (SWI)
319 Faltenbalgflasche aus weichelastischem Hochdruckpolyäthylen für ein Stäube-pulver gegen Insekten und Pilzkrankheiten. (SWI)
320 Beutel für Blumen- und Gemüsesamen. Vierfarbig bedruckt. (GBR)
321 Packungen, Streu- und Sprühdosen für Pflanzenschutz und -nährmittel. (FRA)
322 Tragsäcke aus Kunststoff für ein Sortiment von Gartendüngern. Die als Hinter-grund verwendeten Farbphotos sind in Tiefdruck reproduziert. (GBR)

318 Boîtes de carton ondulé conçues pour du papier d'emballage de viandes. (SWI)
319 Flacon plastique en polyéthylène «haute pression» souple, à soufflets incorporés, pour une poudre insecticide et fongicide à pulvériser. (SWI)
320 Sachets de graines de fleurs et de légumes. Impression polychrome. (GBR)
321 Boîte, bombes aérosol et saupoudreuses pour des produits protecteurs et fertili-sants pour le jardin. (FRA)
322 Sacs portatifs en plastique pour un assortiment d'engrais pour le jardin. Les photos couleur composant le fond sont exécutées en héliogravure. (GBR)

319

320

DESIGNER / GESTALTER / MAQUETTISTE:

318 E + U Hiestand
319 DDB (Aufdruck)/Stephan Bartha,
     Ciba-Geigy (Form)
320 Gerry Barney/David Bristow/
     Terence Griffin/Jenny Sebley
321 C.E.I.-Loewy
322 George Smith

ART DIRECTOR / DIRECTEUR ARTISTIQUE:

318 E + U Hiestand
320 Gerry Barney/David Bristow/
     Terence Griffin/Jenny Sebley
321 C.E.I.-Loewy
322 Milner Gray

AGENCY / AGENTUR / AGENCE – STUDIO:

318 E + U Hiestand
319 Atelier Ciba-Geigy AG
320 Wolff Olins
321 C.E.I.-Loewy
322 Design Research Unit

CLIENT / AUFTRAGGEBER:

318 Feldmann Dutli
319 Ciba-Geigy AG
320 R & G Cuthbert
321 KB Jardin
322 ICI

321

322

323

324

323, 324 Boxes containing refill cups for household paper cup dispensers. Fig. 323: Bright ground colours, harmonizing with the cup colours. Photos in full colour. (USA)
325 Packaging for a range of bathroom fixtures. (GBR)
326 Folding box for paper tissues. Black and pink. (GBR)
327 Plastic pots and cardboard carrier boxes for pre-sprouted hyacinths. Polychrome. (NLD)
328 Package for non-woven disposable dish towels. The check pattern is in two shades of blue on white. (GBR)
329 Transparent plastic wrapper for two rolls of paper towels. Printed in bright colours. (GBR)
330 Pale blue plastic carrier pack for panty diapers. (SWI)
331 Display package for an electric toothbrush. (SWI)

323, 324 Schachteln mit Nachfüllbechern für Haushalt-Papierbecherspender. Abb. 323: Starke Grundfarben, mit den Becherfarben harmonierend. Photos vierfarbig. (USA)
325 Packungen für Badezimmer-Einrichtungen. (GBR)
326 Faltschachtel für Papiertücher. Rosa und Schwarz. (GBR)
327 Plastiktöpfe und Tragkartons für vorbehandelte Hyazinthen. Mehrfarbig bedruckt. (NLD)
328 Packung für nichttextile, wegwerfbare Geschirrtücher. Das karierte Muster ist in zwei Blautönen auf Weiss gedruckt. (GBR)
329 Transparente Plastikhülle für zwei Haushalt-Papierrollen. In leuchtenden Farben bedruckt. (GBR)
330 Hellblaue Plastiktragtasche für Höschenwindeln. (SWI)
331 Schaukarton für eine elektrische Zahnbürste. (SWI)

323, 324 Boîtes contenant des gobelets en carton pour la recharge de distributeurs de ménage. 323, fond en couleurs vives assorties à celles des gobelets. Photos polychromes. (USA)
325 Gamme d'emballages pour articles de salle de bains. (GBR)
326 Boîte pliante pour serviettes en papier. Rose, noir. (GBR)
327 Pots à fleurs en plastique et cartons portatifs pour des jacinthes traitées. Impression polychrome. (NLD)
328 Emballage pour des linges à vaisselle synthétiques à jeter. Motif à carreaux en deux tons bleus sur fond blanc. (GBR)
329 Emballage plastique transparent pour deux rouleaux de papier de ménage. Impression en couleurs éclatantes. (GBR)
330 Sac plastique bleu pâle pour des langes-culottes. (SWI)
331 Carton-présentoir pour une brosse à dents électrique. (SWI)

325

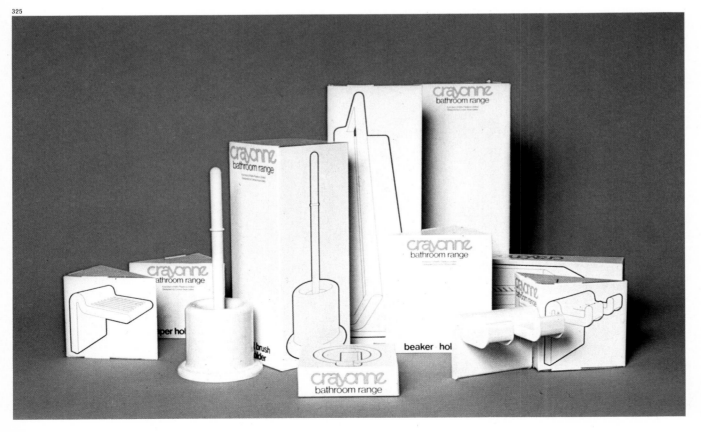

Household, Hardware
Haushalt, Werkzeug
Articles ménagers

326

327

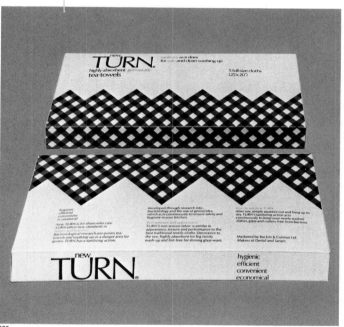

328

serla
Kitchen roll

329

330

331

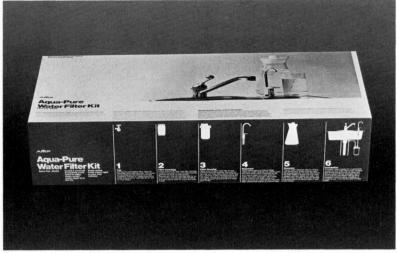

332

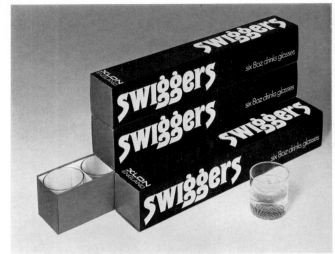

334

333

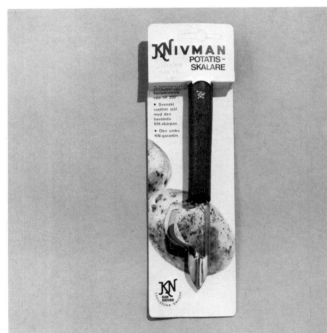

335

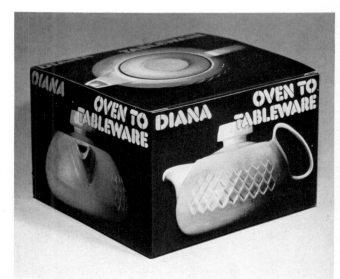

336

332 Box for a water filter kit. Photo black and white, side panel blue. (USA)
333 Folding box for a stainless-steel saucepan. Full colour. (SAF)
334 Slide boxes for glasses. Sleeves black and white, slides red. (GBR)
335 Display carton for a potato peeler. Potato in colour, die-cut "peel" passing through knife. (SWE)
336 Folding box for heat-resistant tableware. Red and orange on black. (AUL)
337 Slide box for a cutlery set. Maroon ground, gold stripe, white lettering. (SPA)
338 Folding box in solid colour, interpackage in expanded polystyrene for a safety razor. (USA)
339 Corrugated cardboard box for a salad server set. Black and white. (ITA)
340 Corrugated cardboard box for an electric mixer. Dark blue and black. (SWI)
341 Glasses serving as holders for perfumed wax candles. Removable labels. (USA)

332 Schachtel für Wasser-Filtergerät. Photo schwarzweiss, Seiten blau. (USA)
333 Faltschachtel für eine Pfanne aus rostfreiem Stahl. Vierfarbig gedruckt. (SAF)
334 Schiebeschachtel für Gläser. Futteral schwarzweiss, Schieber rot. (GBR)
335 Schaukarton für Kartoffelschälmesser. Farbig gedruckt, mit gestanzter Lasche. (SWE)
336 Faltschachtel für feuerfestes Geschirr. Rot und orange auf Schwarz. (AUL)
337 Schiebeschachtel für Besteckgarnitur. Braunroter Grund, Goldstreifen, weisse Schrift. (SPA)
338 Farbige Faltschachtel, Innenpackung aus geschäumtem Polystyrol, für Rasierapparat. (USA)
339 Mikrowellschachtel für elektrisches Handrührwerk. Schwarzweiss. (ITA)
340 Wellkartonschachtel für elektrisches Handrührwerk. Dunkelblau und schwarz. (SWI)
341 In Gläser eingefüllte parfümierte Wachskerzen. Die Etiketten können entfernt werden. (USA)

332 Boîte pour un filtre à eau. Photo noir et blanc, côtés bleus. (USA)
333 Boîte pliante pour une casserole en acier inox. En polychromie. (SAF)
334 Boîtes coulissantes pour verres à boire. Fourreau noir et blanc, partie coulissante rouge. (GBR)
335 Carton-présentoir pour un éplucheur. Pomme de terre en couleur, épluchure en découpe. (SWE)
336 Boîte pliante pour de la vaisselle réfractaire. Rouge et orange sur noir. (AUL)
337 Boîte coulissante pour des couverts. Fond brun-rouge, bande or, lettres blanches. (SPA)
338 Boîte pliante en couleur, emballage intérieur en mousse de polystyrène pour un rasoir. (USA)
339 Boîte de carton micro-ondulé pour un service à salade. Noir et blanc. (ITA)
340 Boîte de carton micro-ondulé pour un batteur-mélangeur électrique. Bleu foncé, noir. (SWI)
341 Bougies de cire parfumée coulées dans des verres. Etiquettes amovibles. (USA)

337

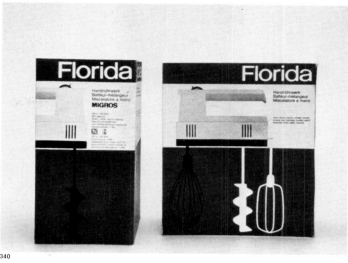

340

338

DESIGNER / GESTALTER / MAQUETTISTE:

332 Eugene J. Grossman/Paul Miller
333 Percy Itzler (Photo: Karl de Haan)
334 Collis Clements
336 Cato Hibberd Hawksby Design (Photo: John Pollard)
337 Julio Arruga Martinez
     (Artist: Julio Arruga Martinez/Francisco Arnò)
338 Nicholas Zarkades/Bruce F. Ray
339 Enzo Mari
340 Studio Pack-Design
341 J. M. Essex (Photo: John Bilecki)

ART DIRECTOR / DIRECTEUR ARTISTIQUE:

332 Eugene J. Grossman
333 Percy Itzler
334 Collis Clements
336 Cato Hibberd Hawksby Design
337 Julio Arruga Martinez
338 Bruce F. Ray
340 Xaver Bürgi
341 J. M. Essex

AGENCY / AGENTUR / AGENCE – STUDIO:

332 Anspach Grossman Portugal, Inc.
333 Young Advertising (Pty) Ltd.
334 Clarke/Clements/Hughes
335 Eco Annonsbyrå AB
336 Cato Hibberd Hawksby Pty Ltd.
337 Publicidad Vila International
338 The Gillette Company
340 Studio Pack-Design
341 Center for Communication Planning

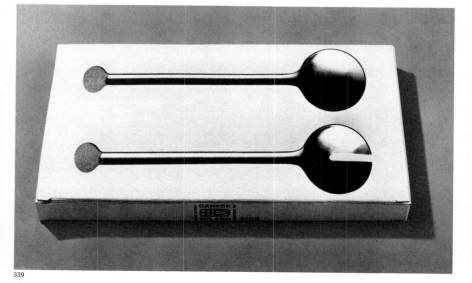

339

341

CLIENT / AUFTRAGGEBER:

332 AMF, Inc.
333 Aloe Stainless Steel
334 Xylon Products Ltd.
336 Diana Pottery Pty Ltd.
337 Industrias Tuperin
338 The Gillette Company
339 Bruno Danese
340 Migros Genossenschaftsbund
341 Earth Rise Designs, Inc.

Household, Hardware, Miscellaneous
Haushalt, Werkzeug, Verschiedenes
Articles ménagers, outillages, divers

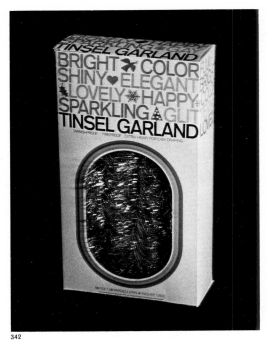

342

343

346

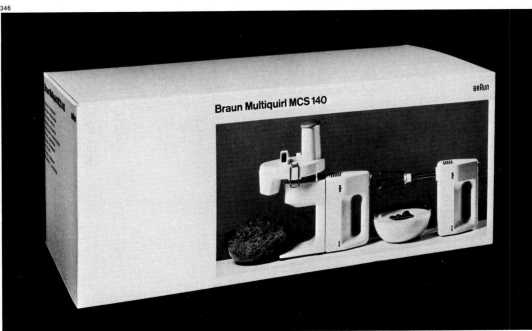

347

350

351

344

345

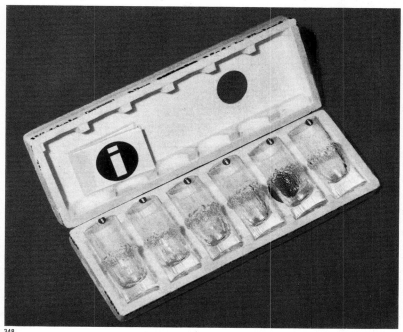

348

349

DESIGNER / GESTALTER / MAQUETTISTE:

342 Harry & Marian Zelenko
343 Studio Pack-Design
344, 348 Tapio Wirkkala
345 Terry Lesnievicz (Photo: Mason Pavlak)
346, 347 Braun Kommunikationsabteilung
349 James C. Douglass
350, 351 Richard Henderson
352 Mervyn Kurlansky (Photo: Peter Higgins/
      Heini Schneebeli)

ART DIRECTOR / DIRECTEUR ARTISTIQUE:

342 Harry & Marian Zelenko
343 Xaver Bürgi
344, 348 Tapio Wirkkala
345 Terry Lesnievicz
346, 347 Braun Kommunikationsabteilung
349 James C. Douglass
350, 351 Richard Henderson
352 Mervyn Kurlansky

AGENCY / AGENTUR / AGENCE – STUDIO:

342 Harry & Marian Zelenko, Inc.
343 Studio Pack-Design
345 Flournoy & Gibbs, Inc.
346, 347 Braun Kommunikationsabteilung
349 Agence Alain Richard SA
350, 351 Richard Henderson Design
352 Pentagram Design Partnership Ltd.

CLIENT / AUFTRAGGEBER:

342 Paper Novelty Manufacturing Co.
343 Trisa Bürstenfabrik
344, 348 Iittala Glassworks
345 Arnold Industries
346, 347 Braun AG
349 Auto-Siphon
350, 351 Wayne Pottery
352 Kenwood Ltd.

342 Box with die-cut window for Christmas-tree decorations. Brightly coloured lettering. (USA)
343 Display box for an electric hair-drying brush. Cardboard and clear acetate. (SWI)
344, 348 Foam plastic box, shown closed and open, containing six liqueur glasses. (FIN)
345 Folding box for a water purifier. Blue and black. (USA)
346, 347 Cardboard boxes for a line of electrical household appliances. The photographs of the contents are reproduced in full colour. Basic colour of box is white. (GER)
349 Corrugated cardboard box for a sodawater syphon bottle. (FRA)
350, 351 Cardboard box for a stoneware pot. Ground colour of box is black, lettering silk-screened, spreading over three sides. Seal red. (AUL)
352 Corrugated cardboard box for an electric kitchen appliance. Four-colour printing. (GBR)

342 Schachtel mit Fenster für Christbaumschmuck. Schrift und Fensterrahmen mehrfarbig. (USA)
343 Ausstellschachtel aus Karton und Acetat für eine elektrische Haartrocknerbürste. (SWI)
344, 348 Schaumstoffschachtel, geschlossen und offen, für sechs Likörgläser. (FIN)
345 Faltschachtel für ein Wasserfiltergerät. Blau und Schwarz. (USA)
346, 347 Kartonschachteln für eine Reihe elektrischer Haushaltgeräte. Die photographischen Abbildungen sind vierfarbig reproduziert. Grundfarbe weiss. (GER)
349 Mikrowellschachtel für eine Siphonflasche. (FRA)
350, 351 Kartonschachtel für Töpfereiware. Grundfarbe der Schachtel ist schwarz. Schrift im Siebdruck über drei Seiten gezogen, Siegel rot. (AUL)
352 Wellpappeschachtel für ein elektrisches Küchengerät. Vierfarbig bedruckt. (GBR)

342 Boîte avec fenêtre en découpe, pour une décoration d'arbre de Noël. Lettres couleur. (USA)
343 Boîte-présentoir pour une brosse-séchoir électrique. Carton et acétate de cellulose. (SWI)
344, 348 Boîte en mousse plastique fermée et ouverte, pour six verres à liqueur. (FIN)
345 Boîte pliante pour un filtre à eau. Bleu et noir. (USA)
346, 347 Boîtes en carton pour une gamme d'appareils électroménagers. La photo du contenu est à chaque fois reproduite en polychromie. Le blanc a été choisi comme couleur de fond. (GER)
349 Boîte en carton micro-ondulé pour un siphon. (FRA)
350, 351 Boîte en carton pour un pot de grès. Le fond de la boîte est noir, le lettrage exécuté en sérigraphie s'étend sur trois côtés. Sceau rouge. (AUL)
352 Boîte en carton micro-ondulé pour un appareil électrique pour la cuisine. Polychromie. (GBR)

352

353

353 Cardboard gift box with transparent inner box of vacuum-formed PVC holding and protecting the contents, two ceramic vases. (GER)
354 Corrugated cardboard box for a decorative glass ball. The cut-out holes allow the contents to be seen. Outside of box is black, inside white. (SWI)
355 Packaging design programme for a line of tableware. The name *Heller* is applied in the same size throughout the range, thus forming different package identities. Red on white. (USA)
356 Sleeves for combs. Gold on white. Cut-out window showing the brand name. (AUS)

353 Faltschachtel mit transparenter, vakuumverformter PVC-Einlage, die zwei keramische Vasen festhält und vor Transportschäden schützt. (GER)
354 Mikrowellkartonschachtel für eine dekorative Glaskugel. Die gestanzten Ausschnitte machen den Inhalt sichtbar. Die Schachtel ist aussen schwarz, innen weiss. (SWI)
355 Packungsprogramm für ein Tischgeschirrsortiment. Der Markenname erscheint auf allen Packungen in der gleichen Grösse, was jeder Schachtel ihre eigene Identität gibt. Rot auf Weiss. (USA)
356 Kartonscheiden für Kämme. Gold auf Weiss. Markenname sichtbar durch gestanztes Oval. (AUS)

353 Carton-cadeau renfermant une boîte transparente en CPV moulé sous vide, qui assure stabilité et protection au contenu – deux vases en céramique. (GER)
354 Boîte de carton micro-ondulé pour une boule de verre décorative. Les hublots ménagés dans la boîte visualisent le contenu. Extérieur de la boîte noir, face interne en blanc. (SWI)
355 Ligne d'emballages réalisée pour une gamme de services de table. Le nom de la marque apparaît au même format sur tous les emballages, ce qui les différencie. Rouge sur blanc. (USA)
356 Etuis à peignes en carton. Or sur blanc. La marque est visible dans l'ovale en découpe. (AUS)

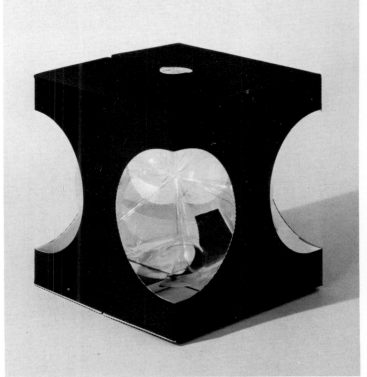

354

355

DESIGNER / GESTALTER / MAQUETTISTE:

353 Villeroy & Boch (Konstruktion:
    Gustav Stabernack)
354 Roberto Niederer
355 Massimo Vignelli
356 J. Skone

ART DIRECTOR / DIRECTEUR ARTISTIQUE:

354 Roberto Niederer
355 Massimo Vignelli
356 O. Habsburg

AGENCY / AGENTUR / AGENCE – STUDIO:

354 Roberto Niederer
355 Vignelli Associates

CLIENT / AUFTRAGGEBER:

353 Villeroy & Boch
354 Roberto Niederer
355 Heller Designs, Inc.
356 Semperit AG

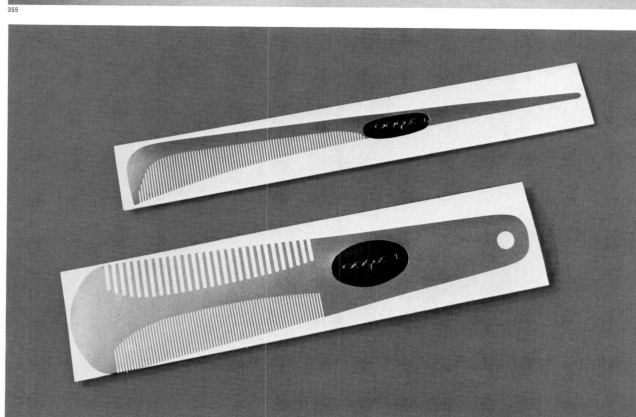

356

Household, Hardware
Haushalt, Werkzeug
Articles ménagers

357

DESIGNER / GESTALTER / MAQUETTISTE:

357 Morten Jersild A/S
358 Sivert Ahringer (Photo: Ateljé von Sterneck)
359 Fumio Hirai/Hamako Yoshizawa
360 Gillian Dathen
361–363 Helfried Hagenberg

ART DIRECTOR / DIRECTEUR ARTISTIQUE:

358 Karlerik Lindgren
359 Fumio Hirai
360 Christopher Timings
361–363 Helfried Hagenberg

AGENCY / AGENTUR / AGENCE – STUDIO:

357 Morten Jersild A/S
358 Sivert Ahringer AB
360 Design Research Unit

CLIENT / AUFTRAGGEBER:

357 Bing & Grøndahl Copenhagen Porcelain
358 AB Orrefors Glasbruk
359 Tokyo Shibaura Electric Co. Ltd.
360 Kabor Ltd.
361–363 Nordlys, Kurt Müller OHG

Household, Hardware, Miscellaneous
Haushalt, Werkzeug, Verschiedenes
Articles ménagers, outillages, divers

358

357 Corrugated cardboard carrier boxes for a line of tableware. (DEN)
358 Packaging for a set of drinking glasses with separate metal handles. The photograph on the lid is printed in full colour. (SWE)
359 Display box for an electric shaver, shown closed and opened to expose the transparent acetate window. (JPN)
360 Label for a line of garden products. Green "K", orange bee. (GBR)
361 – 363 Brown hexagonal folding box for a pepper mill. Fig. 361: Box unfolded. Figs. 362 and 363: Package as shown on display shelf. (GER)

357 Tragkartons aus Mikrowelle für ein Tafelgeschirr-Sortiment. (DEN)
358 Packung für vier Trinkgläser mit abnehmbaren Metallgriffen. Das Photo auf dem Deckel ist vierfarbig gedruckt. (SWE)
359 Ausstellschachtel für einen elektrischen Rasierapparat, geschlossen und geöffnet, um das transparente Acetatfenster freizulegen. (JPN)
360 Etikett für eine Serie von Gartenprodukten. Grün, orange. (GBR)
361 – 363 Braune, sechseckige Faltschachtel für eine Pfeffermühle. Abb. 361: Schachtel ungefalzt. Abb. 362 und 363: Zusammengesteckte Packung und Aufstellung der Packungen zum Verkauf. (GER)

357 Cartons portatifs micro-ondulés pour de la vaisselle. (DEN)
358 Coffret contenant quatre verres à boire et, dans un compartiment séparé, quatre anses métalliques amovibles. Photo du couvercle en polychromie. (SWE)
359 Carton-présentoir pour un rasoir électrique, montré fermé et ouvert pour mettre en évidence la fenêtre transparente en acétate de cellulose. (JPN)
360 Etiquette pour une série de produits de jardinage. Vert et orange. (GBR)
361 – 363 Boîte pliante hexagonale brune pour un moulin à poivre. 361, avant le pliage; 362, boîte pliée; 363, boîtes assemblées en vitrine. (GER)

359

360

361

362

363

Sports, Pastimes,
Tobacco Products

Sport, Freizeit, Rauchwaren

Sports, Loisirs, Tabac

5

364

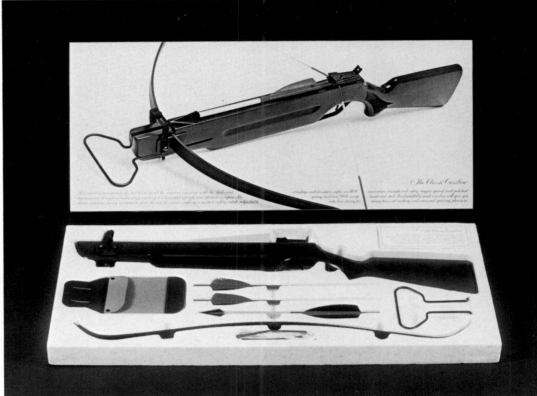

365

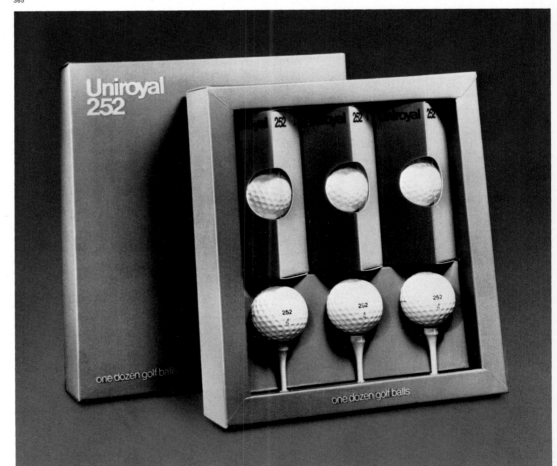

366

DESIGNER / GESTALTER / MAQUETTISTE:

365 David Goodman/Frank Cheatham
    (Photo: Stan Caplan)
366 Richard Edstrom
367 Dyer/Brühwiler
368 Eugene J. Grossman
369 Juan Concepcion
370 Schlechter & Luth, Inc.

ART DIRECTOR / DIRECTEUR ARTISTIQUE:

365 David Goodman
366, 369 Richard Gerstman
367 Rod Dyer/Paul Brühwiler
368 Eugene J. Grossman

AGENCY / AGENTUR / AGENCE–STUDIO:

364 Creative Packaging Co.
365 Porter, Goodman & Cheatham
366, 369 Gerstman & Meyers, Inc.
367 Dyer/Brühwiler
368 Anspach Grossman Portugal, Inc.
370 Schlechter & Luth, Inc.

CLIENT / AUFTRAGGEBER:

364 Shure Brothers, Inc.
365 The Leisure Group, Inc.
366, 369 Uniroyal, Inc.
367 Brown Saltman
368 AMF, Inc.
370 R. J. Reynolds Tobacco Co.

367

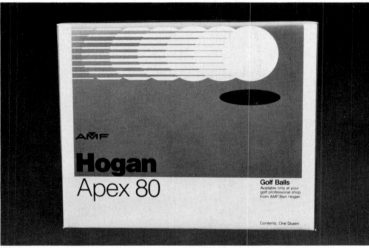

368

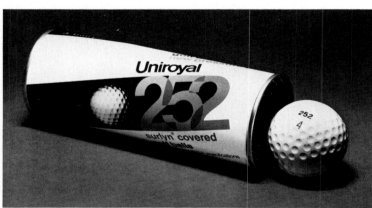

369

370

364 Folding box containing a microphone. Red and silver on black. (USA)
365 Moulded styrofoam package for the dismantled parts of a crossbow kit. Cardboard lid, printed in full colour. (USA)
366 Gift package for a set of 12 golf balls. Green and mustard. (USA)
367 Display carton for a folding chair. Black and red. (USA)
368 Carton for golf balls. Green, black and white. (USA)
369 Metal can for golf balls. Orange, two reds and black on white. (USA)
370 Cigarette package designed especially for female smokers. (USA)

364 Faltschachtel für Mikrophon. Schrift in Rot und Silber auf Schwarz. (USA)
365 Geformte Schaumstoffpackung für die Einzelteile einer Armbrustgarnitur. Kartondeckel vierfarbig bedruckt. (USA)
366 Geschenkpackung für 12 Golfbälle. Grün und senffarbig. (USA)
367 Ausstell-Verpackung für einen Klappstuhl. Schwarz und rot. (USA)
368 Schachtel für Golfbälle. Grün, schwarz und weiss. (USA)
369 Metallbüchse für Golfbälle. Orange, zwei Rottöne und Schwarz. (USA)
370 Zigarettenpackung, speziell für weibliche Raucher konzipiert. (USA)

364 Boîte pliante pour un micro. Rouge et argent sur noir. (USA)
365 Emballage de styrène expansé pour les éléments d'une arbalète. Couvercle en carton, impression polychrome. (USA)
366 Emballage-cadeau pour une série de 12 balles de golf. Vert, moutarde. (USA)
367 Carton illustré pour une chaise pliante. Noir et rouge. (USA)
368 Carton de balles de golf. Vert, noir et blanc. (USA)
369 Etui métallique pour balles de golf. Orange, deux rouges et noir. (USA)
370 Paquet de cigarettes conçu tout spécialement pour les fumeuses. (USA)

371

372

DESIGNER / GESTALTER / MAQUETTISTE:

371, 372 George Tscherny
373 X. Bürgi
374 Christopher Holt
375, 377, 378 Bruno K. Wiese
376 Fernand Maumary
379 Marcel Jacno

ART DIRECTEUR / DIRECTEUR ARTISTIQUE:

371, 372 Robert Hungerford
374 F. H. K. Henrion
375, 377, 378 Bruno K. Wiese
379 Marcel Jacno

AGENCY / AGENTUR / AGENCE–STUDIO:

371, 372 George Tscherny, Inc.
373 Studio Pack Design
374 Henrion Design Association
375, 377, 378 Studio für Visual Design

373

371, 372 Design concept for cigarette packages. (USA)
373 Sleeve-and-tray box for cigars. The sleeve has real wood veneer laminated to its paperboard base. Dark brown wood, "Opal" in gold on red oval, tray red. (SWI)
374 Carton and single pack of a cigarette brand sold duty-free on the planes of an airline. Red ground with dark blue and white. (GBR)
375 Paper-wrapped package of twelve cigarette packs. (GER)
376 Cigarette pack designed for the Nigerian market. (SWI)
377 Package design for mentholated cigarettes. Silver, blue and green. (GER)
378 Flip-top cigarette packs. Left: black and gold. Right: red on white. Coats of arms red, blue and gold. (GER)
379 Paper and foil pack for cigarettes. Printed in two blues and black. (FRA)

371, 372 Gestaltungskonzept für Zigarettenpackungen. (USA)
373 Schiebeschachtel für Zigarren. Echtes Holzfournier ist auf den Karton der Hülle laminiert. Dunkelbraunes Holz, «Opal» in Gold auf rotem Oval, Schieber rot. (SWI)
374 Schachteln für 200 und 20 Zigaretten, die zollfrei in den Flugzeugen einer Fluggesellschaft verkauft werden. Roter Grund mit Dunkelblau und Weiss. (GBR)
375 Papiereingeschlagenes Gebinde für zwölf Schachteln Zigaretten. (GER)
376 Zigarettenpackung, für den nigerischen Markt gestaltet. (SWI)
377 Packungsgestaltung für Menthol-Zigaretten. Silber, blau und grün. (GER)
378 Flip-top Zigarettenpackungen. Links: Schwarz und Gold. Rechts: Rot auf Weiss. Wappen in Rot, Blau und Gold. (GER)
379 Zigarettenpackung aus Papier und Folie. In zwei Blautönen und Schwarz gedruckt. (FRA)

371, 372 Etude esthétique de paquets de cigarettes. (USA)
373 Boîte coulissante pour cigares. Une feuille de placage véritable est laminée à même le carton de la boîte. Bois brun foncé, «Opal» or dans ovale rouge, tiroir rouge. (SWI)
374 Cartouche et paquet d'une marque de cigarettes vendue hors taxe dans les avions d'une compagnie aérienne. Fond rouge, impression bleu foncé et blanc. (GBR)
375 Emballage papier de douze paquets de cigarettes. (GER)
376 Paquet de cigarettes conçu pour le marché nigérien. (SWI)
377 Conception de paquet pour cigarettes au menthol. Argent, bleu et vert. (GER)
378 Paquets de cigarettes à couvercle basculant. A gauche: noir et or; à droite: rouge sur blanc. Armoiries en rouge, bleu, or. (GER)
379 Paquet de cigarettes en papier et papier métallisé. Impression: deux bleus, noir. (FRA)

Sports, Pastimes, Tobacco Products
Sport, Freizeit, Rauchwaren
Sports, Loisirs, Tabac

377

375

374

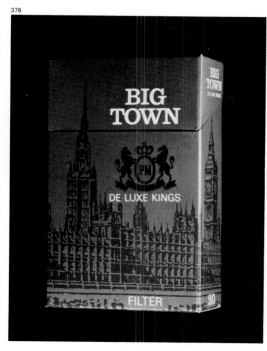

376

378

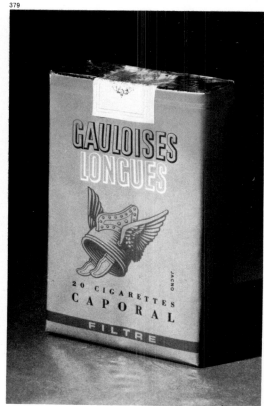

379

135

Sports, Pastimes, Tobacco Products
Sport, Freizeit, Rauchwaren
Sports, Loisirs, Tabac

381

382

383

380

384

136

385

386

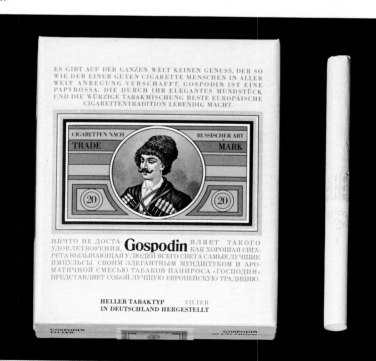

387

388

380 Paper and foil pack for a brand of cigarettes. (FRA)
381 Tin and pouches for pipe tobacco mixtures. (DEN)
382, 383 Cardboard box for five cigars. An outer sleeve which slides down and folds out (Fig. 383) releases the hinged lid of the inner box. Black and gold on white. (NLD)
384 Designs for a series of matchbook covers produced by a food manufacturing company. Bold black outlines, bright colours within. (USA)
385 Matchbook covers. The designs are taken from mineral-water labels (see Fig. 135). (NOR)
386 Cardboard pack for cigarettes. (AUL)
387 Pack for a Russian-type filter cigarette. (GER)
388 Design for a cigarette pack and carton appealing to female smokers. (USA)

380 Packung aus Papier und Folie für eine Zigarettenmarke. (FRA)
381 Dose und Beutel für Pfeifentabak-Mischungen. (DEN)
382, 383 Kartonschachtel für fünf Zigarren. Eine äussere Schiebemanschette, die sich beim Hinunterschieben ausfaltet (siehe Abb. 383), gibt den Klappdeckel der inneren Schachtel frei. In Schwarz und Gold auf Weiss gedruckt. (NLD)
384 Serie von Motiven für die Klappen von Streichholzbriefchen, von einer Firma der Nahrungsmittelbranche herausgegeben. Schwarze Konturen umrahmen leuchtende Farbtöne. (USA)
385 Streichholzbrieflein. Motive von Mineralwasseretiketten übernommen (Abb. 135). (NOR)
386 Kartonschachtel für Zigaretten. (AUL)
387 Packung für Zigaretten nach russischer Art. (GER)
388 Gestaltung von Packungen für eine an Damen appellierende Zigarettenmarke. (USA)

380 Paquet en papier et papier métallisé pour une marque de cigarettes. (FRA)
381 Boîte et blagues à tabac conçues pour une marque de tabac pour la pipe. (DEN)
382, 383 Boîte en carton contenant cinq cigares. En faisant coulisser le tiroir et en le rabattant (fig. 383), on fait apparaître le boîtier intérieur pourvu d'un rabat de fermeture. Noir et or sur blanc. (NLD)
384 Dessins de pochettes d'allumettes réalisées pour une société de produits alimentaires. Personnages délinéés au crayon gras, en noir, avec couleurs vives à l'intérieur. (USA)
385 Pochettes d'allumettes. Sujets: étiquettes de bouteilles d'eau minérale (cf. fig. 135). (NOR)
386 Paquet de cigarettes, en carton. (AUL)
387 Paquet de cigarettes russes à bout filtrant. (GER)
388 Présentation d'une marque de cigarettes pour femmes, paquet et cartouche. (USA)

DESIGNER / GESTALTER / MAQUETTISTE:

389 William Field (Artist: Leroy Hughes)
390, 392, 393 Paul Giambarba
391 William Field (Artist: Stan Malcolm)

ART DIRECTOR / DIRECTEUR ARTISTIQUE:

389–393 William Field

AGENCY / AGENTUR / AGENCE–STUDIO:

390, 392, 393 Studio Giambarba

CLIENT / AUFTRAGGEBER:

389–393 Polaroid Corp.

389

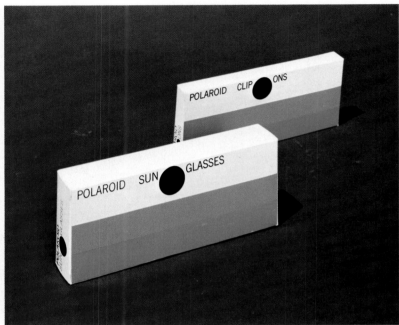

390

389–393 From the packaging design programme of the Polaroid Corporation. (USA)
389 Display boxes in various colours for a camera designed for the youth market.
390 Folding boxes for sun-glasses.
391 Colour-coded cardboard boxes for various types of 4×5″ colour and black-and-white film material for professional photographers.
392 Group of packages for cameras, accessories and films.
393 Cardboard boxes for colour and black-and-white films.

389–393 Beispiele aus dem Packungsgestaltungsprogramm der Polaroid Corporation. (USA)
389 Ausstellschachteln in verschiedenen Farbvarianten für eine Kamera, die hauptsächlich für den Jugendmarkt konzipiert wurde.
390 Faltschachteln für Sonnenbrillen.
391 Farbkodierte Kartonschachteln für verschiedene Arten von Farb- und Schwarzweissfilmmaterial für Berufsphotographen.
392 Gruppe von Packungen für Photoapparate, Zubehör und Filme.
393 Kartonschachteln für Farb- und Schwarzweissfilme.

389–393 Eléments du programme de conditionnement de la Polaroïd Corporation. (USA)
389 Emballages illustrés pour un appareil photo destiné aux jeunes. Diverses couleurs.
390 Cartons pliants pour lunettes de soleil.
391 Cartouches en carton, présentées selon un code-couleur, pour divers types de films 10×13 en couleurs et noir et blanc destinés aux professionnels.
392 Série d'emballages réalisés pour des appareils photo, des accessoires et des films.
393 Boîtes en carton pour films noir-blanc et en couleurs.

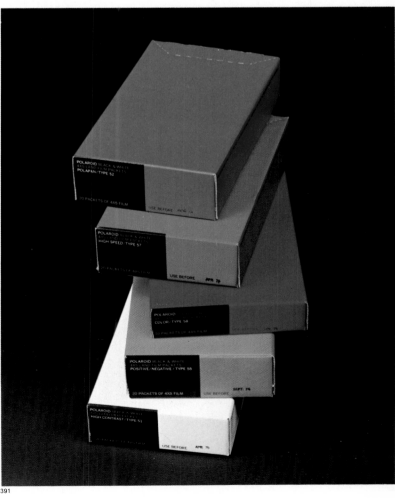

391

392

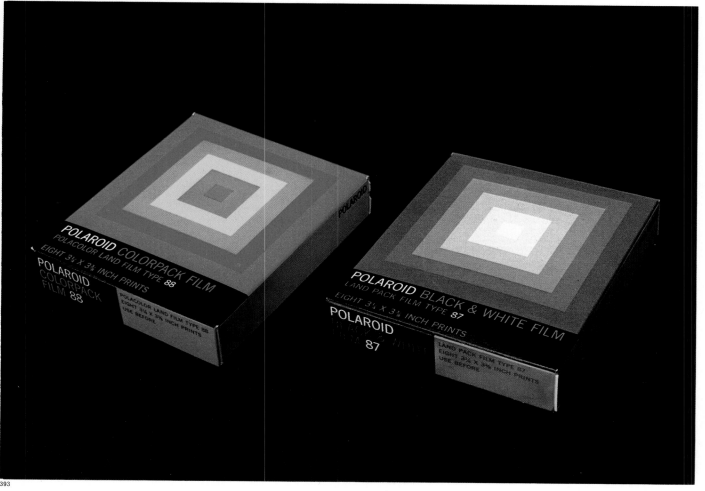

393

394

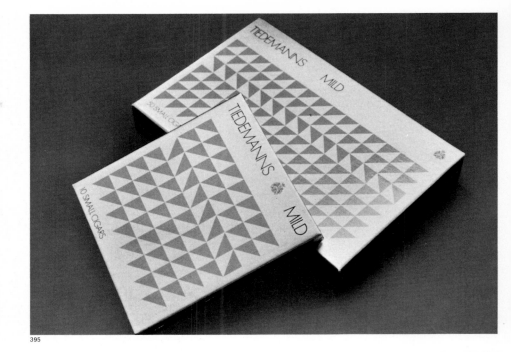

395

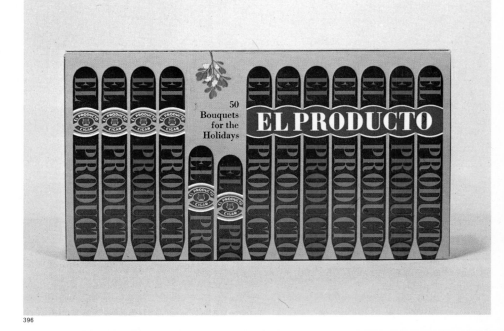

396

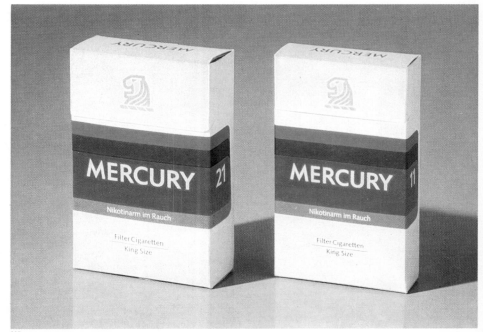

397

394 Flip-top pack for a brand of filter cigarettes. (GER)
395 Set-up boxes for ten and fifty cigarillos. Ochre pattern, lettering dark brown, printed on gold foil. (NOR)
396 Cardboard gift package for fifty cigars. (USA)
397 Flip-top packs for a brand of king-size filter cigarettes. (GER)
398 Soft pack for twenty small cigars. Golden yellow on black. (USA)
399 Gift package for cigars. Red and dark green. (USA)
400 Kit for making filter cigarettes, with its folding box and a box for cigarette papers. (USA)
401 Pouches for a range of Danish pipe tobaccos in various blends. (USA)

394 Klappdeckel-Schachtel für eine Filterzigaretten-Marke. (GER)
395 Schachteln in Festkartonage für zehn und fünfzig Kleinzigarren. Muster in Ocker, Schrift dunkelbraun, auf Goldfolie gedruckt. (NOR)
396 Geschenkschachtel aus Karton für fünfzig Zigarren. (USA)
397 Flip-Top-Kartonschachtel für eine Filterzigaretten-Marke. (GER)
398 Weichpackung für zwanzig kleine Zigarren. Goldgelb auf Schwarz. (USA)
399 Geschenkpackung für Zigarren. Rot und dunkelgrün. (USA)
400 Ausrüstung zum Selbermachen von Filterzigaretten, mit Faltschachtel für Dose und Packung für Zigarettenpapier. (USA)
401 Beutel für verschiedene Mischungen von dänischem Pfeifentabak. (USA)

394 Paquet de cigarettes-filtre; couvercle à rabat. (GER)
395 Boîtes montées pour dix et cinquante cigarillos. Motif ocre, caractères brun foncé; impression sur papier métallisé or. (NOR)
396 Emballage-cadeau en carton, pour cinquante cigares. (USA)
397 Paquets à couvercle basculant pour cigarettes-filtre king-size. (GER)
398 Paquetage sous papier pour vingt cigarillos. Jaune or sur noir. (USA)
399 Emballage-cadeau pour cigares. Rouge et vert foncé. (USA)
400 Accessoires pour cigarettes roulées à la main: boîte de tabac à fumer et boîte pliante qui la contient; boîte de papier à cigarettes. (USA)
401 Blagues pour divers mélanges de tabac danois pour la pipe. (USA)

Sports, Pastimes, Tobacco Products
Sport, Freizeit, Rauchwaren
Sports, Loisirs, Tabac

398

400

399

401

DESIGNER / GESTALTER / MAQUETTISTE:

394, 397 Bruno K. Wiese
395 Bruno Oldani
396, 399 Irv Koons
398 Alan Peckolick
400 Gianninoto Assoc.
401 Photo: Ken Korch

ART DIRECTOR / DIRECTEUR ARTISTIQUE:

395 Bruno Oldani
396, 399 Irv Koons
398 Alan Peckolick
400 John Di Gianni
401 Alan Honig

AGENCY / AGENTUR / AGENCE–STUDIO:

394, 397 Studio für Visual Design
395 Bruno Oldani
396, 399 Irv Koons Assoc., Inc.
398 Lubalin Smith Carnase
400 Gianninoto Associates
401 Mervin & Jesse Levine, Inc.

CLIENT / AUFTRAGGEBER:

394 Zigarettenfabrik Kristinus
395 Tiedemanns Tobakksfabrikk
396, 399 Consolidated Cigar Corp.
397 Zigarettengruppe Brinkmann
398 S.S.C. & B.
400 Brown & Williamson Tobacco Corporation
401 Hollco

402

DESIGNER / GESTALTER / MAQUETTISTE:

402 Martin Causer
403–405 Yusaku Kamekura
406 R. G. Smith/C. C. Woodring
407 Jack Weiss
408 Linda Hinrichs
409 Fred O. Bechlen

ART DIRECTOR / DIRECTEUR ARTISTIQUE:

402 Derek Birdsall
403–405 Yusaku Kamekura
406 Harry Beatty
407 Jack.Weiss
409 Fred O. Bechlen

403

404

407

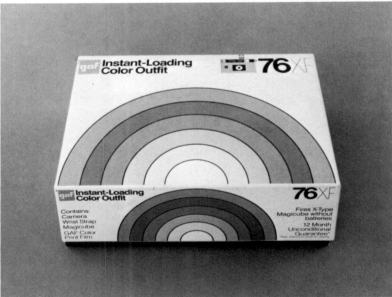

408

402 Packs for colour print films. Grey, white and black with one code colour. (GBR)
403–405 Package designs for a range of photographic and optical equipment manufactured by an optical company. Printed in black or black and grey on silver ground. (JPN)
406 Labels for blank recording cassettes. Part of the co-ordinated package design programme of a department store chain. (USA)
407 Folding box for a 16-mm sample reel for a film studio. Bright red and white. (USA)
408 Box for a camera outfit. Rainbow colours on white. (USA)
409 Boxes for cameras and lenses. Photographic motifs in full colour. Sides black. (JPN)

402 Packungen für Farbfilme. Grau, weiss und schwarz mit einer Erkennungsfarbe. (GBR)
403–405 Packungsgestaltung für eine Serie von photographischen und optischen Geräten. Schwarz oder schwarz und grau bedruckt auf Silbergrund. (JPN)
406 Etikette für unbespielte Tonbandkassetten. Bestandteil des koordinierten Packungsgestaltungsprogrammes einer Warenhauskette. (USA)
407 Faltschachtel für 16mm-Musterfilmrollen eines Filmstudios. Helles Rot und Weiss. (USA)
408 Schachtel für eine Kamera-Ausrüstung. Regenbogenfarben auf Weiss. (USA)
409 Schachteln für Kameras und Objektive. Photographische Motive farbig, Seiten schwarz. (JPN)

402 Emballages de films couleur. Gris, blanc, noir avec une couleur de codage. (GBR)
403–405 Exemples d'emballages pour une gamme d'appareils photo et d'optique fabriqués par une entreprise spécialisée. Noir resp. noir et gris sur fond argent. (JPN)
406 Etiquettes pour cassettes vierges, intégrées dans un programme global de design d'emballage réalisé pour une chaîne de grands magasins. (USA)
407 Boîte pliante d'un studio de cinéma: bobine spécimen, 16 mm. Rouge vif et blanc. (USA)
408 Boîte pour un équipement photo complet. Couleurs arc-en-ciel sur fond blanc. (USA)
409 Emballages d'appareils photo et d'objectifs. Sujets photo polychromes; côtés en noir. (JPN)

Sports, Pastimes, Tobacco Products
Sport, Freizeit, Rauchwaren
Sports, Loisirs, Tabac

142

AGENCY / AGENTUR / AGENCE – STUDIO:

402 Omnific Ltd.
407 The Design Partnership
408 Hinrichs Design Assoc.
409 Koide Advertising Art. Inc./
      Dentsu Advertising Ltd.

CLIENT / AUFTRAGGEBER:

402 Film Corporation of America (U. K.) Ltd.
403–405 Nippon Kogaku K. K.
406 J. C. Penney Co.
407 Ash & Associates
408 G. A. F.
409 Minolta Camera Co. Ltd.

406

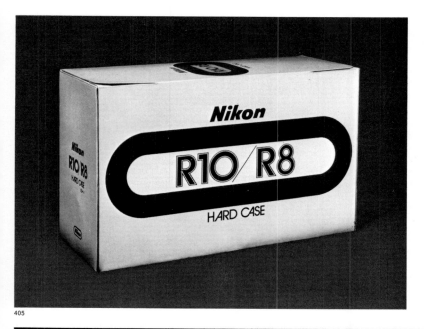

405

409

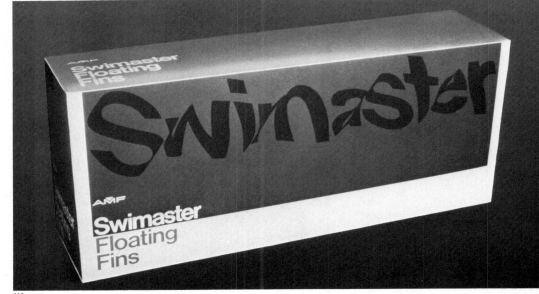

410

410 Carton for swimming fins. Red, white and blue. (USA)
411 Protective container for a marine instrument. (USA)
412 Corrugated cardboard box for an educational kit in social studies. White lettering on light blue. (USA)
413 Boxes containing recording belts used as teaching aids in secretarial and business schools. White lettering on solid colours, such as brown, green or black. (USA)
414 Set-up box for learning games used in schools. (GER)
415 Typographic design for a corrugated cardboard box containing a car radio. Blue and white. (JPN)
416, 417 ''Book laboratory'' with instructions and equipment for experiments in electronics. White, green and transparent plastic, drawing yellow, grey and red. (GER)
418 Box containing an audio-visual educational game used as a teaching aid in social studies. Red, blue, white. (USA)

410 Schachtel für Schwimmflossen. Rot, weiss, blau. (USA)
411 Schutzpackung für ein Schiffsinstrument. (USA)
412 Wellkartonschachtel für Lehrmaterialien in Soziologie-Klassen. Weisse Schrift auf hellblauem Grund. (USA)
413 Stülpdeckel-Schachteln für Endlosbänder, die als Lehrmittel in Handelsschulen gebraucht werden. Weisse Schrift auf einfarbigem Grund (braun, grün, schwarz). (USA)
414 Schachtel für pädagogische Lernspiele für Schulen. (GER)
415 Typographische Gestaltung der Kartonschachtel für ein Auto-Radio. Blau und weiss. (JPN)
416, 417 «Buchlabor» mit Instruktionen und Baukastenelementen für elektronische Experimente. Weisses, grünes und durchsichtiges Plastik. Deckelzeichnung gelb, grau und rot. (GER)
418 Schachtel für ein audio-visuelles pädagogisches Spiel für Soziologieklassen. Rot, blau und weiss. (USA)

410 Carton pour une paire de palmes. Rouge, blanc, bleu. (USA)
411 Emballage de protection: instrument de navigation. (USA)
412 Carton micro-ondulé pour du matériel pédagogique utilisé en sociologie. Texte blanc sur fond bleu clair. (USA)
413 Boîtes contenant des bandes magnétiques sans fin utilisées pour l'enseignement dans les écoles de secrétariat et de commerce. Lettres blanches sur fond couleur uni (brun, vert ou noir). (USA)
414 Boîte rigide pour un jeu éducatif utilisé dans les écoles. (GER)
415 Conception typo d'une boîte en carton micro-ondulé contenant un autoradio. Bleu et blanc. (JPN)
416, 417 «Livre-laboratoire» contenant un manuel d'instruction et l'équipement nécessaire pour se livrer à des expériences d'électronique. Plastique blanc, vert et transparent; dessin de couverture jaune, gris, rouge. (GER)
418 Boîte contenant un jeu éducatif audio-visuel utilisé dans les classes de sociologie. Rouge, bleu, blanc. (USA)

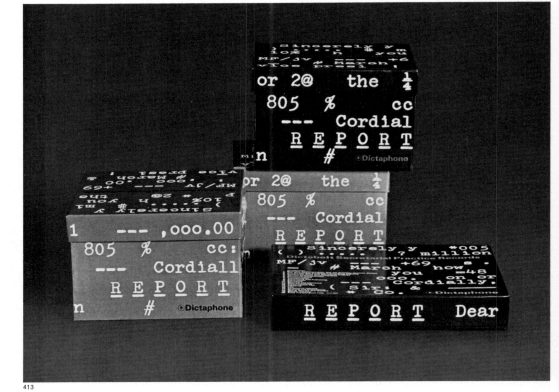

413

416

417

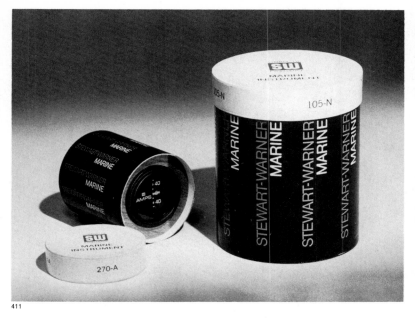

411

412

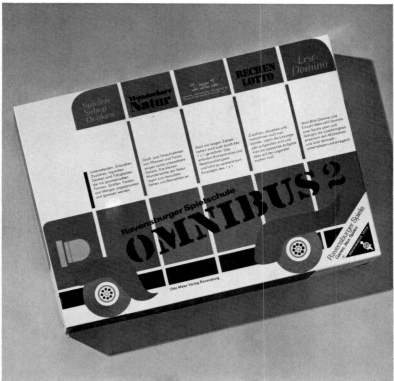

414

415

418

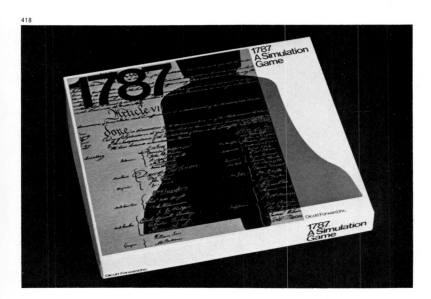

DESIGNER / GESTALTER / MAQUETTISTE:

410 Eugene J. Grossman
411 Howard Knight/Louise Scire
412, 418 Fred Troller
413 Thomas H. Geismar
414 Manfred Burggraf
415 Helmut Schmid
416, 417 Braun Kommunikationsabteilung

ART DIRECTOR / DIRECTEUR ARTISTIQUE:

410 Eugene J. Grossman
411 Howard Knight/Charles MacMurray
412, 418 Robert Kibrick/Seymour Levine
414 Manfred Burggraf
416, 417 Braun Kommunikationsabteilung

AGENCY / AGENTUR / AGENCE – STUDIO:

410 Anspach Grossman Portugal, Inc.
411 Charles MacMurray & Associates
412, 418 Fred Troller Associates
413 Chemayeff & Geismar Associates, Inc.
414 Graphisches Atelier Otto Maier Verlag
415 Nippon International Agency
416, 417 Braun Kommunikationsabteilung

CLIENT / AUFTRAGGEBER:

410 AMF, Inc.
411 Stewart Warner Corp.
412, 418 Olcott Forward, Inc.
413 Dictaphone Corp.
414 Otto Maier Verlag
415 Sanyo Electric
416, 417 Braun AG

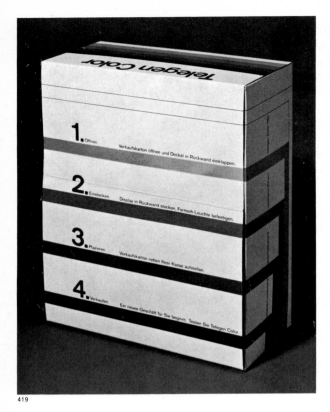

419

420

419 Display box for a television lamp. Yellow, orange, red and purple stripes on white ground. (GER)
420 Box with cut-out window for a game with coloured wood blocks. (SWI)
421 Cardboard tube for a wooden toy. Purple, red and white. (SWI)
422 Hinged double box of corrugated cardboard, containing butane camping cooker and lamp. Lettering white and yellow on bright red. (FRA)
423 Box for a toy racing car. (GBR)
424 Design for a folding box containing an adult game. (USA)
425 Folding box for an optical filter. Cardboard laminated with aluminium foil by the *Dufex* process. Lettering blue and black. (GBR)
426 Package design for a movie camera sold by a department store. (USA)
427 Carton for a multimedia teaching aid, containing buttons, food units, etc., for a game to be played in a school TV programme. (CAN)

419 Auslage-Packung für eine Fernsehlampe. Streifen in Gelb, Orange, Rot und Violett auf weissem Grund. (GER)
420 Schachtel mit gestanztem Fenster für ein Baukastenspiel mit farbigen Holzklötzen. (SWI)
421 Kartonrolle für ein hölzernes Spielzeug. Violett, rot und weiss. (SWI)
422 Doppel-Klappschachtel aus Wellkarton für Butan-Zeltlagerkocher und -lampe. Schrift weiss und gelb auf Rot. (FRA)
423 Schachtel für einen Spielzeug-Rennwagen. (GBR)
424 Gestaltung einer Packung für ein Spiel für Erwachsene. (USA)
425 Faltschachtel für einen optischen Filter. Im *Dufex*-Verfahren mit Alumini-umfolie kaschierte Aussenseite. Schrift blau und schwarz. (GBR)
426 Packung für eine Filmkamera. Hausmarke eines Warenhauses. (USA)
427 Schachtel für ein Multimedia-Lehrmittel, das Knöpfe, Nahrungsmittel-Einheiten usw. für ein Spiel im Schulfernsehen enthält. (CAN)

419 Emballage de vitrine pour une lampe d'ambiance pour téléviseurs. Bandes jaunes, orange, rouges et pourpres sur fond blanc. (GER)
420 Boîte à fenêtre découpée à l'emporte-pièce. Jeu de cubes. (SWI)
421 Tube en carton pour un jouet en bois. Pourpre, rouge, blanc. (SWI)
422 Boîte double en portefeuille, en carton micro-ondulé, contenant un réchaud de camping à gaz butane et une lampe tempête. Lettres blanches et jaunes sur fond rouge vif. (FRA)
423 Emballage pour un jouet (bolide de course). (GBR)
424 Etude de boîte pliante pour un jeu pour adultes. (USA)
425 Boîte pliante pour un filtre optique. Carton revêtu d'une pellicule d'alumi-nium (procédé *Dufex*). Texte bleu et blanc. (GBR)
426 Conception de l'emballage pour une caméra de grand magasin. (USA)
427 Carton pour un jeu multimédias contenant des boutons, des unités alimen-taires, etc., utilisé dans les programmes de la télévision scolaire. (CAN)

423

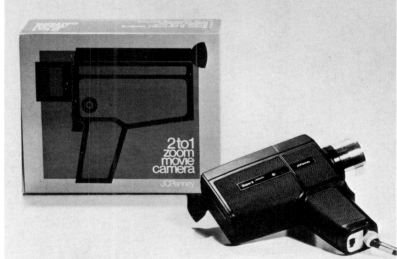

426

Sports, Pastimes, Tobacco Products
Sport, Freizeit, Rauchwaren
Sports, Loisirs, Tabac

421

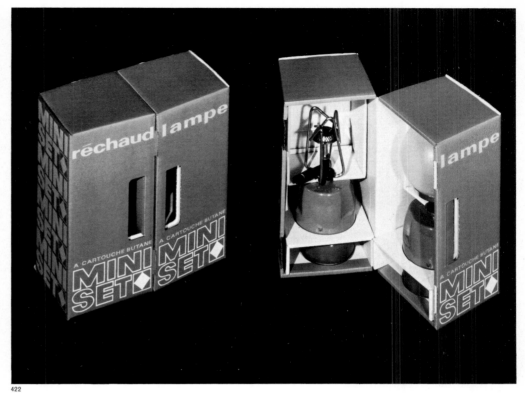

422

424

425

427

DESIGNER / GESTALTER / MAQUETTISTE:

419 Kristian Roth
420 Ferdi Afflerbach
   (Photo: Peer Clahsen)
423 Baden Warner/Vernon Daglish
424 Richard Schneider
425 David Bromige/Graham Southworth
426 R. G. Smith/C. C. Woodring
427 Burton Kramer/Pat Valentine

CLIENT / AUFTRAGGEBER:

419 Telegen
420, 421 Kurt Naef
422 A. D. G. – Camping Gaz
423 The Educational Supply Assoc.
424 Innovative Playthings, Inc.
425 B. D. B. Engineers
426 J. C. Penney Co.
427 Ontario Educational Communications Authority

ART DIRECTOR / DIRECTEUR ARTISTIQUE:

419 Kristian Roth
420, 421 Ferdi Afflerbach
423 Harold & Mary Brend
424 Richard Schneider
425 David Bromige/Graham Southworth
426 Harry Beatty
427 Burton Kramer

AGENCY / AGENTUR / AGENCE – STUDIO:

420, 421 Ferdi Afflerbach
422 Form Technic International
423 Brend Design Associates
424 Schneider Studio
425 Graham Southworth, David Bromige & Associates
427 Burton Kramer Assoc. Ltd.

Sports, Pastimes, Tobacco Products
Sport, Freizeit, Rauchwaren
Sports, Loisirs, Tabac

428 Folding boxes for a range of wooden toys. Black and white on mustard yellow. (SWI)
429 Carton for an educational game based on static electricity. Red, white, blue, black. (ISR)
430 Package with transparent top for a recorder. (USA)
431 Folding boxes with die-cut windows for a series of educational toys, such as articulated chains of balls, tiles, etc., which can be brought into various positions. (SWI)
432 Set-up box for a board game. Black, yellow, red and white on silver ground. (AUL)
433 Designs for cardboard folding boxes for a range of wooden toy vehicles. The colour scheme, bright orange and black on white, identifies the entire range. (SWI)
434 Cardboard boxes for an extensive system of toy construction sets. (DEN)

428 Faltschachteln aus einer Serie für Holzspielzeuge. Schwarzweiss auf Senfgelb. (SWI)
429 Schachtel für ein Lernspiel, auf Elektrostatik basierend. Rot, weiss, blau, schwarz. (ISR)
430 Packung mit transparentem Stülpdeckel für eine Blockflöte. (USA)
431 Faltschachteln mit ausgestanzten Fenstern für eine Serie von Spielzeugen mit erzieherischem Wert, wie Gelenkketten aus Kugeln, Plättchen usw., die sich formen lassen. (SWI)
432 Kartonschachtel für Brettspiel. Schwarz, gelb, rot und weiss auf Silbergrund. (AUL)
433 Gestaltung der Kartonschachteln für eine Serie von hölzernen Spielzeug-Kraftwagen. Das Farbschema, leuchtendes Orange und Schwarz auf Weiss, identifiziert die ganze Serie. (SWI)
434 Kartonschachteln für ein ausgedehntes Spielzeug-Baukastensystem. (DEN)

428 Boîtes pliantes pour une gamme de jouets en bois. Noir-blanc sur jaune moutarde. (SWI)
429 Carton pour un jeu éducatif à base d'électricité statique. Rouge, blanc, bleu, noir. (ISR)
430 Emballage au couvercle transparent pour un flageolet. (USA)
431 Boîtes pliantes, avec fenêtres découpées à l'emporte-pièce, pour une série de jeux éducatifs (assemblages articulés de boules, plaquettes, etc., à géométrie variable). (SWI)
432 Boîte montée pour un jeu de table. Noir, jaune, rouge, blanc sur fond argent. (AUL)
433 Conception de cartons pliants pour une série de jouets en bois (véhicules divers). Le motif couleur — orange lumineux et noir sur blanc — sert à identifier la gamme. (SWI)
434 Boîtes en carton pour un jeu de construction intégré en un système complet. (DEN)

428

429

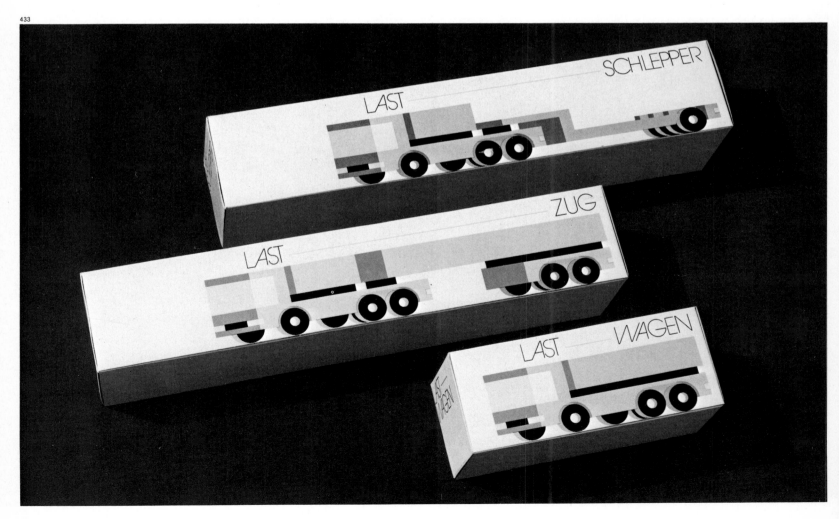

433

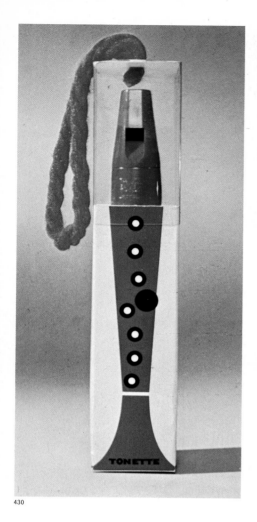

430

431

432

DESIGNER / GESTALTER / MAQUETTISTE:

428, 431 Ferdi Afflerbach (Photo: Walter Grunder)
429 Dror Ben Dov
430 Lothar Klaschik
432 R. Cato
433 Ferdi Afflerbach
434 Niels Hartmann/Folkmar Roll

ART DIRECTOR / DIRECTEUR ARTISTIQUE:

428, 431, 433 Ferdi Afflerbach
429 Dror Ben Dov/A. Kalderon

AGENCY / AGENTUR / AGENCE – STUDIO:

428, 431, 433 Ferdi Afflerbach
429 KV Design International Ltd.
434 Dot Zero Design Group AS

CLIENT / AUFTRAGGEBER:

428, 431, 433 Kurt Naef
429 Orda Industries Ltd.
430 Chicago Musical Instrument Co.
432 Random International PTY Ltd.
434 Lego System

434

435 Packages of corrugated cardboard for plastic saving boxes given away by a bank. (SWI)
436 Packaging system for display and permanent storage of tape cassettes, film strips, records and teaching guides for an audio-visual teaching aid programme. (USA)
437, 438 Boxes for a range of mechanical toys which help children improve their spelling, sense of perception, etc. Photographic illustrations. (USA)
439 Box for a psychological game based on the male/female confrontation. (USA)
440 Set-up box for a Chinese draughts game. (USA)
441 Set-up box for a silhouette puzzle. (USA)
442 Design for a tube containing a skiing game. (USA)
443 Typographic design for a box containing a game. (USA)
444 Design of the lid and interior of a set-up box containing a board game. Plastic insert provides bins for chips and cards. Polychrome printing. (NLD)

435 Wellkartonschachteln für Sparkassen aus Kunststoff. Werbegeschenk einer Bank. (SWI)
436 Packungssystem für die Präsentation und Aufbewahrung von Tonbandkassetten, Filmstreifen, Platten und Textmaterial eines audiovisuellen Lehrmittel-Programmes. (USA)
437, 438 Schachteln für eine Serie von mechanischen Spielzeugen, die beim Buchstabierenlernen helfen, das Wahrnehmungsvermögen von Kindern schärfen usw. (USA)
439 Schachtel für ein psychologisches Spiel, das auf der Mann/Frau-Konfrontation basiert. (USA)
440 Stülpdeckelschachtel für ein chinesisches Brettspiel. (USA)
441 Stülpdeckelschachtel für ein Silhouetten-Zusammensetzspiel. (USA)
442 Kartonrolle für ein Skiabfahrts-Spiel. (USA)
443 Typographische Gestaltung einer Schachtel für ein Wortspiel. (USA)
444 Gestaltung von Deckel und Innenteil einer Kartonschachtel für ein Brettspiel. Kunststoffeinsatz für Spielstein- und Kartenfächer. Mehrfarbendruck. (NLD)

435 Emballages de carton micro-ondulé pour les tirelires en plastique d'une banque. (SWI)
436 Système d'emballage pour la présentation et le stockage des cassettes, films, disques et manuels utilisés dans un programme pédagogique audio-visuel. (USA)
437, 438 Boîtes pour une gamme de jouets mécaniques destinés à améliorer la perception et l'orthographe des enfants, etc. Illustrations photographiques. (USA)
439 Boîte pour un jeu psychologique basé sur la confrontation des sexes. (USA)
440 Boîte montée, pour un jeu de dames chinois. (USA)
441 Boîte montée, pour un puzzle de silhouettes. (USA)
442 Emballage cylindrique d'un jeu de ski de descente. (USA)
443 Conception typographique de la boîte renfermant un jeu de société. (USA)
444 Conception du couvercle et de l'intérieur d'une boîte montée contenant un jeu de table. Des casiers sont aménagés dans le fond plastique pour les jetons et cartes. Polychromie. (NLD)

435

DESIGNER / GESTALTER / MAQUETTISTE:

435 Pierre Miedinger
436 James L. Neill
437 Tomoko Miho
439 Howard Saunders/Tom Lewis
440, 443 Edward C. Kozlowski
441 William R. Tobias (Photo: Leonard Soned)
442 Terry Rose
444 Anton Beeke

ART DIRECTOR / DIRECTEUR ARTISTIQUE:

437, 438 John Massey
439 Joe Y. Takahashi
440, 443 Edward C. Kozlowski
441 William R. Tobias
442 Terry Rose

AGENCY / AGENTUR / AGENCE – STUDIO:

435 Gérard Miedinger
436 Source, Inc.
437, 438 Center for Advanced Research in Design
439 Communications, Research, Machines, Inc.
440, 443 Edward C. Kozlowski Design, Inc.
442 Terry Rose
444 Studio Hausemann & Hötte N. V.

436

437
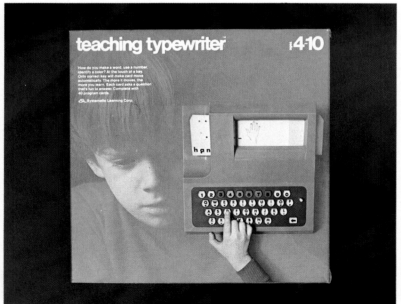

438

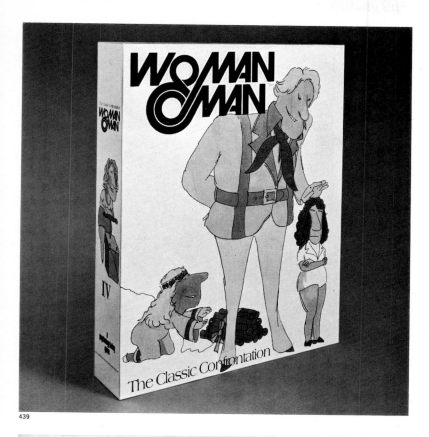

439

CLIENT / AUFTRAGGEBER:

442

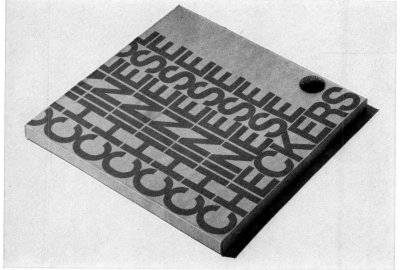

440

443

441

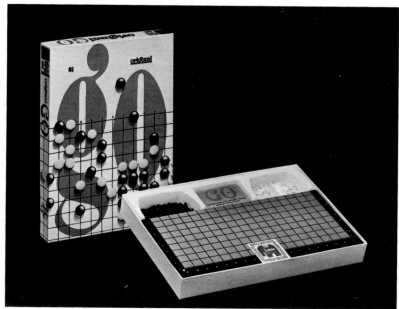

444

151

Stationery
Carrier Bags
Wrapping Paper

Papeteriewaren
Tragtaschen
Einwickelpapiere

Articles de papeterie
Sacs portatifs
Papiers d'emballage

6

445

446

448

447

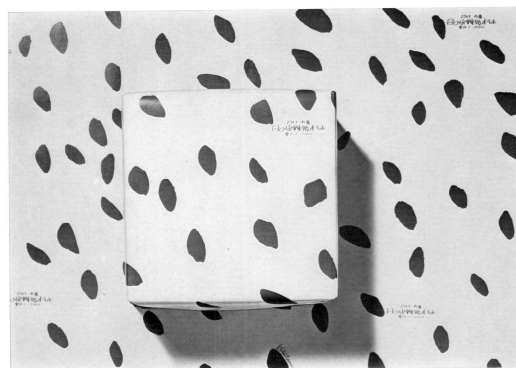

449

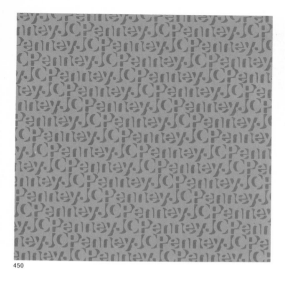

450

451

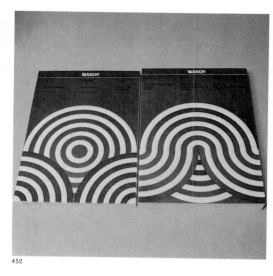

452

453

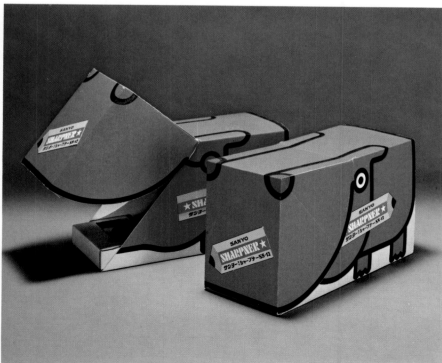

454

445 Wrapping paper for photocopying paper. (GBR)
446 Carrier bag issued during the Christmas season by a department store. Blue and red on green, lettering white. (USA)
447 Design for paper bags and wrapping paper. The initials LEB stand for London Electricity Board. White on orange. (GBR)
448 Cartons with hinged lids for stationery. Colourful designs, plastic finish. (USA)
449 Wrapping paper for confectionery. (JPN)
450 Wrapping paper for a department store chain, making decorative use of its logotype. (USA)
451, 452 Blocks of writing and typing paper. Part of a co-ordinated packaging design programme for a department store. (SWI)
453 Slipcase for a colour atlas with supplement. (GER)
454 Package design for a pencil sharpener. (JPN)

445 Einwickelpapier für Photokopiermaschinen-Papier. (GBR)
446 Tragtasche eines Warenhauses für die Weihnachtssaison. Blau und Rot auf Grün, Schrift weiss. (USA)
447 Muster für Papiertüten und Einwickelpapier. «LEB» sind die Initialen des London Electricity Board. Weiss auf Orange. (GBR)
448 Schachteln mit Scharnierdeckeln für Briefpapier. Farbenfrohe Muster, mit Plastik laminiert. (USA)
449 Einwickelpapier für eine Konditorei. (JPN)
450 Einwickelpapier für eine Warenhauskette, mit dekorativer Anwendung des Namenszuges. (USA)
451, 452 Schreib- und Schreibmaschinenpapier-Blöcke. Aus dem koordinierten Packungsprogramm eines Warenhauses. (SWI)
453 Schuber für Farbatlas und Ergänzungsausgabe. (GER)
454 Gestaltung der Packung für einen Bleistiftspitzer. (JPN)

445 Papier d'emballage pour papier de photocopie. (GBR)
446 Sac en papier d'un grand magasin à l'occasion de Noël. Bleu et rouge sur vert, texte blanc. (USA)
447 Motif pour cornets et papier d'emballage. «LEB» est l'abréviation de «London Electricity Board». Blanc sur orange. (GBR)
448 Cartons à couvercle rabattant pour du papier à lettres. Sujets hauts en couleur à pelliculage plastique. (USA)
449 Papier d'emballage pour une confiserie. (JPN)
450 Papier d'emballage pour une chaîne de grands magasins: utilisation décorative du logo. (USA)
451, 452 Blocs de papier à lettres et de papier machine. La décoration en est intégrée dans le programme d'emballage global conçu pour le grand magasin qui les vend. (SWI)
453 Etui cartonné pour un atlas et son supplément. (GER)
454 Conception de l'emballage d'un taille-crayon. (JPN)

Stationery / Papeteriewaren
Articles de papeterie

Wrapping Paper

DESIGNER / GESTALTER / MAQUETTISTE:

455 Piero Dorazio/Gene Davis/Toshinobu Onosato
456 Frank Beauland
457 Alan Fletcher/Colin Forbes
458, 459 Stan Richards/Steve Stanley
460 Alfred Leung

ART DIRECTOR / DIRECTEUR ARTISTIQUE:

458, 459 Steve Stanley
460 Henry Steiner

455

457

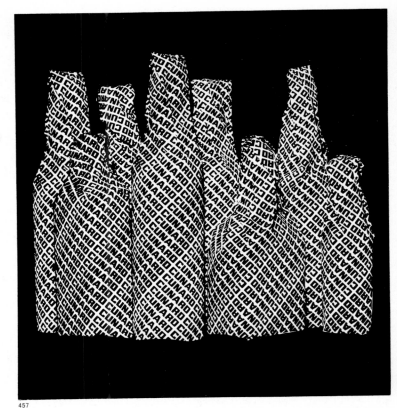

456

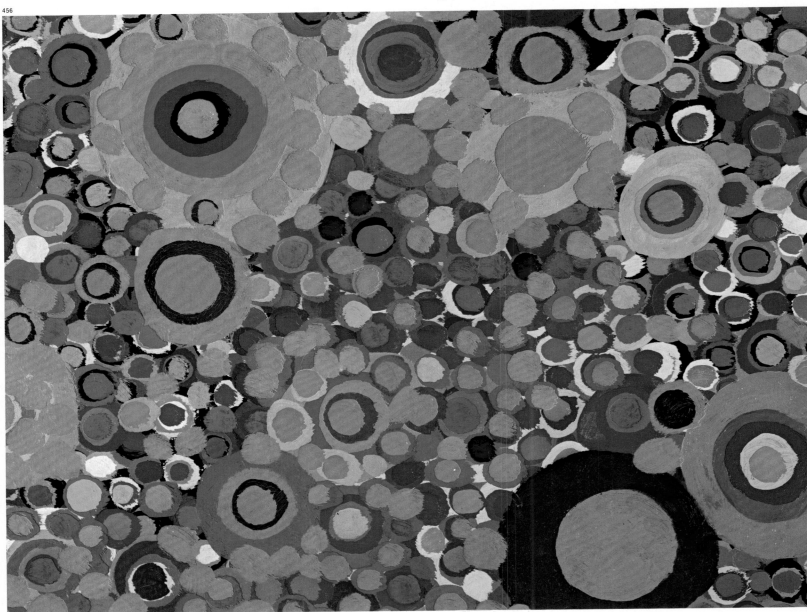

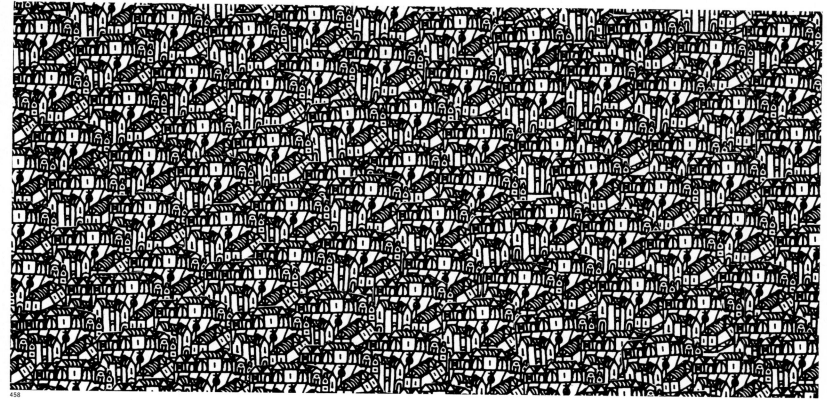

458

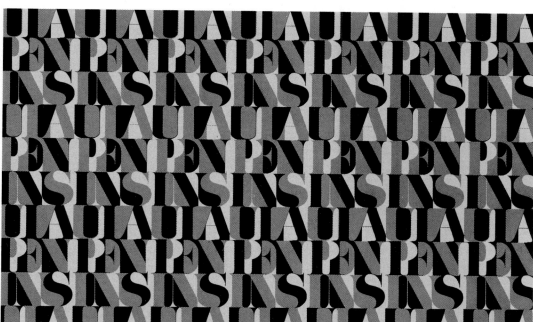

460

459

AGENCY / AGENTUR / AGENCE – STUDIO:

457 Pentagram
458, 459 Stan Richards & Assoc.
460 Graphic Communication Ltd.

CLIENT / AUFTRAGGEBER:

456 Neiman-Marcus
457 Cunard Line
458, 459 Canterbury Press
460 The Peninsula Hotel

455, 456 Examples and detail in actual size (Fig. 456) from a limited series of gift wrapping papers designed and painted by internationally known artists. The designs were commissioned by a department store. Fig. 455 shows framed originals and the wrapping papers as they were used. (USA)
457 Wrapping paper used in duty-free shops on the holiday cruisers of a shipping company. (GBR)
458, 459 Pattern made from the trade mark of a publishing house and example of its application on an envelope. (USA)
460 Wrapping-paper design for the shops of a hotel. The pattern is derived from repetition of "Peninsula", the name of the hotel. Maroon and brown on ochre. (HKG)

455, 456 Beispiele und Ausschnitt in Originalgrösse (Abb. 456) aus einer limitierten Serie von Geschenkpapieren für ein Warenhaus, mit deren Entwürfen und Ausführung international bekannte Kunstmaler beauftragt wurden. Abb. 455 zeigt gerahmte Originale und daneben die Verwendung der Papiere. (USA)
457 Einwickelpapier für die zollfreien Läden auf den Schiffen einer Schiffahrtsgesellschaft. (GBR)
458, 459 Ein aus der Schutzmarke eines Verlagshauses abgeleitetes Muster und seine Anwendung auf einem Umschlag. (USA)
460 Einwickelpapier für die Läden eines Hotels. Das Muster ist durch Repetition des Hotelnamens «Peninsula» entstanden. Weinrot und dunkelbraun auf ockerfarbigem Papier. (HKG)

455, 456 Exemples et détail grandeur nature (fig. 456) d'une gamme limitée des papiers d'emballage de cadeaux créés (et peints) pour un grand magasin par des artistes de réputation internationale. La fig. 455 présente les originaux encadrés et l'usage auquel ils étaient destinés. (USA)
457 Papier d'emballage utilisé dans les magasins hors taxe des paquebots de croisière d'une compagnie de navigation. (GBR)
458, 459 Motif de réseau maillé réalisé à l'aide de la marque déposée d'un éditeur, et enveloppe où il figure. (USA)
460 Papier d'emballage conçu pour les boutiques d'un grand hôtel. Motif créé par la répétition du nom de l'hôtel, «Peninsula». Marron et brun sur ocre. (HKG)

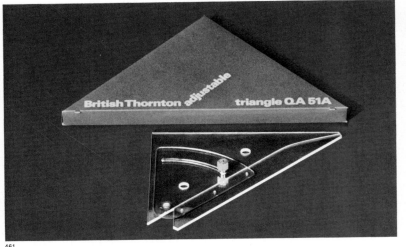

461

462

DESIGNER / GESTALTER / MAQUETTISTE:

461 Christopher Ludlow
462 Archie Boston
463 Morton Chapman
464–467 Michael Peters & Partners
468 Mervyn Kurlansky
469 Mike Stanard

ART DIRECTOR / DIRECTEUR ARTISTIQUE:

461 Norman Stevenson
462 Don Weller
463 Morton Chapman
464–467 Ian Butcher/Geoff Hockey
468 Mervyn Kurlansky
469 Ray Peterson

463

464

AGENCY / AGENTUR:

461 Stevenson/Ward
462 Botsford Ketchum, Inc.
463 Joseph Magnin
464–467 Michael Peters & Partners
468 Pentagram
469 Container Corp. of America

CLIENT / AUFTRAGGEBER:

461 British Thornton Ltd.
462 Pentel
463 Joseph Magnin
464–467 Winsor & Newton Ltd.
468 Rank Xerox Corp.
469 Dayton's Department Store

468

465

469

466

461 Folding box for an adjustable triangle. Colour of package is blue, lettering white. (GBR)
462 Display box with die-cut window for a set of watercolour paints. Full-colour printing. (USA)
463 Gift boxes of various sizes for a department store. Printed in metallic colours. (USA)
464–467 Examples from a range of folding boxes and labels for a line of drawing inks. The full-colour drawings illustrate and designate the colours of the contents. Fig. 465 shows the complete assortment. (GBR)
468 Plastic bottle and folding box for materials used in photocopying machines (see also Fig. 445). (GBR)
469 Gift box design for a department store. (USA)

461 Faltschachtel für einen verstellbaren Winkel. Farbe der Packung ist blau, Schrift weiss. (GBR)
462 Ausstellpackung mit ausgestanztem Fenster für ein Wasserfarbensortiment. Mehrfarbig bedruckt. (USA)
463 Geschenkschachteln in verschiedenen Grössen für ein Warenhaus. In metallischen Farben bedruckt. (USA)
464–467 Beispiele aus einer Serie von Faltschachteln und Etiketten für ein Sortiment von Zeichentuschen. Die farbigen Illustrationen beziehen sich auf die Farbe des Inhalts. Abb. 465 zeigt das ganze Sortiment. (GBR)
468 Plastikflasche und Faltschachtel für Materialien zur Bedienung von Photokopiermaschinen (siehe auch Abb. 445). (GBR)
469 Geschenkschachtel-Gestaltung für ein Warenhaus. (USA)

461 Boîte pliante pour un triangle de panne pliable. Emballage bleu, lettrage blanc. (GBR)
462 Emballage de présentation pour un assortiment de peintures à l'eau. Fenêtre découpée à l'emporte-pièce. Polychromie. (USA)
463 Boîtes-cadeaux de différentes dimensions pour un grand magasin. Impression en couleurs métallisées. (USA)
464–467 Exemples d'une ligne de boîtes pliantes et d'étiquettes pour un assortiment d'encres à dessin. Les dessins polychromes servent d'illustrations et de repères pour les différentes couleurs. Assortiment complet à la fig. 465. (GBR)
468 Bouteille plastique et boîte pliante pour des fournitures pour photocopieurs (cf. aussi la fig. 445). (GBR)
469 Conception de boîte-cadeau pour un grand magasin. (USA)

467

**Stationery / Papeteriewaren
Articles de papeterie**

470

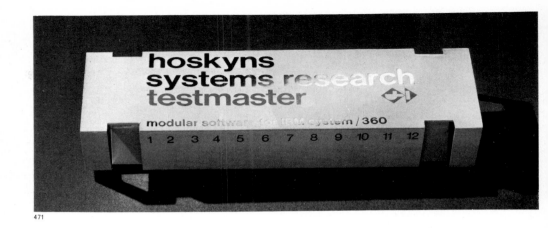

471

473

476

470 Box design based on the logotype of a department store chain. Red and white. (USA)
471 Folding box for punched cards used in computers. (GBR)
472 Four sides of a package for a letter stamping device. Full-colour photographic illustrations. (SWI)
473 Box for a slide rule. Black and white on red. (GBR)
474 Design for a sleeve-and-tray box containing products of a paper mill. Olive, gold and white. (FIN)
475 Wrapping paper used by a night club for gift purposes. Pattern black on white with occasional red dots. (JPN)
476 Take-out carrier bags and boxes for a delicatessen store. White lettering on blue, red tags. (USA)
477 Cardboard folding box and plastic boxes for a range of typewriter ribbons. (AUS)
478 Special Christmas gift package design for a portable typewriter. In red tones. (GBR)

470 Mit dem Firmensignet einer Warenhauskette gestaltete Packung. In Rot und Weiss. (USA)
471 Faltschachtel für in Computern verwendete Lochkarten. (GBR)
472 Vier Seiten der Packung für einen Schriftband-Prägeapparat. Mehrfarbige, photographische Illustrationen. (SWI)
473 Schachtel für Rechenschieber. Schwarz, weiss auf Rot. (GBR)
474 Schieberschachtel für Produkte einer Papierfabrik. In Olivgrün, Gold und Weiss. (FIN)
475 Geschenk-Packpapier für einen Nachtclub. Muster schwarz auf Weiss mit verstreuten roten Punkten. (JPN)
476 Tragtaschen und -schachteln für ein Delikatessengeschäft. Weisse Schrift auf Blau, rote Anhängeetiketten. (USA)
477 Packungen für Schreibmaschinen-Farbbänder. (AUS)
478 Spezielle Weihnachtsgeschenk-Verpackung für eine tragbare Schreibmaschine, in Rottönen. (GBR)

470 Décoration de boîte inspirée du logo d'une chaîne de grands magasins. Rouge et blanc. (USA)
471 Boîte pliante pour cartes perforées d'ordinateurs. (GBR)
472 Les quatre côtés de l'emballage d'une machine à étamper les lettres. Illustrations photo en polychromie. (SWI)
473 Emballage de règle à calcul. Noir, blanc sur rouge. (GBR)
474 Conception de boîte coulissante pour les produits d'une papeterie. Olive, or et blanc. (FIN)
475 Papier d'emballage utilisé par un night-club pour des cadeaux. Motif noir sur un fond blanc parsemé de points rouges. (JPN)
476 Sacs en papier et boîtes utilisés par un traiteur. Lettres blanches sur fond bleu, étiquettes rouges. (USA)
477 Carton pliant et boîtes en plastique pour une gamme de rubans de machines à écrire. (AUS)
478 Emballage spécial de Noël pour une machine à écrire portable. Tons rouges. (GBR)

Stationery / Papeteriewaren
Articles de papeterie

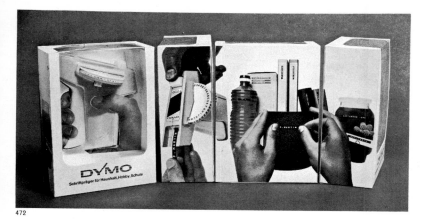

472

474

475

477

478

DESIGNER / GESTALTER / MAQUETTISTE:

479 Carlos Danielsson
480 Jerry Braude
481 Gary C. Springer
482 Josse Goffin
483 Paul Rand

479 Label design for an aerosol tube containing a cleaner for typewriters and adding machines. Black lettering on white label. (SWE)
480 Cardboard tubes used as gift boxes by a boutique. Brown kraft paper laminated to board. Caps black, rough hempen strings. (USA)
481 Folding cartons for data processing cards. (USA)
482 Gift boxes and bags for a department store. (BEL)
483 Examples from the packaging design programme of IBM. The use of the logotype as the only unifying graphic element allows sufficient variety throughout the range to avoid undesirable monotony. (USA)

479 Etikettgestaltung für eine Aerosoldose, die ein Reinigungsmittel für Schreib- und Rechenmaschinen enthält. Schwarze Schrift auf weissem Grund. (SWE)
480 Geschenkpackungen in Rollenform für eine Boutique. Röhre mit braunem Papier laminiert, Deckel und Boden schwarz, rauhe Hanfschnur. (USA)
481 Faltschachteln für Datenverarbeitungs-Lochkarten. (USA)
482 Geschenkschachteln, -tüten und -tragtaschen für ein Warenhaus. (BEL)
483 Beispiele aus dem Packungsgestaltungs-Programm der Firma IBM. Die konsequente Anwendung des Namenszuges als einziges verbindendes graphisches Element erlaubt genügend Spielraum für Variationen, um unerwünschte Monotonie zu vermeiden. (USA)

479 Conception d'étiquette pour un flacon atomiseur contenant un produit de nettoyage pour machines à écrire et calculatrices. Lettres noires sur étiquette blanche. (SWE)
480 Emballages cylindriques utilisés comme boîtes-cadeaux par une boutique de modes. Carton revêtu de papier kraft brun, couvercle et fond noirs, ficelles grossières de chanvre. (USA)
481 Boîtes pliantes en carton pour cartes perforées d'ordinateurs. (USA)
482 Boîtes et sacs en papier pour les cadeaux d'un grand magasin. (BEL)
483 Exemples du programme d'emballage intégré d'IBM. Le recours au seul logo pour l'identification des divers emballages se justifie par sa souplesse d'adaptation, qui bannit toute idée de monotonie dans la présentation de ces produits. (USA)

480

479

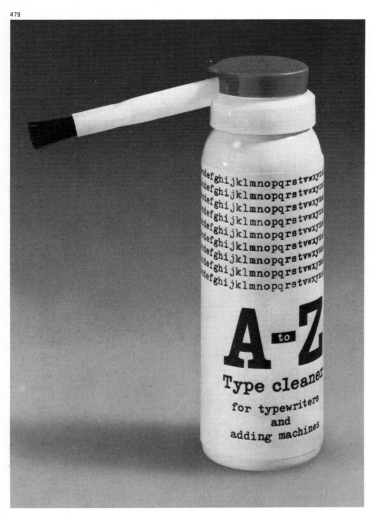

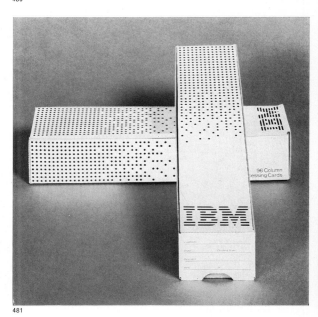

481

ART DIRECTOR / DIRECTEUR ARTISTIQUE:

481 Thomas F. Coleman
482 Michel Michiels
483 Eliot Noyes

AGENCY / AGENTUR / AGENCE – STUDIO:

479 Bergengren Reklam AB
480 Jerry Braude & Associates
481, 483 IMB Rochester Design Center

CLIENT / AUFTRAGGEBER:

479 Spray Kemi AB
480 Zane
481, 483 IBM Corp.
482 Innovation SA

482

483

DESIGNER / GESTALTER / MAQUETTISTE:

484 Dwight Frazier/Paul Hauge
485 Gianni Marazzi
486 Yosei Kawaji/Jutaro Ito
487 Sheila Wolk
488 Wolfgang Stegelmann
489 Massimo Vignelli
490 Bruno Oldani
491 Donald & Anne Crews
492 Max Schneider
493 Burton Kramer

ART DIRECTOR / DIRECTEUR ARTISTIQUE:

484 Dwight Frazier/Paul Hauge
485 Gianni Marazzi
486 Tokihiko Kimata
488 Wolfgang Stegelmann
490 Bruno Oldani
491 Donald & Anne Crews
492 Fritz Girardin
493 Burton Kramer

484

485

489

490

AGENCY / AGENTUR / AGENCE – STUDIO:

484 Frazier/Hauge & Assoc.
485 Studio G. M. D.
487 Sheila Designs
488 Graphik Studio Hamburg
489 Vignelli Assoc.
490 Bruno Oldani
491 Donald & Anne Crews
493 Burton Kramer Assoc. Ltd.

CLIENT / AUFTRAGGEBER:

484 Picture Company
485 Motta Panettoni S. p. A.
486 Keio Plaza Hotel
487 Cats & Things Ltd.
488 Philips/Phonogram Tongesellschaft m. b. H.
489 Bloomingdales
490 Fernando Menk Blumenboutique
491 17th Citizens' Committee
492 Swissair
493 Royal Ontario Museum

486

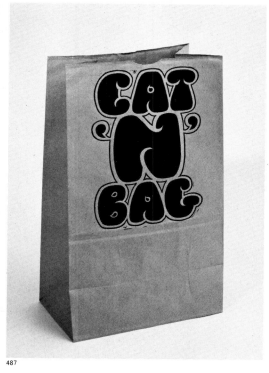

487

488

491

492

493

484 Design for a Christmas wrapping paper. (USA)
485 Carrier bag issued by a chocolate manufacturer for the Easter season. Yellow tulip, pink circle on white. (ITA)
486 Carrier bag for a hotel. (JPN)
487 Brown paper bag with black imprint for a pet shop. (USA)
488 Paper carrier bag containing a promotional gift bottle of whisky. Dark brown bag, lettering white and black. (GER)
489 Carrier bags and re-usable gift boxes for a department store. The only firm identification on the boxes is on a removable elastic vinyl band. (USA)
490 Design for boxes and carrier boxes for flower arrangements from a florist's. Polychrome. (NOR)
491 Carrier bag used for promotional purposes during a congressional election campaign. (USA)
492 Carrier bag for duty-free purchases aboard the aircraft of an airline. Red and blue on white. (SWI)
493 Carrier bag for a museum shop. Black and white. (CAN)

484 Einwickelpapier für Weihnachtsgeschenke. (USA)
485 Tragtasche, von einer Schokoladenfabrik für die Ostersaison herausgegeben. Gelbe Tulpe, rosa Kreis auf Weiss. (ITA)
486 Tragtasche für ein Hotel. (JPN)
487 Papiersack mit schwarzem Aufdruck für Tierhandlung. (USA)
488 Papiertragtasche für eine Flasche Whisky als Werbegeschenk. Weisse und schwarze Schrift auf Dunkelbraun. (GER)
489 Tragtaschen und wiederverwendbare Geschenkschachteln eines Warenhauses. Der Firmenname auf den Schachteln ist auf ein entfernbares elastisches Vinylband aufgedruckt. (USA)
490 Gestaltung von Schachteln und Tragschachteln für die Blumenarrangements einer Blumenboutique. Mehrfarbig. (NOR)
491 Tragtasche, die den Wählern während einer Wahlkampagne zu Werbezwecken ausgehändigt wurde. (USA)
492 Tragtasche für zollfreie Einkäufe an Bord von Flugzeugen. Rot und Blau auf Weiss. (SWI)
493 Tragtasche für den Laden eines Museums. (CAN)

484 Papier d'emballage pour cadeaux de Noël. (USA)
485 Sac en papier créé pour la saison de Pâques par un fabricant de chocolats. Tulipe jaune, cercle rose sur blanc. (ITA)
486 Sac en papier pour un hôtel. (JPN)
487 Sac en papier brun, texte noir, pour un salon de chats. (USA)
488 Sac en papier brun foncé pour un cadeau publicitaire – une bouteille de whisky. Texte imprimé en noir et blanc. (GER)
489 Sacs en papier et boîtes-cadeaux réutilisables pour un grand magasin, dont le nom ne figure que sur une bande élastique amovible en résine vinylique. (USA)
490 Motif décoratif des boîtes et cartons portables pour les arrangements floraux d'un fleuriste. En polychromie. (NOR)
491 Sac en papier avec un motif électoral utilisé pendant la campagne de nomination d'un député au Congrès. (USA)
492 Sac en papier pour les achats hors taxe à bord des appareils d'une compagnie aérienne. Rouge et bleu sur blanc. (SWI)
493 Sac en papier pour le kiosque d'un musée. Noir et blanc. (CAN)

494

496

495

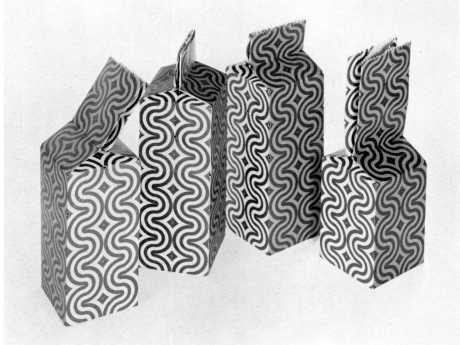

499

ARTIST / KÜNSTLER / ARTISTE:

494, 495, 501 Eiichi Hasegawa
497 · Eiichi Hasegawa/Yasuo Shigehara
498, 500 Eiichi Hasegawa/Kyouko Umino

DESIGNER / GESTALTER / MAQUETTISTE:

494, 495, 497, 501 Eiichi Hasegawa/Kyouko Umino
496 Shozo Kakutani
498, 500 Eiichi Hasegawa
499 Kozo Miyama/Shinzi Saijo
502 Osamu Nakabayashi

ART DIRECTOR / DIRECTEUR ARTISTIQUE:

494, 495, 497, 498, 500, 501 Eiichi Hasegawa
496 Shozo Kakutani
499 Kozo Miyama
502 Masao Sano

AGENCY / AGENTUR / AGENCE – STUDIO:

494, 495, 497, 498, 500, 501 Madison Ad and Creative Agency
496 Kakutani Design Office
499 Honshu Insatu Shiki Co. Ltd.

CLIENT / AUFTRAGGEBER:

494, 495, 497, 498, 500, 501 Toga Folk Art Shop
496 Sanyudo
499 Honshu Paper Board Printing Co. Ltd.
502 Fashion Tokyo Ltd.

494, 495, 498 Designs in traditional Japanese woodcut style for the carrier bags and set-up boxes of a shop specializing in Japanese folk art. Printed in black and white. (JPN)
496 Two sides of a paper carrier bag commissioned by a confectionery establishment. (JPN)
497 Tubular containers with the same motifs as shown in Figs. 494, 495, 498 and 500. (JPN)
499 General-purpose gift bags. Several crease lines at regular intervals along the length of the bags allow the size to be adapted to the volume of the contents. Wine-red and grey-green. (JPN)
500, 501 Set-up boxes with traditional Japanese motifs for food products sold by a speciality store. Printed in black and white (see also Fig. 497). (JPN)
502 Carrier bag for a fashion store. The trade mark is derived from the initials F and T. (JPN)

Stationery, Carrier Bags

497

498

500

501

494, 495, 498 Motive in traditioneller japanischer Holzschnittmanier für die Tragtaschen und Karton-schachteln eines Spezialgeschäftes für japanische Volkskunst. Einfarbig schwarzweiss bedruckt. (JPN)
496 Zwei Seiten von Tragtaschen aus Papier, für ein Konditorei-Spezialgeschäft. (JPN)
497 Runde Behälter mit denselben Motiven wie in Abb. 494, 495, 498 und 500. (JPN)
499 Mehrzweck-Geschenksäcke. In regelmässigen Abständen über die Länge der Säcke verteilte Falt-linien erlauben das Anpassen der Sackgrösse an das Volumen des Inhalts. Weinrot und grüngrau. (JPN)
500, 501 Stülpdeckelschachteln mit traditionellen japanischen Motiven für Nahrungsmittelprodukte eines Spezialgeschäftes. Schwarzweiss bedruckt (siehe auch Abb. 497). (JPN)
502 Tragtasche für ein Modegeschäft. Die Schutzmarke ist von den Initialen F und T abgeleitet. (JPN)

494, 495, 498 Décoration de sacs en papier et de boîtes montées, dans le style traditionnel de l'estampe japonaise gravée sur bois, pour un magasin d'art populaire japonais. Impression noir-blanc. (JPN)
496 Deux côtés d'un sac en papier créé pour une confiserie spécialisée. (JPN)
497 Récipients cylindriques décorés des motifs des fig. 494, 495, 498 et 500. (JPN)
499 Sachets-cadeaux à usage général. Une série de plis préformés dans le sens de la longueur permettent d'adapter le volume de ces sachets à leur contenu. Rouge vineux et gris vert. (JPN)
500, 501 Boîtes montées décorées de motifs japonais traditionnels, pour les produits spécialisés d'un maga-sin de comestibles. Impression noir et blanc (cf. aussi la fig. 497). (JPN)
502 Sac en papier pour un magasin de modes. La marque déposée est dérivée des initiales F et T. (JPN)

502

503

504

506

507

DESIGNER / GESTALTER / MAQUETTISTE:

503 Eiichi Ishizeki
504 Takao Yamada
505 Kreativ-Team Ulrich + Fehlmann
506 K. Friedeberger
507 Saul Bass & Assoc.
508 Tomoko Miho/Karen Kutner
509 John Rieben

ART DIRECTOR / DIRECTEUR ARTISTIQUE:

503 Mitsuo Mihira
504 Takao Yamada
505 Kreativ-Team Ulrich + Fehlmann
507 Art Goodman
508 John Massey/EAnn Thut
509 John Rieben

Stationery, Carrier Bags

Cosmetics, Toiletries

Kosmetik, Toilettenartikel

Produits cosmétiques
articles de toilette

7

510

511

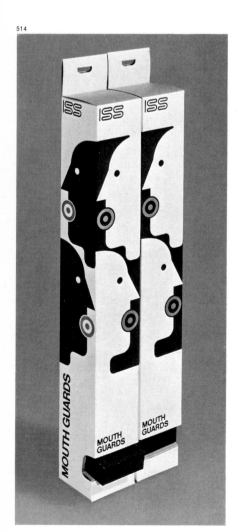

514

515

DESIGNER / GESTALTER / MAQUETTISTE:

510 Gio Rossi
512 Joseph Messina
513 John Alcorn
514 Emery, Fowler-Brown Pty Ltd.
515 Kimiko Tsuchikura
516 E + U Hiestand

ART DIRECTOR / DIRECTEUR ARTISTIQUE:

512 Constance von Collande
513 Murray Jacobs
515 Haruyo Tahira
516 E + U Hiestand

AGENCY / AGENTUR / AGENCE – STUDIO:

510 Milano & Grey
511 Design & Layout Concept – Dieter Hütt
512 Elizabeth Arden Creative Packaging Dept.
513 Wells, Rich, Greene, Inc.
514 Emery, Fowler-Brown Pty Ltd.
516 E + U Hiestand

CLIENT / AUFTRAGGEBER:

510 Beecham Italia S. p. A.
511 Marbert
512 Elizabeth Arden, Inc.
513 Menley & James Laboratories, Inc.
514 Industrial Safety Services
515 Kobayashi Kose Co. Ltd.
516 ABM Au Bon Marché

512

513

516

510 Aerosol container in several colours for a deodorant. (ITA)
511 Boxes for shaving soap, after-shave lotion and cream. Black label on silver embossed board. (GER)
512 Gift pack of soap and eau de cologne for men, with a transparent lid. (USA)
513 Package from a range of cosmetics, here for a cleansing lotion. The photograph runs over two sides of the box. (USA)
514 Dispenser package for mouth pastilles, with a tab for wall hanging. (AUL)
515 Box and powder compact contained in it. (JPN)
516 Bottles and container from a range of men's cosmetics sold by a chain of department stores. (SWI)

510 Mehrfarbige Deodorant-Spraydose. (ITA)
511 Verpackungen für Rasierseife, Rasierwasser und Hautcreme. Schwarzes Etikett auf geprägtem Silberkarton. (GER)
512 Geschenkpackung mit einer Seife und einer Flasche Kölnischwasser für Herren. Deckel durchsichtig. (USA)
513 Packung aus einem Sortiment von Kosmetikartikeln, hier für eine Reinigungsmilch. (USA)
514 Spenderpackung zum Aufhängen für Tabletten gegen Ansteckung. Mehrfarbig. (AUL)
515 Faltschachtel und Puderdose. (JPN)
516 Flaschen und Dosen aus dem Herren-Kosmetiksortiment einer Warenhauskette. (SWI)

510 Bombe aérosol pour un désodorisant. Diverses couleurs. (ITA)
511 Conditionnements pour du savon à barbe, de la lotion après rasage et de la crème pour la peau. Etiquette noire sur carton avec gaufrage argent. (GER)
512 Assortiment-cadeau sous couvercle transparent, consistant en un savon et une eau de Cologne pour messieurs. (USA)
513 Exemple d'une gamme d'emballages pour cosmétiques, ici pour un démaquillant. La photo occupe deux faces du carton. (USA)
514 Emballage polychrome de pastilles pour une haleine fraîche, faisant fonction de distributeur, avec suspension murale. (AUL)
515 Boîte et poudrier qu'elle contient. (JPN)
516 Flacons et conditionnements cylindriques pour une gamme de cosmétiques messieurs distribués par un grand magasin. (SWI)

Cosmetics, Toiletries
Kosmetik, Toilettenartikel
Produits cosmétiques

Cosmetics, Toiletries
Kosmetik, Toilettenartikel
Produits cosmétiques, Articles de toilette

DESIGNER / GESTALTER / MAQUETTISTE:

517, 519 Schwartz & Wassyng
518 Edward C. Kozlowski
520 Fujiko Suzuki
522 Dante Vernice

ART DIRECTOR / DIRECTEUR ARTISTIQUE:

517, 519 Adam Grodin
518 Edward C. Kozlowski
520 Katsu Kimura
522 Dante Vernice

517, 519 Bottle with chrome-coloured plastic cap and smoky brown transparent plastic package for a men's eau de cologne. (USA)
518 White plastic bottle for a product meant to strengthen bleached and dyed hair. Black lettering on white. (USA)
520 Jars, bottles and folding boxes for a range of cosmetic products. (JPN)
521 Bottle and folding box for an eau de cologne. (SPA)
522 Sample packages for lipsticks. The colour is revealed through the die-cut window. (ITA)

517, 519 Flasche für ein Kölnischwasser für Herren und durchsichtige, braungetönte Plastikschachtel, in der sie verkauft wird. (USA)
518 Weisse Plastikflasche für einen Haarfestiger mit natürlichem, organischem Protein zur Behandlung von gebleichtem oder gefärbtem Haar. Schwarze Schrift. (USA)
520 Dosen, Flaschen und Faltschachteln für eine Kosmetika-Reihe. (JPN)
521 Flasche und Packung für ein Kölnischwasser. (SPA)
522 Musterpackungen für Lippenstifte. Die Farbe ist sichtbar im ausgestanzten Fenster. (ITA)

517, 519 Flacon d'eau de Cologne avec son bouchon plastique couleur de chrome et son emballage plastique transparent teinté en brun. (USA)
518 Bouteille plastique blanche pour un fortifiant à base de protéines organiques naturelles pour cheveux teints ou décolorés. Lettres noires sur fond blanc. (USA)
520 Pots, flacons et boîtes pliantes pour une gamme de cosmétiques. (JPN)
521 Flacon et boîte pliante pour une eau de Cologne. (SPA)
522 Emballages pour échantillons de rouges à lèvres. La couleur transparaît dans les fenêtres découpées à l'emporte-pièce. (ITA)

518

517

519

AGENCY / AGENTUR / AGENCE – STUDIO:

517, 519 Shulton, Inc.
518 Edward C. Kozlowski Design, Inc.
520 Packaging Direction Co. Ltd.
522 Studio Vernice Design & Packaging

CLIENT / AUFTRAGGEBER:

517, 519 Jacqueline Cochran, Inc.
518 Josh, Inc.
520 Japan Elfinese Co. Ltd.
521 Perfumeria Parera SA
522 Margaret Astor

520

521

522

DESIGNER / GESTALTER:

523 Ernest R. Smith
524 Catherine Levine
525 Migros Genossenschaftsbund,
     Abt. Verpackung ·

ART DIRECTOR:

523 Stanley Kohlenberg
524 Kurt Weihs
525 H. Uster
526 J. Behaeghel

AGENCY / AGENTUR:

523 Lubalin Smith Carnase
524 Lois/Chajet Design Group, Inc.
525 Migros Genossenschaftsbund,
     Abt. Verpackung
527 Design & Layout Concept –
     Dieter Hütt

CLIENT / AUFTRAGGEBER:

523 Spectrum Cosmetics, Inc.
524 Glemby Hair Salons
525 Migros Genossenschaftsbund
526 Olivin Cosmetics

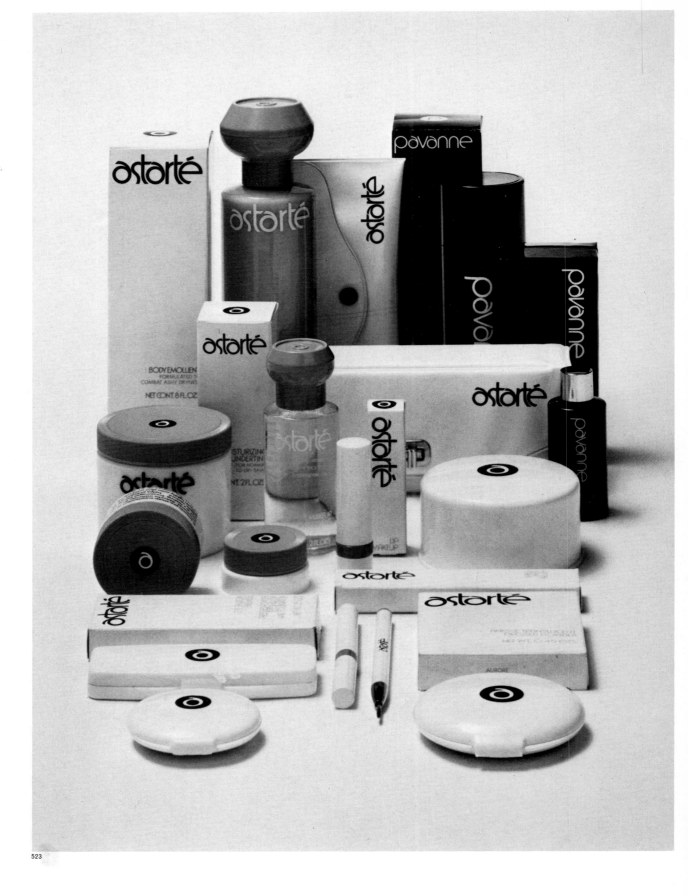

523

523 Bottles, jars, tubes and folding boxes from an extensive range of cosmetics. (USA)
524 Bottles and tubes for shampoos and hair conditioners, with a folding box for a hair dryer. Black and white. (USA)
525 Folding box and tube for a sun-tan cream. Red, white, orange and brown on ochre. (SWI)
526 Range of deodorant sprays, part of a redesign programme undertaken by this brand. (BEL)
527 Bottle for a perfume. Brown plastic cap with light brown velvet ribbon. (GER)

523 Flaschen, Dosen, Tuben und Faltschachteln aus einer reichhaltigen Kosmetik-Reihe. (USA)
524 Dosen und Tuben für Haarwasch- und -festigungsmittel und Packung für einen Haartrockner. Schwarzweiss. (USA)
525 Faltschachtel und Tube für eine Selbstbräunungscreme. Rot, weiss, orange und braun auf Ocker. (SWI)
526 Dosen aus dem Sortiment einer Deodorant-Marke. Beispiele aus einem Neugestaltungsprogramm. (BEL)
527 Flasche für ein Parfüm. Brauner Verschluss aus Kunststoff mit einem hellbraunen Samtband. (GER)

523 Flacons, pots, tubes et boîtes pliantes pour une gamme étendue de cosmétiques. (USA)
524 Flacons et tubes pour des shampooings et fixateurs pour cheveux; carton pliant pour un séchoir. Noir, blanc. (USA)
525 Boîte pliante et tube de crème solaire. Rouge, blanc, orange et brun sur ocre. (SWI)
526 Gamme de sprays désodorisants conçus dans le cadre d'un nouveau programme de conditionnement de la marque. (BEL)
527 Flacon de parfum. Bouchon plastique brun, col agrémenté d'un ruban de velours brun clair. (GER)

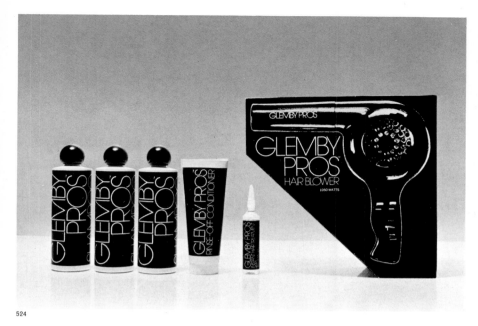

524

526

525

527

Cosmetics, Toiletries
Kosmetik, Toilettenartikel
Produits cosmétiques, Articles de toilette

Cosmetics, Toiletries
Kosmetik, Toilettenartikel
Produits cosmétiques, Articles de toilette

DESIGNER / GESTALTER / MAQUETTISTE:

528, 530 Roland Peterson/Jerry Dior
529 Greub + Gerisch (Photo: Pius Rast)
531 Les Mason
532–534 Ira Schwartz (Artist: Charles Boyd)
536, 537 Design-Studio Halm

ART DIRECTOR / DIRECTEUR ARTISTIQUE:

528, 530 Roland Peterson
531 Les Mason
532–534 Ira Schwartz

AGENCY / AGENTUR / AGENCE – STUDIO:

528, 530 Peterson & Blyth Associates, Inc.
529 Alwin Frank
531 Hayes Advertising Pty Ltd.
532–534 Schwartz/Wassyng

CLIENT / AUFTRAGGEBER:

528, 530 Corand Company
529 Jean Bollhalter & Co.
531 Preservene Pty Ltd.
532–534 Fabergé, Inc.
535 Elizabeth Arden, Inc.
536, 537 Haarmann & Reimer GmbH

528

529

530

531

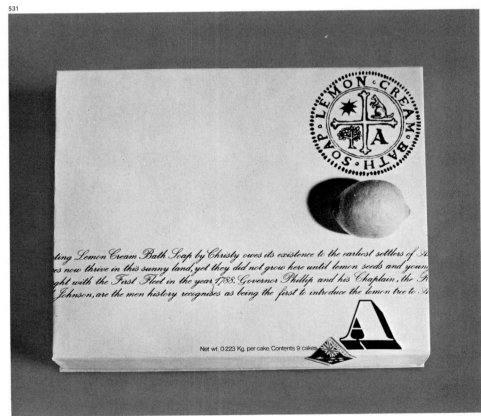

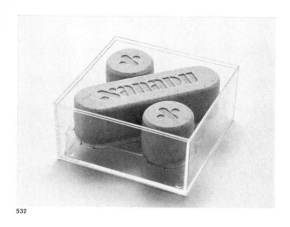

532

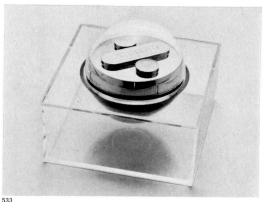

533

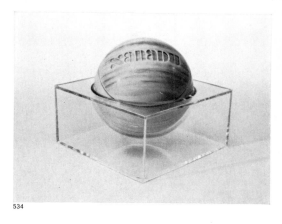

534

535

528 Gift pack for an eau de cologne. Lettering in gold and white on a black ground. (USA)
529 Folding box for a vitamin cream bath. Printed in gold and black on white. (SWI)
530 Bottle styling and folding box for a bath oil. From a gift range with three fragrances. Lettering and seal gold and white, black ground. (USA)
531 Package for nine cakes of lemon cream bath soap. Label blue and red, yellow lemon, black lettering on white. (AUL)
532–534 Display packs in transparent plastic for a range of cosmetic products. Fig. 533 won a gold medal in the 1970 New York Art Directors Show. (USA)
535 Plastic bottle in two colours for a foam bath. Bottle of polypropylene, cap of polystyrene. (GBR)
536, 537 Folding box and complete gift pack in the form of a casket for a perfume atomizer. (GER)

528 Geschenkpackung für ein Kölnischwasser. Schrift in Gold und Weiss auf schwarzem Grund. (USA)
529 Faltschachtel für ein Vitamin-Creme-Bad. Gedruckt in Gold und Schwarz auf weissem Grund. (SWI)
530 Flaschengestaltung und Faltschachtel für ein Badeöl. Aus einer Geschenkreihe mit drei Duftnoten. Schrift und Siegel in Gold und Weiss auf schwarzem Grund. (USA)
531 Verpackung für neun Stück Zitronen-Creme-Badeseifen. Der Text bezieht sich auf die Einführung der Zitrone in Australien im Jahre 1788. Etikett blau und rot, Zitrone gelb, Schrift in Schwarz auf Weiss. (AUL)
532–534 Schaupackungen für Kosmetika. Abb. 533 Goldmedaille 1970 des New York Art Directors Club. (USA)
535 Zweifarbige Plastikflasche für ein «Meerwasser»-Schaumbad. Flasche aus Polypropylen. (GBR)
536, 537 Faltschachtel und Geschenkpackung in Form einer Miniaturkassette für einen Parfüm-Zerstäuber. (GER)

528 Emballage-cadeau pour une eau de Cologne. Lettrage or et blanc sur fond noir. (USA)
529 Boîte pliante pour une crème de bain aux vitamines. Impression or et noir sur blanc. (SWI)
530 Etude de flacon et boîte pliante pour une huile de bain. La gamme complète, présentée sous ce genre d'emballage-cadeau, comprend trois parfums. Texte et sceau or et blanc sur noir. (USA)
531 Emballage pour neuf savons de bain à la crème au citron. Etiquette bleu, rouge, citron jaune, texte noir sur blanc. (AUL)
532–534 Emballages de présentation en plastique transparent pour une ligne de cosmétiques. Celui de la fig. 533 a remporté une médaille d'or à l'Art Directors Show, New York 1970. (USA)
535 Flacon plastique bicolore pour un bain de mousse. Flacon en polypropylène, bouchon en polystyrène. (GBR)
536, 537 Boîte pliante et emballage-cadeau complet en forme de cassette, pour un flacon vaporisateur de parfum. (GER)

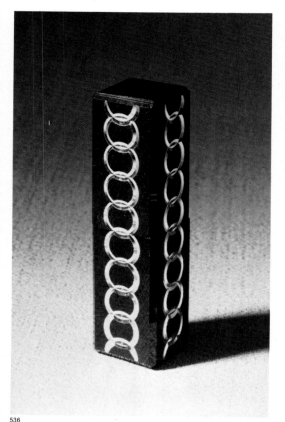

536

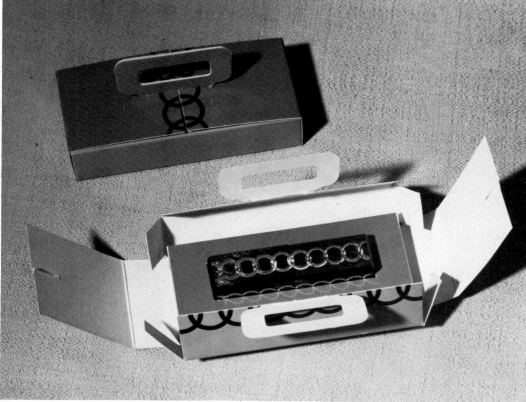

537

538 Carton for a hair lotion. (USA)
539 Project for a folding box for a toilet water from a range of cosmetics. Black and grey "M" on white ground. (JPN)
540 Aerosol container for a hair spray. (FRA)
541 Bottle design for an after-shave lotion. (USA)
542 Scent bottle for a hotel. Black and white. The bottle is not available on the market but is used exclusively as a gift presented to hotel guests. The packing includes the wrapping paper shown in the background. (FRA)
543 Folding boxes for eye make-up products. Iris of eye in bright colours. (ITA)
544 Bottles for a range of cosmetic oils with four different fragrances. The design of the label is the same throughout (blossoming spray orange, lilac, green and brown on beige), the fragrances are distinguished only by the colours and names on the caps. (USA)

538 Verpackung für ein Haarpflegemittel. Schwarzweiss. (USA)
539 Entwurf einer Faltschachtel für ein Toilettenwasser aus einem Kosmetiksortiment. Buchstabe «M» in Schwarz und Grau auf weissem Grund. (JPN)
540 Aerosol-Behälter für einen Haarlack. Mehrfarbig. (FRA)
541 Flaschengestaltung für ein Rasierwasser. Geschenkartikel. (USA)
542 Parfümflasche des Hôtel du Cap d'Antibes. Schwarzweiss. Die Flasche ist nicht im Handel erhältlich, sondern dient ausschliesslich als Präsent für Hotelgäste. Zur Verpackung gehört ausserdem das hier im Hintergrund abgebildete Einwickelpapier. (FRA)
543 Faltschachteln für Augen-Make-up. Augen und Schrift mehrfarbig auf Weiss. (ITA)
544 Verpackungen für kosmetische Öle mit Ambra-, Sandelholz-, Moschus- und Zibet-Duftessenzen. Die graphisch einheitlich gestalteten Packungen (Blütenzweige orange, lila, grün und braun auf beigem Hintergrund) unterscheiden sich durch verschiedenfarbige Etiketten. Auf der Rückseite wurde eine kurze Erklärung über das Herkunftsland aufgedruckt. (USA)

538 Carton pour une lotion capillaire. Noir et blanc. (USA)
539 Projet de boîte pliante pour une eau de toilette figurant dans une ligne de cosmétiques. «M» noir et gris sur blanc. (JPN)
540 Bombe aérosol pour une laque pour les cheveux. En polychromie. (FRA)
541 Etude de flacon pour une lotion après rasage. (USA)
542 Flacon de parfum de l'Hôtel du Cap d'Antibes. Noir sur blanc. Ce flacon n'est pas commercialisé, mais réservé exclusivement aux cadeaux de la direction pour la clientèle de l'hôtel. A l'arrière-plan, le papier d'emballage allant de pair avec le flacon. (FRA)
543 Boîtes pliantes pour des produits de maquillage pour les yeux. Iris polychromes. (ITA)
544 Flacons pour une ligne d'huiles cosmétiques parfumées à l'ambre, au santal, au musc et à la civette. Motif d'étiquette unitaire (rameau fleuri orange, lilas, vert, brun sur beige). Les différents parfums se distinguent par la couleur de l'étiquette. (USA)

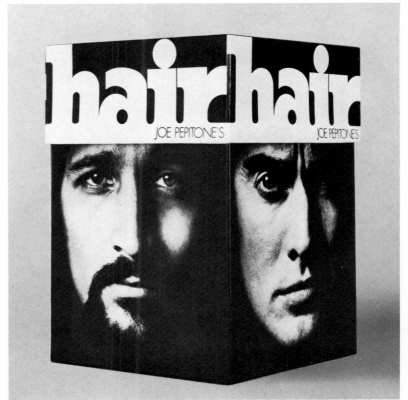

538

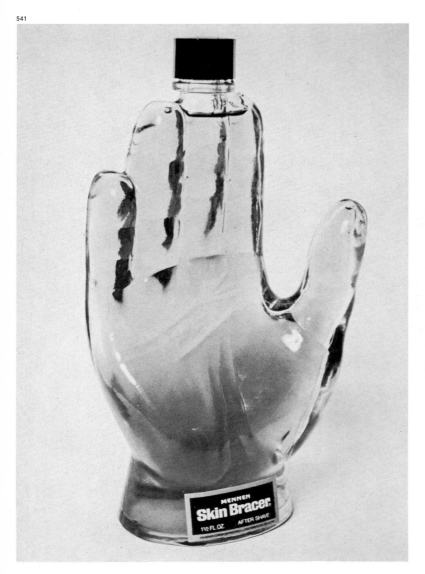

541

542

539

540

ART DIRECTOR / DIRECTEUR ARTISTIQUE:

538 Peter Coutroulis
539 Hiroichi Nakano
540 R. C. Garamond
542 Heinz Kroehl/Peter Offenberg
543 Annegret Beier
544 James Thomas

AGENCY / AGENTUR / AGENCE – STUDIO:

538 The Old School, Inc.
541 Case & McGrath, Inc.
542 Kroehl Design Gruppe
543 Lubalin Delpire & Cie.
544 James Thomas Design

CLIENT / AUFTRAGGEBER:

538 One Touch of Glamour, Inc.
539 Kanebo Cosmetics, Inc.
540 Arona
541 The Mennen Company
542 Hôtel du Cap d'Antibes
543 Saipo (L'Oréal)
544 Sunshine Natural Products

543

544

Cosmetics, Toiletries
Kosmetik, Toilettenartikel
Produits cosmétiques, Articles de toilette

545

DESIGNER / GESTALTER / MAQUETTISTE:

545 Shigeru Akizuki
546 Naomi Hosoya/Kyoko Manabe
547 Carlos Rocha
548 E + U Hiestand
549 Tom Wachs
550 Eugene J. Grossman
551 Fritz Gottschalk

CLIENT / AUFTRAGGEBER:

545 Kanebo Cosmetics, Inc.
546 Albion Cosmetics
547 Intermarca
548 Dr. G. Dralle
549 Will Ross, Inc.
550 Sterling Drug
551 Syntex Ltd.

ART DIRECTOR / DIRECTEUR ARTISTIQUE:

546 Naomi Hosoya
547 Carlos Rocha
548 E + U Hiestand
550 Eugene J. Grossman
551 Fritz Gottschalk

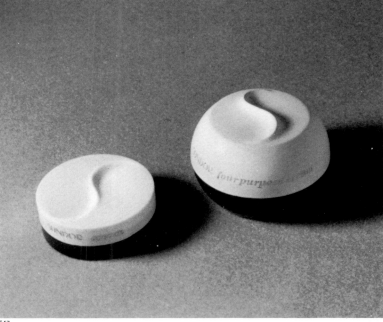

546

547

Cosmetics, Toiletries
Kosmetik, Toilettenartikel
Produits cosmétiques, Articles de toilette

AGENCY / AGENTUR / AGENCE – STUDIO:

545 Akizuki Design Office
547 Hora Publicidade
548 E + U Hiestand
549 International Paper Company
550 Anspach Grossman Portugal, Inc.
551 Gottschalk & Ash Ltd.

549

550

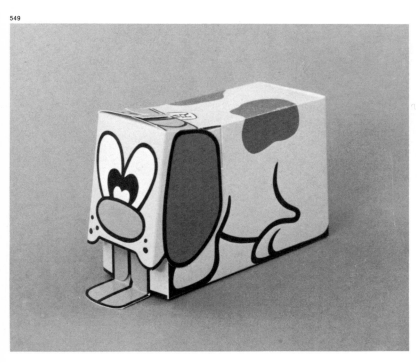

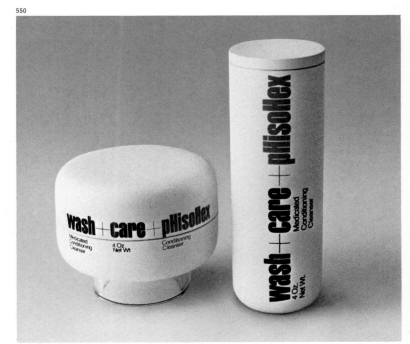

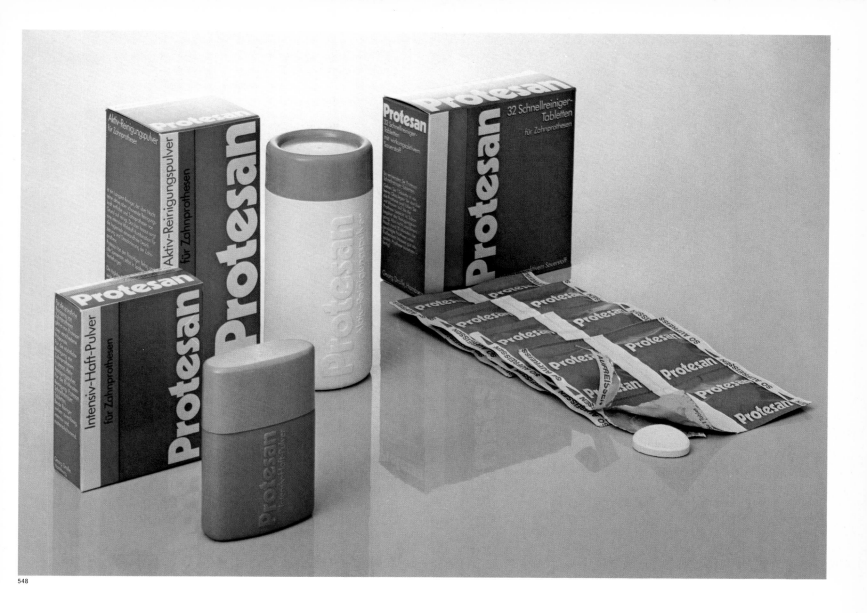

548

551

545 Range of folding boxes for toilet soaps. (JPN)
546 Jar for a cold cream. Lettering white and blue on black, silver lid. (JPN)
547 Powder compact and jar of four-purpose cream from a cosmetic range. White lids with golden lettering round the edge, black containers. (POR)
548 Range of boxes, containers and packs for products for the care of false teeth. (GER)
549 Folding box containing soap, a cloth, toothpaste and toothbrush handed to children on arrival in a hospital, a small gift which they can also take with them when they leave. (USA)
550 Polypropylene jar and blow-moulded squeeze bottle for a skin conditioning cream and lotion. Lettering in black and olive green. (USA)
551 Bottles and jars from a range of cosmetics. (CAN)

545 Aus einer Serie von Toilettenseifen. (JPN)
546 Creme-Dose aus einer Kosmetikreihe. Schrift weiss und schwarz, Deckel in Silber. (JPN)
547 Puder- und Cremedosen aus einem Kosmetiksortiment. Deckel weiss mit goldener Schrift am Rande, Dose dunkelblau. (POR)
548 Einheitlich gestaltete Packungsfamilie mit Faltschachteln, Dosen und Beuteln für Produkte, die der Pflege von Zahnprothesen dienen. (GER)
549 Faltschachtel mit Seife, Handtuch, Zahnpasta und Zahnbürste, die im Krankenhaus an Kinder abgegeben wird und die sie nach ihrer Entlassung mitnehmen dürfen. (USA)
550 Dose und Flasche für eine Creme und Lotion zur Reinigung und Pflege der Haut. Beide Behälter sind aus Polypropylen. Schwarze und grüne Schrift. (USA)
551 Flaschen und Dosen für eine Serie kosmetischer Produkte. (CAN)

545 Gamme d'emballages pour savons de toilette. (JPN)
546 Pot de cold-cream. Texte blanc et bleu sur noir, couvercle argent. (JPN)
547 Poudrier et pot de crème à quatre usages figurant dans une gamme de cosmétiques. Couvercles blancs, lettrage or sur le rebord, récipients noirs. (POR)
548 Gamme de boîtes, cartons et sachets pour des produits d'entretien de dentiers. (GER)
549 Boîte pliante avec un savon, une serviette, un dentifrice et une brosse à dents, remise aux enfants lors de leur entrée à l'hôpital. On permet qu'ils l'emportent chez eux. (USA)
550 Pot en polypropylène et bouteille souple obtenue par moulage creux, pour une crème et une lotion servant au traitement de la peau. Lettres noires et vert olive. (USA)
551 Flacons et pots figurant dans une gamme de cosmétiques. (CAN)

552

553

DESIGNER / GESTALTER / MAQUETTISTE:

552 Xaver Bürgi
553 Shunsaku Sugiura
554 E + U Hiestand
556 Raila Alanen
557 Raymond Bellamare
558, 560 Dieter Zembsch
559 Studio de Photo Lancôme

ART DIRECTOR / DIRECTEUR ARTISTIQUE:

552 Xaver Bürgi
553 Shigeyoshi Aoki
554 E + U Hiestand
557 Raymond Bellamare
558, 560 Dieter Zembsch

AGENCY / AGENTUR / AGENCE – STUDIO:

552 Studio Pack Design
554 E + U Hiestand
555 Agnes Gay
556 SEK Advertising
557 Raymond Bellamare
558, 560 Dieter Zembsch
559 Studio de Photo Lancôme

CLIENT / AUFTRAGGEBER:

552 Paul Müller SA
553 Shiseido Co. Ltd.
554 Acopharm/Milopa
555 Lorsa SA – L'Oréal
556 Berner Oy
557 Natur, Inc.
558, 560 Mann & Schröder, Chem. Fabrik
559 Lancôme SA

555

557

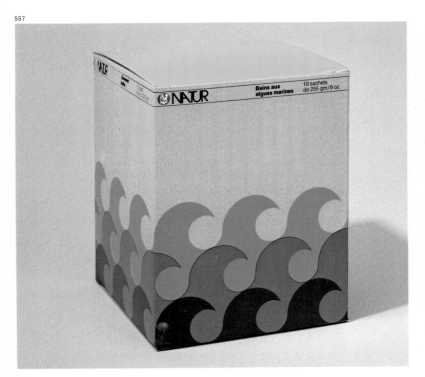

558

554

556

552 Bottles and tubes for a range of cosmetic products. The forms remain the same, the various articles are distinguished by discreet colour coding. (SWI)
553 Bottle, jar and folding box for men's cosmetics. (JPN)
554 Tubes, containers and folding boxes for a range of products specially developed for baby care. (SWI)
555 Bottles for shampoos on a herb basis, here containing camomile, chestnut-leaf, hawthorn and sage essences. (FRA)
556 Aerosol containers for a deodorant cologne marketed in three different fragrances. (FIN)
557 Carton for a seaweed bath additive. (CAN)
558, 560 Bottle in the form of a preserves jar and a medicine bottle with a jute wrapper for bath salts. (GER)
559 Package containing a cleansing emulsion, a freshening lotion and a day cream. (SWI)

552 Flaschen und Tuben für eine Reihe kosmetischer Produkte, die sich bei gleichbleibender Form durch dezente Farbabstufungen untereinander unterscheiden. (SWI)
553 Flasche, Dose und Faltschachtel für Kosmetikartikel. (JPN)
554 Tuben, Behälter und Schachteln für Produkte, die speziell für die Säuglingspflege entwickelt wurden. (SWI)
555 Flaschen für auf pflanzlicher Basis entwickelte Haarwaschmittel (hier Kamille, Kastanie, Weissdorn und Salbei). (FRA)
556 Aerosol-Flaschen für ein Deodorant, der in drei verschiedenen Duftnoten erhältlich ist. (FIN)
557 Verpackung für ein Meeralgen-Bademittel. (CAN)
558, 560 Flasche in Form eines Einmachglases und in Jute verpacktes Medizinglas für Badezusätze. (GER)
559 Verpackung für eine Reinigungsemulsion, ein Erfrischungswasser und eine Tagescreme. (SWI)

552 Flacons et tubes pour une ligne de cosmétiques. Formes unitaires; identification au moyen d'un code-couleur discret. (SWI)
553 Flacon, pot et carton pliant étudiés pour des cosmétiques pour messieurs. (JPN)
554 Tubes, récipients et cartons pliants pour une gamme de produits spécialisés pour les soins à donner aux bébés. (SWI)
555 Bouteilles de shampooings aux essences de plantes (ici: camomille, feuille de châtaignier, aubépine et sauge). (FRA)
556 Flacons atomiseurs pour trois variétés d'une eau de Cologne désodorisante agrémentée de divers parfums. (FIN)
557 Carton pour un bain aux algues marines. (CAN)
558, 560 Conditionnements de sels de bains affectant la forme d'un bocal à conserves et d'un flacon médicinal enrobé de jute. (GER)
559 Emballage contenant une émulsion détergente, une lotion rafraîchissante et une crème de jour. (SWI)

559

560

561

562

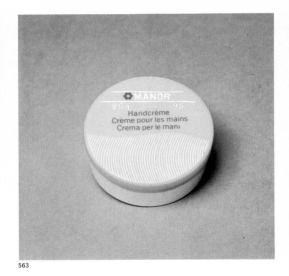

563

565

566

DESIGNER / GESTALTER / MAQUETTISTE:

561–563 E + U Hiestand
564 Max Schneider
565 Atelier Sommer
566 Monica Grimburg-Flood
567, 569 R. Joseph Hutchcroft
568 Heinz Grunwald
570 Tom Robbins/Jim Thomas

ART DIRECTOR / DIRECTEUR ARTISTIQUE:

561–563 E + U Hiestand
564 Max Schneider
566 Gerard Rosenfeld
567, 569 Pat Jeronimus
570 Tom Robbins

AGENCY / AGENTUR / AGENCE – STUDIO:

561–563 E + U Hiestand/H. M. Eggmann
564 Hermann & Schneider Creativ Team
565 Atelier Sommer
566 House of Harley Art Dept.
567, 569 Center for Advanced Research in Design
568 Neish, Tutt, Grunwald

568

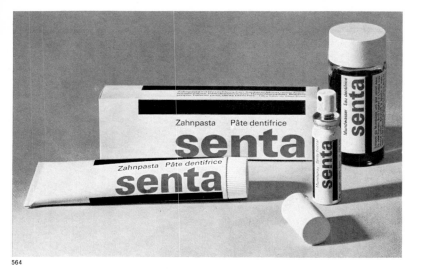

564

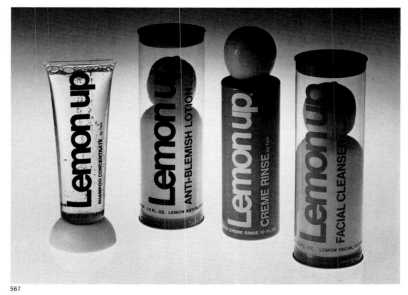

567

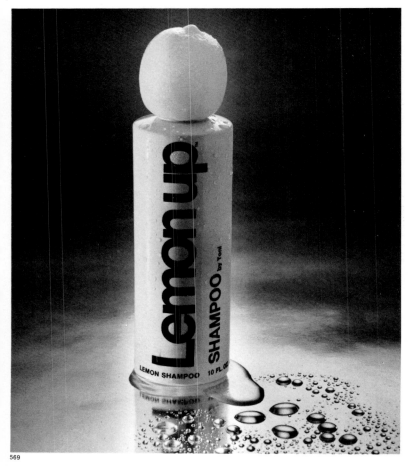

569

CLIENT / AUFTRAGGEBER:

561–563 Maus Frères SA
564 Labocentro AG
565 Beiersdorf AG
566 House of Harley
567, 569 The Gillette Company
568 Prue Acton Cosmetics
570 Polly Bergen

561–563 From the perfumery assortment of a chain of department stores. The fine linear pattern suggests hair or the pores of the skin. Standard shapes with special colouring for the various products. (SWI)
564 Packaging for toothpaste and mouth hygiene products. (SWI)
565 Plastic bottles in green, white and brown from a relaunch programme for sun-tan products. Yellow cap, label printed in black on yellow and orange shades. (GER)
566 Bottle and carton for a cologne. (GBR)
567, 569 Plastic tubes and containers with a lemon-shaped cap for a lemon shampoo and skin cleansing products. (USA)
568 Containers and cartons for a range of cosmetic products. (AUL)
570 Two-in-one cosmetics gift package. (USA)

561–563 Beispiele aus einem Parfümeriesortiment einer Warenhauskette, in dem das feine Linienmotiv den Gefühlswert dieser Produktgattung widerspiegeln soll. Standardformen mit spezieller Produkt- und Verschlusseinfärbung. (SWI)
564 Packungen für Zahnpasta und Produkte für Mundhygiene. (SWI)
565 Plastikflaschen in Grün, Weiss und Braun für Sonnenschutzmittel. Verschluss gelb, Etikett gelb und orange, schwarze Schrift. (GER)
566 Flasche und Packung für ein Kölnischwasser. (GBR)
567, 569 Plastiktube und -packungen mit zitronenförmigem Verschluss für Haarwasch- und Hautreinigungsmittel. (USA)
568 Behälter und Faltschachteln für Kosmetikartikel. (AUL)
570 Zwillings-Geschenkpackung für Kosmetika, von einer Firma der amerikanischen Verpackungsindustrie entwickelt. (USA)

561–563 Extraits de l'assortiment de parfumerie d'une chaîne de grands magasins. La linéarité délicate du motif doit évoquer les cheveux resp. les pores de la peau. Formes standards, couleurs repères. (SWI)
564 Emballages de dentifrice et de produits pour l'hygiène orale. (SWI)
565 Flacons plastiques en vert, blanc et brun pour une nouvelle campagne de lancement de produits solaires. Bouchon jaune, texte des étiquettes noir sur jaune et tons orange. (GER)
566 Flacon et carton pour une eau de Cologne. (GBR)
567, 569 Tubes plastiques et leurs étuis à bouchon en forme de citron pour un shampooing au citron et des détergents cutanés. (USA)
568 Récipients et cartons pour une ligne de cosmétiques. (AUL)
570 Emballage-cadeau bipartite pour des cosmétiques. (USA)

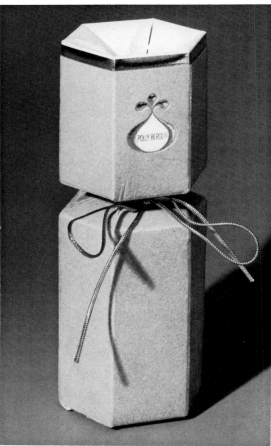

570

571

572

573

571 Plastic container for a beauty lotion. (USA)
572 Soap package with diaphragm closure. (USA)
573 Bottle design for a new scent. Orange ribbon. (FRA)
574 Bottle styling for a toilet water for men. Cap and lettering black. (GER)
575 Bottle styling and label for a hair tonic with a masculine note. Cap and label black. (GER)
576 Tubes, jars and containers for a range of hair lotions, skin tonics and shaving cream for men. The tubes and jars fit into special sewn sleeves made of plastic. (JPN)
577 Folding boxes for a range of soaps with flower fragrances. The package on the left is orange and brown on white, that on the right pink and blue on white. Yellow band printed brown. (GBR)

571 Plastikbehälter für ein Schönheitswasser. (USA)
572 Seifenpackung mit Rosettenverschluss. (USA)
573 Flacon mit orangem Band für ein Parfum. (FRA)
574 Flaschenentwurf für ein Toilettenwasser für Herren. Verschluss und Schrift in Schwarz. (GER)
575 Flaschenentwurf und Graphik für ein Haartonikum mit speziell männlicher Note. Etikett und Verschluss in Schwarz. (GER)
576 Serie von Tuben, Dosen und Flaschen für Herrenkosmetika. (JPN)
577 Packungen für Toilettenseifen, mit natürlichen Geruchstoffen aus schottischem Heidekraut und südenglischen Veilchen gemacht. Linke Packung orange und braun auf Weiss, rechte Packung rosa und blau auf Weiss. Gelbe Banderole mit braunem Aufdruck. (GBR)

571 Conditionnement plastique d'une lotion de beauté. (USA)
572 Emballage de savon pourvu d'une fermeture à soufflet. (USA)
573 Etude de flacon de parfum. Ruban orange. (FRA)
574 Conception de flacon pour une eau de toilette pour messieurs. Capuchon et lettrage noirs. (GER)
575 Flacon et étiquette pour un tonique capillaire répondant aux goûts masculins. Capuchon de fermeture et étiquette noirs. (GER)
576 Tubes, pots et flacons pour une ligne masculine: lotions capillaires, toniques pour la peau, crème à raser. Etuis cousus en plastique. (JPN)
577 Emballages pliants pour une gamme de savons parfumés aux herbes (bruyères d'Ecosse, violettes du sud de l'Angleterre). A gauche, orange et brun sur blanc; à droite, rose et bleu sur blanc. Bande jaune à impression en brun. (GBR)

DESIGNER / GESTALTER / MAQUETTISTE:

571 Edward C. Kozlowski
572 Glenn Matsuyama
574, 575 Bruno K. Wiese
576 Bunshichi Toyoi/Hirozo Saida
577 Ronald Lampitt

576

574

ART DIRECTOR / DIRECTEUR ARTISTIQUE:

571 Herbert R. Nubel/Edward C. Kozlowski
572 Tom Robbins
574, 575 Bruno K. Wiese
576 Haruyo Tahira
577 Peter Windett

AGENCY / AGENTUR / AGENCE – STUDIO:

571 Edward C. Kozlowski Design, Inc.
573 Publicis Conseil
574, 575 Studio für Visual Design
577 Peter Windett Associates

CLIENT / AUFTRAGGEBER:

571 Dorothy Gray, Inc.
573 Parfums Caron
576 Kobayashi Kose Co. Ltd.
577 Crabtree & Evelyn Truc Int., Inc.

575

577

578 Folding box with full-colour photographic illustration for a teething lotion. (USA)
579 Folding box for a tinting shampoo. Hair in full colour, white lettering. (FRA)
580 Bottle styling and folding box design for hair conditioners and shampoos. "Rainbows" in pastel shades. (FRA)
581 Jar and cartons for cosmetics made with herbs. (USA)
582 Tube, container and cartons for cosmetics showing the rainbow that can be created when the cartons are displayed in rows. (SWI)
583 Bottles (with special closure) and cartons for anti-dandruff hair tonics and shampoos. Light blue and white on dark blue. (GER)
584 Package for a combination of make-up and lipstick. Polychrome treatment. (ITA)
585 Folding box (turquoise and lavender) and bottle for a beauty lotion. (JPN)

578 Farbige Faltschachtel für eine Baby-Lotion zur Linderung der Beschwerden beim Zahnen. (USA)
579 Verpackung für ein Haarfärbemittel. Haar in Brauntönen, weisse Schrift. (FRA)
580 Flaschen- und Faltschachtelgestaltung für Haarfestiger und Shampoos. «Regenbogen» in Pastelltönen. (FRA)
581 Töpfchen und Faltschachteln für Kosmetika. (USA)
582 Tube, Behälter und Schachteln für Kosmetikartikel. Durch Aneinanderreihen der Packungen kann ein Regenbogenmuster gebildet werden. (SWI)
583 Flaschen (mit Spezialverschluss) und Schachteln für ein Haarwasser und Shampoo gegen Schuppen. Hellblau und weiss auf Dunkelblau. (GER)
584 Packungen für ein Sortiment von verschiedenen Schminkprodukten. Mehrfarbig. (ITA)
585 Faltschachtel (türkise und lavendelfarbig) und Flasche für ein Hautpflegemittel. (JPN)

578 Boîte pliante pour une lotion contre les troubles de la dentition des bébés. Photo polychrome. (USA)
579 Carton pliant pour un shampooing colorant. Cheveux polychromes, texte en blanc. (FRA)
580 Flacons et emballages cartonnés pour un shampooing et conditionneur et un revitalisant capillaire. Arc-en-ciel aux tons pastels. (FRA)
581 Pot et cartons pour cosmétiques aux herbes. (USA)
582 Tube, récipient et cartons pour cosmétiques. Les cartons rangés côte à côte composent un arc-en-ciel. (SWI)
583 Flacons à capuchons d'exécution spéciale et cartons pour des lotions revitalisantes et shampooings antipelliculaires. Bleu clair et blanc sur bleu foncé. (GER)
584 Emballages pour un assortiment de produits de maquillage et un rouge à lèvres. En polychromie. (ITA)
585 Boîte pliante (turquoise et lavande) et flacon conçus pour une lotion de beauté. (JPN)

579

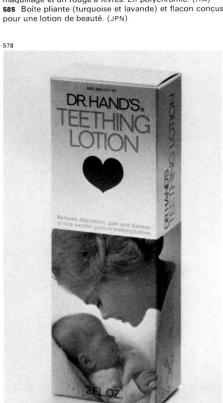

578

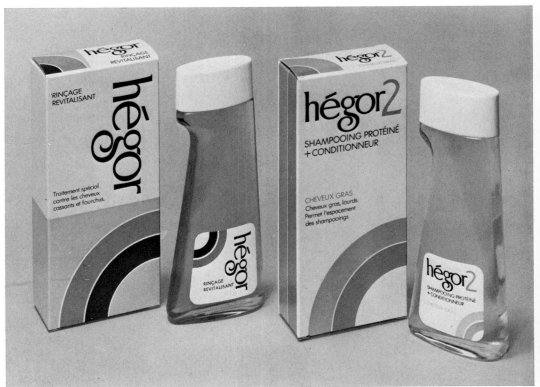

580

DESIGNER / GESTALTER / MAQUETTISTE:

578, 580 Joe Lombardo
579 Annegret Beier (Photo: Hans Mauli)
581 Lynn Shook (Artist: Julie Ann Ach)
582 Richard Sigg
583 Hartmut Staats/Ursula Reimer
584 Dante Vernice
585 Isao Iwasaki

ART DIRECTOR / DIRECTEUR ARTISTIQUE:

578 John S. Blyth
579 Annegret Beier
580 Ronald Peterson
581 Tom Robbins
582 Felix Burkard
583 Hartmut Staats
584 Dante Vernice
585 Isao Iwasaki

AGENCY / AGENTUR / AGENCE – STUDIO:

578, 580 Peterson & Blyth Assoc., Inc.
579 Delpire-Advico SA
582 Idema (Juvena SA)
583 Communicative Design –
      Staats Design Studio
584 Studio Vernice

CLIENT / AUFTRAGGEBER:

578 Denver Chemical Manufacturing Co.
579 L'Oréal SA
580 Laboratoire Lachartre SA
581 Holiday Magic
582 Juvena SA
583 Thera GmbH
584 Margaret Astor
585 Kokuryudo Co. Ltd.

583

581

584

582

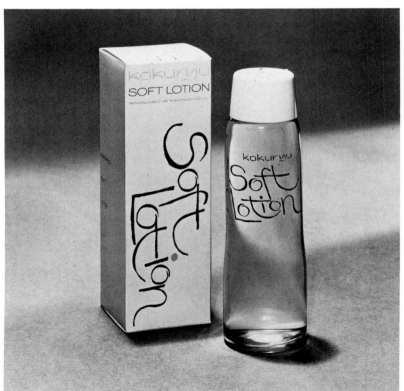

585

191

586 Aerosol container for a deodorant based on vitamin E. Black and white on cream. (USA)
587 Bottle, tube and cartons for an after-shave lotion and shaving cream. Bottle and tube in brown and white. (GER)
588 Bottles, cartons and wrappers for herbal shampoos, lotions and soaps. Designs on soap wrappers and labels green, brown and orange, cartons printed white and gold on black. (CAN)
589 Screw-cap bottles for nail varnish. (JPN)
590 Three packages for after-shave lotion fitted together to form a hexagon. The top is formed by the bottle caps. (JPN)
591, 592 Tube and folding box for a toothpaste. Red and blue on white. (FRA)
593 Package and bottle for a hair lotion for men. See also Fig. 590. (JPN)

586 Spraydose für ein Deodorant mit Vitamin E. Schwarzweiss auf beigem Hintergrund. (USA)
587 Flasche, Tube und Schachteln für einen Herrenkosmetik-Artikel. Flasche und Tube in Braun und Weiss. (GER)
588 Flaschen und Packungen für Kosmetikartikel, die mit pflanzlichen Extrakten hergestellt werden. Seifen-Einwickelpapier grün, braun und orange gedruckt auf weissem Grund. Packungen in Weiss und Gold auf Schwarz. (CAN)
589 Flaschenentwürfe für Nagellack. (JPN)
590 Drei zu einem Sechseck zusammengefügte Packungen für ein Rasierwasser. Die Oberfläche ist mit der Verschlusskappe der Flasche identisch. (JPN)
591, 592 Tube und Faltschachtel für eine Zahnpasta. Rot und blau auf weissem Grund. (FRA)
593 Packung und Flasche für ein Haarwasser für Herren. Siehe auch Abb. 590. (JPN)

586 Bombe aérosol pour un déodorant à base de vitamine E. Noir et blanc sur fond crème. (USA)
587 Flacon, tube et cartons pour une lotion après rasage et une crème à raser. Flacon et tube brun et blanc. (GER)
588 Bouteilles, cartons et emballages de shampooings, lotions et savons à base d'extraits de plantes. Motifs des emballages de savons et des étiquettes en vert, brun et orange. Impression des cartons : blanc et or sur noir. (CAN)
589 Flacons de vernis à ongles, capuchons vissables. (JPN)
590 Trois emballages de lotion après rasage assemblés de manière à former un hexagone, dont le dessus est constitué par les capuchons des flacons. (JPN)
591, 592 Tube et carton qui le contient, pour un dentifrice. Rouge et bleu sur blanc. (FRA)
593 Emballage et conditionnement d'une lotion capillaire pour messieurs. Cf. aussi la fig. 590. (JPN)

587

586

588

DESIGNER / GESTALTER / MAQUETTISTE:

586 Herb Lubalin (Artist: Tom Carnase)
587 Manfred Geicher
588 John K. Sallinen
589 Yoshiaki Uchinuma
590, 593 Hitoshi Iho/Yoshiaki Uchinuma
591, 592 J. Nathan-Garamond

ART DIRECTOR / DIRECTEUR ARTISTIQUE:

586 Arnie Arlow
588 John K. Sallinen
589 Yoshiaki Uchinuma
590, 593 Hitoshi Iho/Yoshiaki Uchinuma
591, 592 R. Excoffon

AGENCY / AGENTUR / AGENCE – STUDIO:

586 Lubalin Smith Carnase
587 Markenkonzeption
588 J. K. Sallinen & Associates
589 Momotani Ltd. Design Dept.
590, 593 Honsvu Printing Co. Ltd.
591, 592 Agence U & O

CLIENT / AUFTRAGGEBER:

586 The Mennen Company
587 Farina Gegenüber
588 Upper Canada Soap & Candle Makers
589 Momotani Juntenkan Ltd.
590, 593 Suzuken Bikagaku Ltd.
591, 592 Klérdence

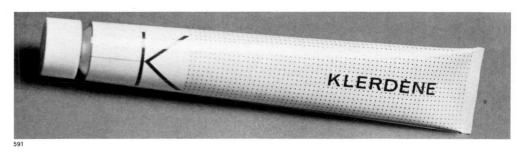

591

589

592

590

593

Cosmetics, Toiletries
Kosmetik, Toilettenartikel
Produits cosmétiques, Articles de toilette

594

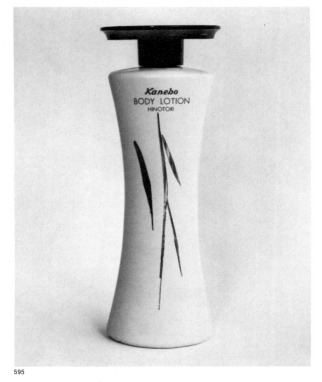

595

DESIGNER / GESTALTER / MAQUETTISTE:

594 Contini Sjöstedt Univas
595 Masahichi Awashima/Shigeru Akizuki
596 Dieter Zembsch
597 Eric Brenzinger
598 Tadayoshi Iwaya/Masayoshi Nakajo/
    Mitsuo Mihira
599 Naomi Hosoya
600 Shigeru Akizuki
601 Shozo Nishigori
602 Akira Takahashi

ART DIRECTOR / DIRECTEUR ARTISTIQUE:

594 Contini Sjöstedt Univas
595 Hiroichi Uakano
596 Dieter Zembsch
597 Eric Brenzinger
598 Tadayoshi Iwaya
599 Haruyo Tahira
600 Shigeru Akizuki
601 Naomi Hosoya
602 Akira Takahashi

AGENCY / AGENTUR / AGENCE – STUDIO:

594 Contini Sjöstedt Univas
596 Dieter Zembsch
597 Recherche et Design
598 Kao Soap Company
599, 601 Albion Cosmetics Design Room
600 Akizuki Design Office

CLIENT / AUFTRAGGEBER:

594 F. Uhlmann-Eyraud SA
595, 600, 602 Kanebo Cosmetics, Inc.
596 Mann & Schröder, Chem. Fabrik
597 Laboratoires Cazé
598 Kao Soap Co. Ltd.
599, 601 Albion Cosmetics

596

597

598

599

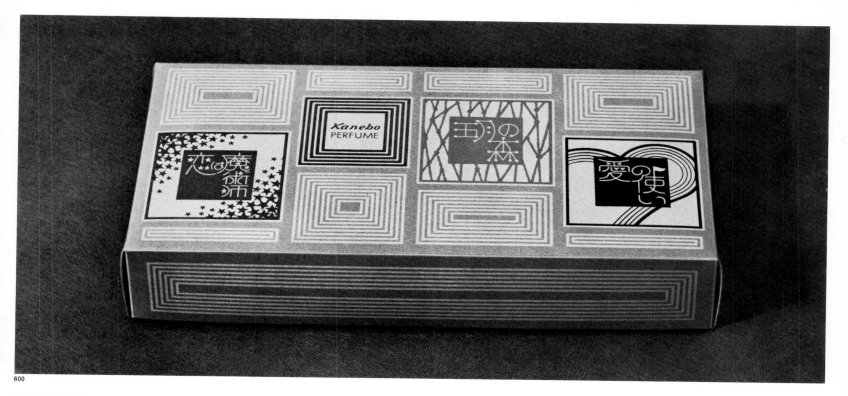

600

601

602

594 Plastic bottle for a shampoo for babies. (SWI)
595 Bottle for a body lotion. (JPN)
596 Plastic bottle for a bath oil containing herbal essences, for use in the sauna. Tag in colour. Bottle shaped to ensure a firm grip. (GER)
597 From a range of deodorant products — here soap and spray — sold only by chemists. Graphics in dark and light green and turquoise. (FRA)
598 Plastic tubes for a hair lotion. Pink on white. (JPN)
599 Bottle and carton for a perfume. Carton with embroidered effect in beige and pale blue-grey shades. (JPN)
600 Gift pack for three perfumes — "May Woods", "The Messenger of Love" and "Love is a Magician". (JPN)
601 Package for cakes of scented soap. (JPN)
602 Folding boxes for a range of beauty products. Black and pink on silver. (JPN)

594 Kunststoff-Flasche für ein Baby-Haarwaschmittel. (SWI)
595 Flasche für ein Körperpflegemittel. (JPN)
596 Kunststoff-Flasche für ein Bademittel, das sich auch, wie auf dem angehängten Etikett vermerkt, gut für eine Badeschwitzkur in der Sauna eignet. (GER)
597 Zwei Beispiele aus einer Verpackungsreihe für Toilettenartikel, die nur zum Verkauf in Apotheken bestimmt sind. Schrift und Graphik in Dunkelgrün, Hellgrün und Türkis auf weissem Grund. (FRA)
598 Kunststofftuben für ein Haartonikum. Rosa auf Weiss. (JPN)
599 Flacon und Schachtel für ein Parfüm. Schachtel mit Stickerei-Effekt in beigen und hellen Blaugrautönen. Verschluss und Schriftzeichen schwarz. (JPN)
600 Geschenkpackung für drei Parfüms: «Maiwald», «Der Liebesbote» und «Die Liebe ist eine Zauberin». (JPN)
601 Packung für eine parfümierte Seife. (JPN)
602 Faltschachteln für kosmetische Produkte. Schwarz und rosa auf Silber. (JPN)

594 Flacon plastique pour un shampooing pour bébés. (SWI)
595 Flacon pour une lotion pour les soins de beauté du corps. (JPN)
596 Flacon plastique pour une huile de bain à base d'essences de plantes recommandée également pour le sauna. Etiquette en couleurs. Le relief donné au flacon assure une prise en main confortable. (GER)
597 Spray et savon déodorants vendus seulement en pharmacie. Lettrage et motif en vert clair et foncé et en turquoise. Eléments d'une gamme complète. (FRA)
598 Tubes plastiques pour une lotion capillaire. Rose sur blanc. (JPN)
599 Flacon et emballage pour un parfum. Carton illustré d'un motif de broderie exécuté en beige et en bleu gris pâle. Bouchon et texte en noir. (JPN)
600 Emballage-cadeau pour trois parfums: «Forêt en mai», «Messager d'amour» et «L'Amour est un magicien». (JPN)
601 Emballage de savons parfumés. (JPN)
602 Boîtes pliantes pour une gamme de cosmétiques. Noir et rose sur argent. (JPN)

Cosmetics, Toiletries
Kosmetik, Toilettenartikel
Produits cosmétiques, Articles de toilette

DESIGNER / GESTALTER / MAQUETTISTE:

603 Robert Burns (Photo: Bert Bell)
604 Felix Burkard
605 Théodore Stamatakis
606 Henry Robertz
607 E + U Hiestand
609 Jeissing Beiersdorf

ART DIRECTOR / DIRECTEUR ARTISTIQUE:

603 Robert Burns
604 Felix Burkard
605 Théodore Stamatakis
607 E + U Hiestand
608 Création Robert Ricci, Marc Lalique

AGENCY / AGENTUR / AGENCE – STUDIO:

603 Burns, Cooper & Weatherstone Ltd.
605 Création Stama
606 Henry Robertz Design
607 E + U Hiestand
608 Edifrance
609 Jeissing Beiersdorf

CLIENT / AUFTRAGGEBER:

603 Kimberly Clark, Ltd.
604 Elizabeth Arden, Inc.
605 S.H.D.V.
606 Jovan, Inc.
607 Dr. G. Dralle
608 Nina Ricci
609 Masius & D'Arcy-MacManus

603

604

605

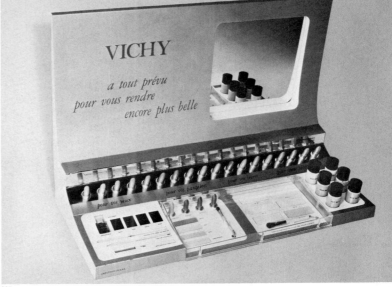

606

607

609

608

603 Front and end-on views — which register for shelf display — of folding-box packages for sanitary napkins. (CAN)
604 Christmas gift box for a men's cosmetic; paper cover in gold and brown, with plastic seal in red and gold. (USA)
605 Display unit for lipsticks and facial make-up. (FRA)
606 Bottle with atomizer for an eau-de-cologne spray, cap and design silver; folding box in matt silver with colour photograph. (USA)
607 Bottle styling and folding boxes for two versions of a hair lotion. (GER)
608 Bottle styling for a perfume. (FRA)
609 Aerosol packages for a mild deodorant. (GER)

603 Vorder- und Seitenansicht von Faltschachteln für Damenbinden. (CAN)
604 Weihnachtsgeschenkpackung für ein Herrenkosmetikprodukt; Papier-Kaschierung in Braun auf Hell- und Altgold, Plastik-Siegel in Rot und Gold. (USA)
605 Auslagesteller für ein Sortiment von Kosmetikprodukten. (FRA)
606 Kölnischwasser-Flacon mit Aerosolzerstäuber. Verschlusskappe und Aufdruck in Silber. Faltschachtel mit Farbphotographie in mattiertem Silber. (USA)
607 Flaschen und Faltschachteln für zwei Haarwasser. (GER)
608 Fläschchen für ein Parfüm. (FRA)
609 Aerosoldosen für ein mildes Antitranspirant. (GER)

603 Faces avant et latérale, se prêtant à l'exposition en magasin, d'emballages de bandes hygiéniques. (CAN)
604 Emballage-cadeau d'un cosmétique pour messieurs conçu en fonction des ventes de Noël. Revêtement papier or et brun, sceau plastique or et rouge. (USA)
605 Présentoir pour rouges à lèvres et produits de maquillage. (FRA)
606 Flacon atomiseur d'eau de Cologne. Capuchon et impression argent. Carton d'emballage argent mat, photo couleur. (USA)
607 Conception de flacons et cartons pour deux lotions capillaires. (GER)
608 Etude de flacon pour un parfum. (FRA)
609 Bombes aérosols pour un désodorisant léger. (GER)

Cosmetics, Toiletries
Kosmetik, Toilettenartikel
Produits cosmétiques, Articles de toilette

610

611

DESIGNER / GESTALTER / MAQUETTISTE:

610 Eugene J. Grossman
611 Takehiko Umekawa
612 Shigeo Morita
613 Shunsaku Sugiura/Kunio Hachimura/Suichi Ikeda
614 Oliver Waley/Jean Vitrac
615 Shigeya Sakai

ART DIRECTOR / DIRECTEUR ARTISTIQUE:

610 Eugene J. Grossman
611, 612, 615 Yasui Kumai
613 Shigeyoshi Aoki
614 Oliver Waley

613

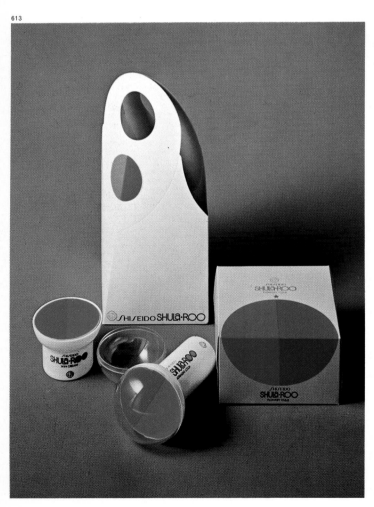

614

612

610 Aerosol containers and tube for a range of men's cosmetics (face wash, shaving foam and protein hair shampoo). (USA)
611 Gift pack containing a perfume and a face powder. (JPN)
612 Pack for a beauty soap. (JPN)
613 Tube, jar, carton and carrier bag for a range of cosmetics developed specially for teenagers. (JPN)
614 Bottles for a perfume and toilet water from a range of cosmetics. The caps in matt black plastic are designed in imitation of the bulbous towers of Russian churches. The name "Nitchevo" means "Nothing" in Russian. (FRA)
615 Gift packs for a range of translucent facial soaps. Folding boxes of several sizes in various designs and colours. (JPN)

610 Dosen und Tube für eine Reihe von Herren-Kosmetikprodukten. Von links nach rechts: Gesichtsseife, Rasierschaum und Haarwaschmittel mit Protein. (USA)
611 Geschenkpackung enthaltend Parfüm und Gesichtspuder. (JPN)
612 Packung für eine Toilettenseife. (JPN)
613 Tube, Dose, Faltschachtel und Tragtasche für ein Sortiment Kosmetikprodukte, das speziell für Teenager entwickelt wurde. (JPN)
614 Flaschen für ein Toilettenwasser und ein Parfüm. Die mattschwarzen Kunststoff-Schraubverschlüsse sind den russischen Kirchturmspitzen, den «Zwiebeln», nachgeahmt. «Nitchevo» bedeutet auf russisch «Nichts». (FRA)
615 Geschenkpackungen für durchscheinende Gesichtsseifen, die unter dem Namen «Honigkuchen» hergestellt werden. (JPN)

610 Flacons atomiseurs et tube pour une ligne de cosmétiques pour messieurs (spray détergent pour les soins du visage, mousse à raser, shampooing aux protéines). (USA)
611 Emballage-cadeau pour un parfum et de la poudre de riz. (JPN)
612 Emballage pour un savon de toilette. (JPN)
613 Tube, pot, carton et sac en papier pour une gamme de cosmétiques visant une clientèle de jeunes. (JPN)
614 Flacons pour un parfum et une eau de toilette figurant dans une ligne de cosmétiques. Capuchons plastiques noir mat imitant les coupoles en forme de bulbes des églises russes. «Nitchevo» = «rien». (FRA)
615 Emballages-cadeaux pour les savons faciaux translucides «Rayon de miel». Boîtes pliantes de formats et coloris divers. (JPN)

AGENCY / AGENTUR / AGENCE — STUDIO:

610 Anspach Grossman Portugal, Inc.
611—613, 615 Shiseido Cosmetics, Advert. Dept.
614 London Design Unit

CLIENT / AUFTRAGGEBER:

610 Sterling Drug
611—613, 615 Shiseido Cosmetics Co. Ltd.
614 Juvena SA

615

Cosmetics, Toiletries
Kosmetik, Toilettenartikel
Produits cosmétiques, Articles de toilette

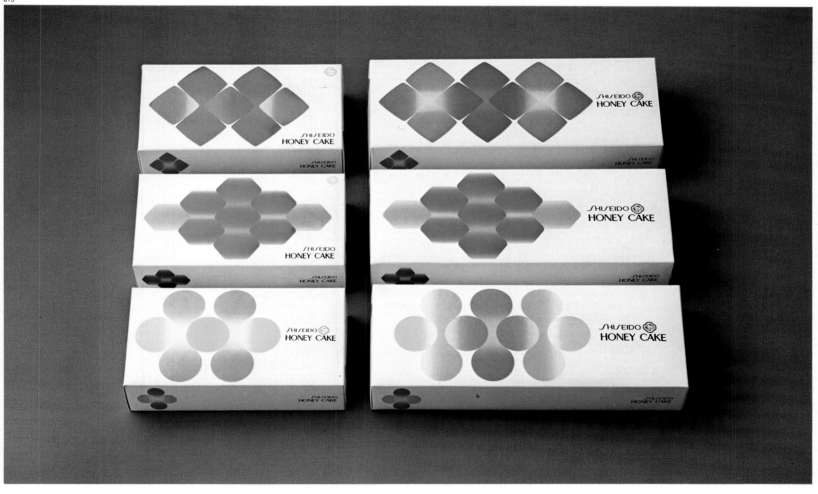

DESIGNER / GESTALTER / MAQUETTISTE:

616 Felix Burkard/Niklaus Schmid
617 Masakazu Yamashita
619 Sunsho Machi/Michiko Nakayama
621 Penny Johnson

ART DIRECTOR / DIRECTEUR ARTISTIQUE:

616 Felix Burkard
617 Yasui Kumai
619 Haruyo Tahira
621 Penny Johnson

AGENCY / AGENTUR / AGENCE – STUDIO:

617 Shiseido Cosmetics, Advert. Dept.
621 Penny Johnson

CLIENT / AUFTRAGGEBER:

616 Elizabeth Arden, Inc.
617 Shiseido Cosmetics Co. Ltd.
618 Elizabeth Arden, Inc.
619 Kobayashi Kose Co. Ltd.
620 Courrèges SA
621 World of Beauty Club

Cosmetics, Toiletries
Kosmetik, Toilettenartikel
Produits cosmétiques, Articles de toilette

617

616

618

619

620

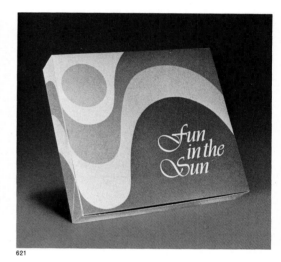

621

616 Bottles with wooden caps and carton for men's cologne. (USA)
617 Gift packages for a large range of cosmetic products. (JPN)
618 Gift package and carton for men's cosmetics. (SWI)
619 Bottles for perfume and toilet water. (JPN)
620 Bottles for perfume and toilet water. The bottle in the spherical silver gift pack is of a white opaque glass enclosed in Perspex. The caps are silver. (FRA)
621 Folding box for a sun-tan cream. Shades of yellow and light brown. (USA)

616 Flaschen mit Holzverschluss und Verkaufspackung für ein Kölnischwasser für Herren. (USA)
617 Verkaufsbereit aufgemachte Geschenkschachteln für die Kosmetikprodukte eines grossen Sortiments. (JPN)
618 Geschenkpackung und Schachtel für Herren-Kosmetika. (SWI)
619 Flacons für Parfüms und Gesichtswasser. (JPN)
620 Flacons für Parfüm und Toilettenwasser. Das Flacon in der silbernen Geschenkkugel ist aus weissem Milchglas, das mit einer dicken Plexiglashülle umgeben wurde. Die anderen Flacons sind ganz- oder teilversilbert. (FRA)
621 Packung für ein Sonnenschutzmittel. Gelbe und hellbraune Töne. (USA)

616 Flacons aux capuchons en bois et emballage de vente pour une eau de Cologne pour messieurs. (USA)
617 Emballages-cadeaux pour une gamme étendue de produits de cosmétiques. (JPN)
618 Emballage-cadeau et carton, pour des cosmétiques pour messieurs. (SWI)
619 Flacons pour un parfum et une eau de toilette. (JPN)
620 Flacons pour un parfum et une eau de toilette. Le flacon dans l'emballage-cadeau sphérique est en verre dépoli blanc entouré d'une couche de Perspex plastique. Capuchons argentés. (FRA)
621 Emballage de crème solaire. Jaunes et bruns rouges. (USA)

Pharmaceutical Products
Pharmazeutische Produkte
Produits pharmaceutiques

8

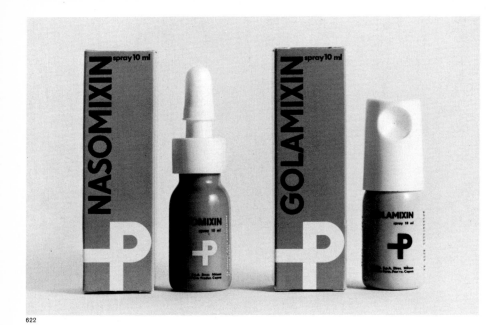

622

Pharmaceutical Products
Pharmazeutische Produkte
Produits pharmaceutiques

DESIGNER / GESTALTER / MAQUETTISTE:

622 Claudio Platania
623 Kerstin Bartelmae (Photo: Ingo Kilian)
625 David Enock/Stan Eisenmann
626 Hans W. Vocke
627 John J. J. Janos
628 Charles Goslin
629 Ronald Baum (Artist: Bruno-Mease)
630 Juan Concepcion/Larry Riddell

ART DIRECTOR / DIRECTEUR ARTISTIQUE:

622 Alfredo Mastellaro
623 Kerstin Bartelmae
625 Eisenman & Enock, Inc.
626 Peter D. Asmussen
627 John J. J. Janos
629 J. Robert Parker
630 Richard Gerstman

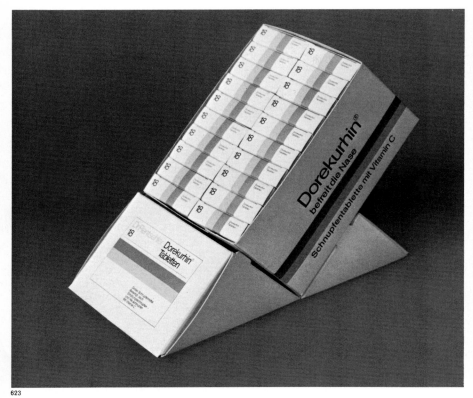

623

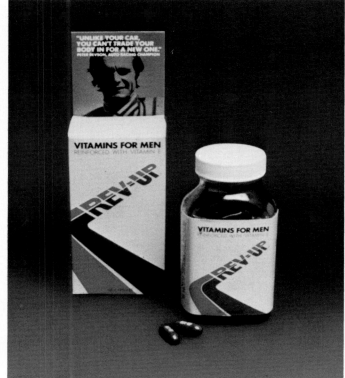

625

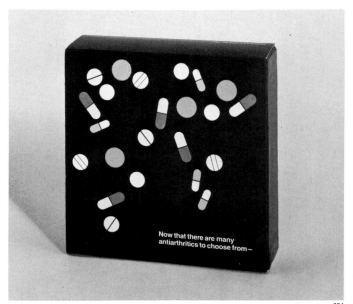

624

626

627

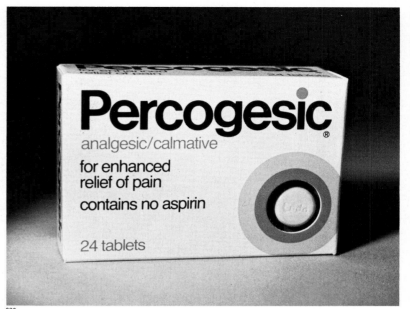

630

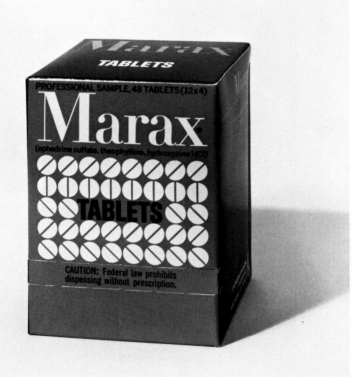

628

AGENCY / AGENTUR / AGENCE – STUDIO:

622 Ufficio Pubblicità
623 Design Bartelmae
625 Levine, Huntley, Schmidt, Plapler, Beaver, Inc.
626 Atelier Vocke
627 Hertz Walpole Advertising
628 Barnett/Goslin/Barnett
629 Smith Kline & French Laboratories
630 Gerstman & Meyers, Inc.

CLIENT / AUFTRAGGEBER:

622 Pierrel S. p. A.
623 Dr. Rentschler
626 Beiersdorf AG
627, 629 Smith Kline & French Laboratories
628 Pfizer, Inc.
630 Endo Laboratories

622 Folding boxes and plastic containers for a nose and throat spray. (ITA)
623 Display unit with boxes of tablets against colds and nasal congestion. (GER)
624 Sleeve containing a set-up box with a sample of *Butazolidin* as the most widely prescribed short-term antiarthritic. Brightly coloured tablets and capsules on a black ground. (USA)
625 Folding box, leaflet and bottle for vitamin tablets for men. Design in red and blue. (USA)
626 Box to take printed matter on the *Beiersdorf* medical programme. Orange and blue stripes, black lettering. (GER)
627 Folding box for capsules to relieve coughs and colds. (AUL)
628 Folding box, with tear-off strip to permit use as a dispenser, for a professional sample of ephedrine tablets. (USA)
629 Packs for the equipment needed in various medical tests. (USA)
630 Folding box for analgesic and calmative tablets. Printed yellow, brown and black. An actual tablet is visible under cellophane in the circle at bottom right, the purpose being to underline the effectiveness of the single tablet. (USA)

622 Faltschachteln und Aerosoldosen aus Plastik für einen Nasen- und Rachenspray. (ITA)
623 Display-Behälter mit Faltschachteln für Schnupfentabletten. (GER)
624 Ärztemuster für *Butazolidin,* das meist verschriebene Mittel gegen Arthritis. Farbige Pillen. (USA)
625 Als Display-Schachtel erweiterte Verkaufspackung und Flasche für ein Aufbaupräparat für Männer. Streifen und Schrift blau und rot auf Weiss. (USA)
626 Schachtel, die Unterlagen über das medizinische Programm von *Beiersdorf* enthält. Streifen orange und blau, Schrift schwarz. (GER)
627 Faltschachtel für Kapseln gegen Erkältungskrankheiten mit Husten. (AUL)
628 Faltschachtel als Ärztepackung für rezeptpflichtige Tabletten. (USA)
629 Verpackungen, die zur Aufnahme von Testausrüstungen für die Bestimmung von verschiedenen Krankheitserregern dienen. (USA)
630 Faltschachtel für ein ohne Rezept erhältliches schmerzstillendes Beruhigungsmittel. Gelb, braun und schwarz auf weissem Grund. Im Kreis rechts unten ist jeweils eine Originaltablette, durch Cellophan geschützt, deutlich sichtbar. Dies soll die Wirksamkeit der einzelnen Tablette hervorheben. (USA)

622 Cartons pliants et aérosoliseurs en plastique pour applications buccale et nasale. (ITA)
623 Présentoir garni de boîtes de comprimés contre les rhinites. (GER)
624 Boîte coulissante destinée au médecin pour *Butazolidin* en tant que remède contre l'arthrite. (USA)
625 Boîte pliante, élément de présentation et flacon de vitamines pour hommes. Composition de la boîte et de l'étiquette en rouge et bleu sur blanc. (USA)
626 Boîte de classement pour la documentation médicale fournie par *Beiersdorf.* Bandes orange et bleues, lettres noires. (GER)
627 Boîte de capsules contre la toux et le rhume. (AUL)
628 Boîte pliante utilisable comme distributeur de comprimés d'éphédrine, une fois la bande de protection arrachée. Echantillon médical. (USA)
629 Emballages d'équipements utilisés dans divers tests de laboratoire. (USA)
630 Boîte pliante pour un remède à effet analgésique et calmant présenté sous forme de comprimés. Impression jaune, marron, noir sur blanc. Dans le cercle, en bas, à droite, est logé un vrai comprimé sous le cellophane, pour démontrer qu'un seul comprimé est déjà très efficace. (USA)

Pharmaceutical Products
Pharmazeutische Produkte
Produits pharmaceutiques

632

631 Folding box for hair treatment capsules. Black and white. (JPN)
632 Folding boxes embodying the standardized design principles of a pharmaceutical company. The standing boxes have the Z emblem in the upper third, the name of the product in the middle and the indications on the lower third. The dosage and other particulars are given on the sides. (SWI)
633 Cylindrical pharmaceutical packages in display stands. (USA)
634 Boxes for expanding bandages. Use on various parts of the body is illustrated on the boxes. The available types of bandages are also colour coded. (USA)
635 Horizontal boxes for tubes, from the same range as the boxes shown in Fig. 632. The three divisions are here arranged from left to right. (SWI)
636 Folding boxes for psychotropic drugs. (SWI)

631 Faltschachtel für Haarwuchskapseln. Schwarzweiss. (JPN)
632 Einheitlich gestaltete Faltschachteln für alle Produkte einer Arzneimittelfabrik. Bei stehenden Packungen erscheint das Z-Signet Ton in Ton, das mittlere Drittel ist dem Präparatnamen vorbehalten, während das untere Drittel die Indikationen angibt. Die Seitenflächen enthalten Dosierung sowie Angaben über die Zusammensetzung des Präparats. (SWI)
633 Dosen und Display-Ständer für Pharmaka. (USA)
634 Packungen für dehnbare Bandagen. Die Anwendungen bei den entsprechenden Körperteilen sind graphisch dargestellt und unterscheiden sich zusätzlich durch verschiedene Farben. (USA)
635 Liegende Packungen der gleichen Marke wie in Abb. 632. Hier wird die Dreiteilung von links nach rechts abgewickelt. (SWI)
636 Faltschachteln für Psychopharmaka. (SWI)

631 Boîte pliante pour capsules favorisant la repousse des cheveux. Noir et blanc. (JPN)
632 Boîtes pliantes reflétant la conception standardisée des emballages d'une société pharmaceutique: Z dans le tiers supérieur, nom du produit au milieu, indications dans le tiers inférieur. Posologie et composition sur les côtés. (SWI)
633 Présentoir et boîtes cylindriques contenant des produits pharmaceutiques. (USA)
634 Boîtes de pansements extensibles pour diverses parties du corps. Identification par les illustrations et le code-couleur. (USA)
635 Boîtes pliantes horizontales. Même marque que celles de la fig. 632, avec la même organisation graphique tripartite, mais cette fois-ci de gauche à droite et non pas de haut en bas. (SWI)
636 Boîtes pliantes pour drogues psychotropes. (SWI)

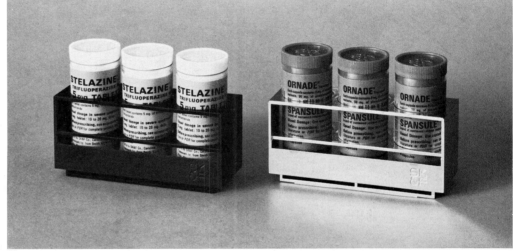
633

631

634

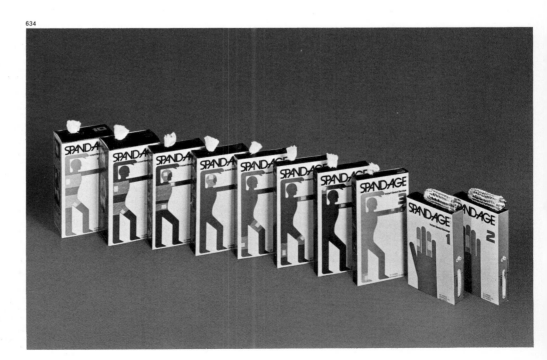

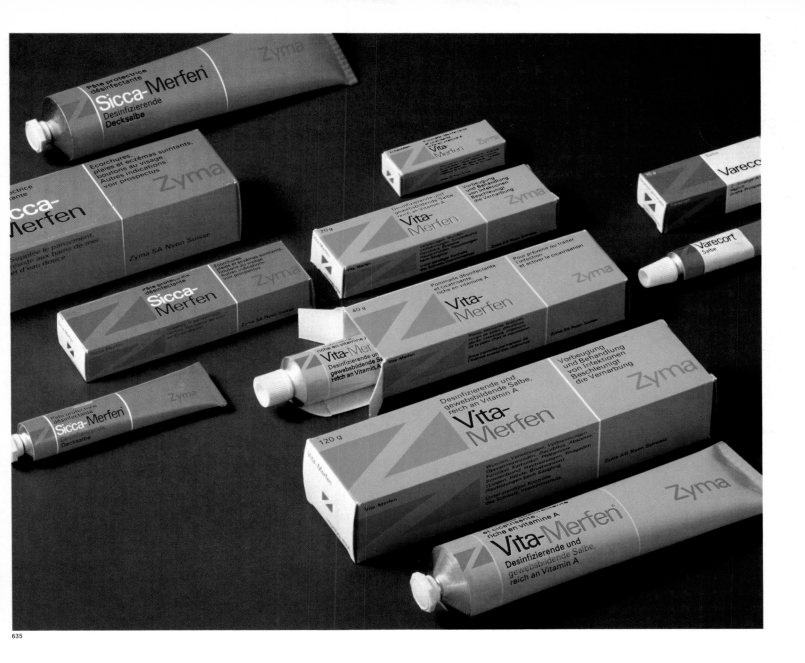

635

636

DESIGNER / GESTALTER / MAQUETTISTE:

631 Helmut Schmid
632, 635 Hansruedi Widmer
633 Ronald Baum
634 Harry & Marion Zelenko
636 Sylvia Goeschke

ART DIRECTOR / DIRECTEUR ARTISTIQUE:

632, 635 Hansruedi Widmer
633 Warren Blair
634 Herb Perry
636 Jacques Hauser

AGENCY / AGENTUR / AGENCE – STUDIO:

631 Nippon International Agency
632, 635 Devico Design
633 Smith Kline & French Laboratories
634 Zelenko Associates, Inc.
636 Humbert & Vogt

CLIENT / AUFTRAGGEBER:

631 Taiho Pharmaceutical Co. Ltd.
632, 635 Zyma SA
633 Smith Kline & French Laboratories
634 Medi-Tech International Corp.
636 Hoffmann-La Roche AG

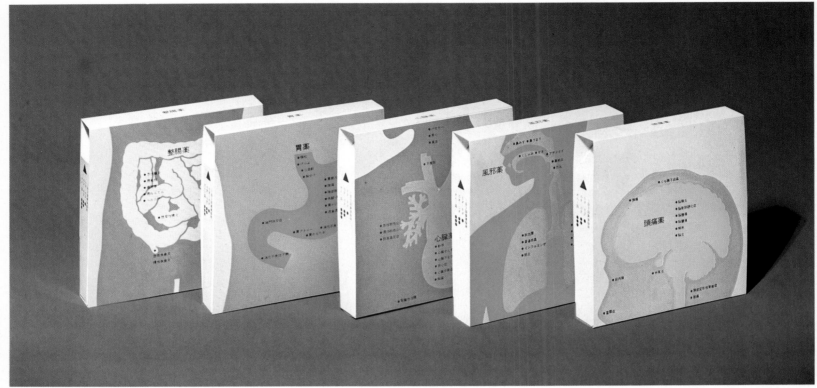

637

637 Series of folding boxes of standardized format for various pharmaceutical products. (JPN)
638 Folding boxes for a fortifying medicine. When packed in a transparent wrapper, they produce a striking display effect. (JPN)
639 Sleeve-and-tray packing for cleaning substances for contact lenses. Combination of board and plastic with an embossed pattern on the lid. (USA)
640 Folding box and plastic bottle with dosage measuring cap for a liquid tranquillizer. (GBR)
641 Family of packs for a range of pharmaceuticals. (FRA)
642, 643 Folding boxes for a range of medicines. (GBR)
644 Carton with built-in dosage measuring system for a kidney diet for dogs. (SWI)
645 Clinical package for an analgesic and febrifuge. Blue "A", black type matter. (GER)

637 Serie von im Format einheitlichen Faltschachteln für verschiedene pharmazeutische Produkte. (JPN)
638 Faltschachteln für ein pharmazeutisches Aufbaupräparat. Die aufeinandergestapelten Packungen ergeben einen markanten Display-Effekt. (JPN)
639 Schiebeschachtel für Reinigungs- und Pflegemittel für Kontaktlinsen. Kombination von Plastik und Karton mit blindgeprägtem Muster auf dem Deckel. (USA)
640 Faltschachtel und Plastikflasche mit Messbecher für ein flüssiges Beruhigungsmittel. (GBR)
641 Packungsfamilie für verschiedene Pharmazeutika. (FRA)
642, 643 Faltschachteln für verschiedene Medikamente des gleichen Herstellers. (GBR)
644 Packung für eine Nierendiätkost für Hunde. (SWI)
645 Klinikpackung für ein Mittel gegen Schmerzen. Blaues «A» auf weissem Grund, Text schwarz. (GER)

637 Série de boîtes pliantes de format standardisé conçues pour divers produits pharmaceutiques. (JPN)
638 Boîtes pliantes pour un fortifiant. Empilées sous un emballage transparent, elles composent une silhouette humaine qui constitue un effet de présentation original. (JPN)
639 Boîte coulissante pour des produits de nettoyage et d'entretien pour verres de contact. Combinaison de carton et de plastique, motif gaufré à même le couvercle. (USA)
640 Boîte pliante et flacon plastique avec gobelet doseur pour un tranquillisant liquide. (GBR)
641 Famille d'emballages de produits pharmaceutiques. (FRA)
642, 643 Boîtes pliantes pour une série de médicaments. (GBR)
644 Carton avec mesurette incorporée, pour un régime des néphrites canines. (SWI)
645 Emballage clinique pour un analgésique et fébrifuge. «A» bleu sur fond blanc, typo en noir. (GER)

638

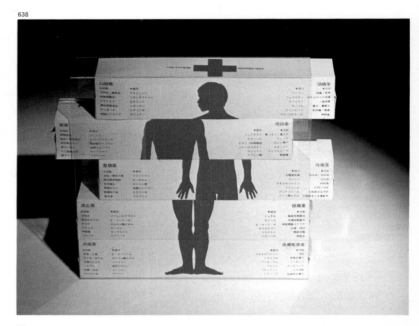

639

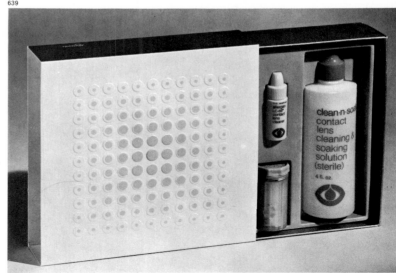

Pharmaceutical Products
Pharmazeutische Produkte
Produits pharmaceutiques

640

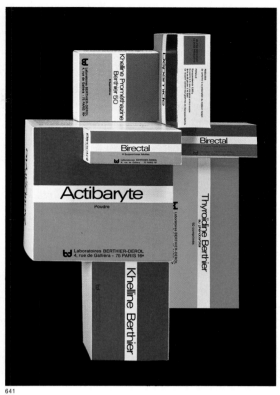

641

DESIGNER / GESTALTER / MAQUETTISTE:

637, 638 Ryuichi Arkai
639 House of Packaging, Inc.
641 Christian Schmutz/Laurent Ceppi
642, 643 FHK Henrion
644 X. Bürgi
645 Erich Unger

ART DIRECTOR / DIRECTEUR ARTISTIQUE:

637, 638 Ryuichi Arkai
641 Christian Schmutz
642, 643 FHK Henrion
644 Sandoz AG

AGENCY / AGENTUR:

641 Création 3 SA
642, 643 HDA International

CLIENT / AUFTRAGGEBER:

639 Allergan Pharmaceuticals
640 Winthrop Laboratories
641 Berthier-Derol Laboratoires
642, 643 Porto 1
644 Sandoz AG
645 Steiner Arzneimittel

642

643

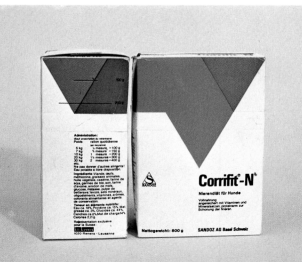

644

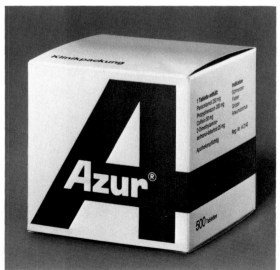

645

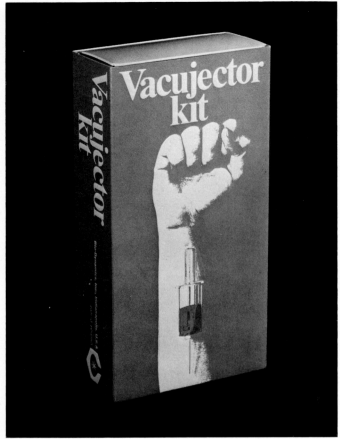

646

647

646 Sliding box for an injection kit. Red on grey. (USA)
647 Pack containing folding boxes of capsules for the control of blood sugar in diabetic patients. (USA)
648 Folding boxes containing five disposable syringes filled with a penicillin product used for intramuscular injections. (USA)
649, 650 Bottle and range of folding boxes for medicines against coughs and colds for adults and children. (CAN)
651 Display unit for folding boxes containing an antiseptic paint for use on cuts, burns, scalds, etc. (USA)

646 Schiebeschachtel für eine Injektionsausrüstung. Rot auf Grau. (USA)
647 Verpackung für Faltschachteln mit Kapseln, die zur Regulierung des Blutzuckers bei Diabetikern dienen. (USA)
648 Faltschachtel für fünf wegwerfbare Spritzen. Sie enthalten ein Medikament mit Penicillin, das zur intramuskulären Injektion verwendet wird. (USA)
649, 650 Flasche und Faltschachteln für Medikamente gegen Erkältungskrankheiten für Erwachsene und Kinder. (CAN)
651 Verkaufshelfer mit Faltschachteln für einen antiseptischen Anstrich für Schnittwunden, Verbrennungen usw. (USA)

646 Boîte coulissante pour un équipement d'injection. Rouge sur gris. (USA)
647 Emballage regroupant diverses boîtes pliantes pour des capsules destinées à régulariser le taux de sucre sanguin des diabétiques. (USA)
648 Boîtes pliantes contenant cinq seringues à jeter d'un médicament à base de pénicilline applicable par injection intramusculaire. (USA)
649, 650 Bouteille et série de boîtes pliantes pour des remèdes contre la toux et les refroidissements chez les adultes et les enfants. (CAN)
651 Emballage de présentation recevant des boîtes pliantes d'une teinture antiseptique pour les coupures, brûlures, etc. (USA)

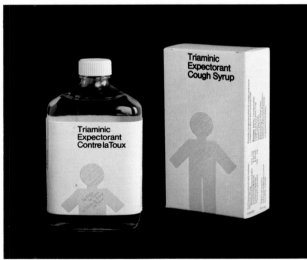

649

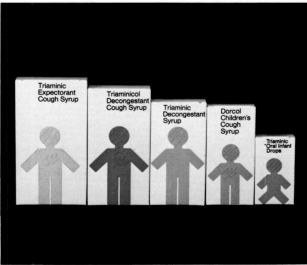

650

648

DESIGNER / GESTALTER / MAQUETTISTE:

646 Barry Doss (Photo: Joe McGuire)
647 Charles Goslin
648 Brian Sadgrove
    (Photo: Specialized Photographic)
649, 650 Stuart Ash
651 Brian Sadgrove/Andrew Fowler-Brown

ART DIRECTOR / DIRECTEUR ARTISTIQUE:

646 Barry Doss
647 Charles Goslin
648, 651 Brian Sadgrove
649, 650 Gottschalk & Ash Ltd.

AGENCY / AGENTUR / AGENCE – STUDIO:

646 The Design Group, Inc.
647 Barnett/Goslin/Barnett
648, 651 Brian Sadgrove, Inc.
649, 650 Gottschalk & Ash Ltd.

CLIENT / AUFTRAGGEBER:

646 Bio-Dynamics, Inc.
647 U.S. Vitamin Corp.
648, 651 F. H. Faulding & Co. Ltd.
649, 650 Anca Laboratories

651

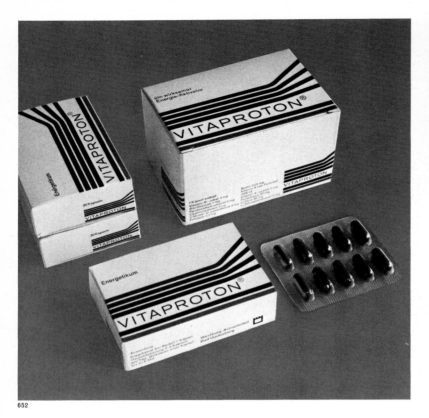

652

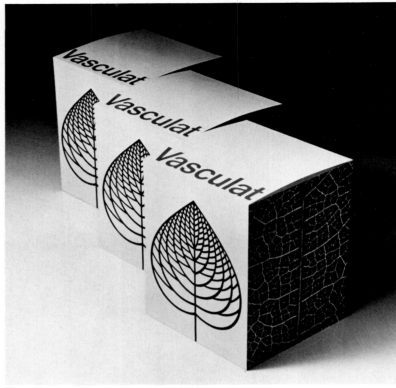

653

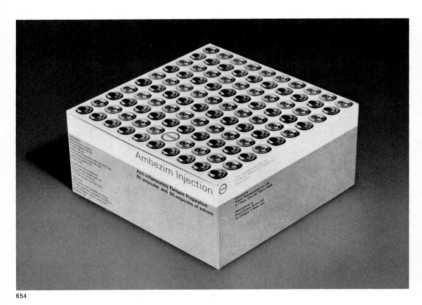

654

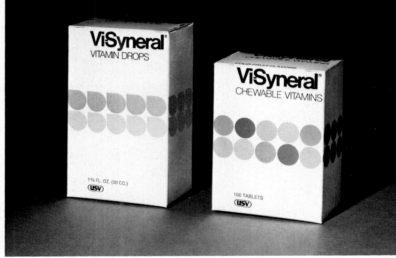

655

DESIGNER / GESTALTER / MAQUETTISTE:

652 Nikolaus Müller-Behrendt
653 Heinz Kroehl/Peter Offenberg
654, 658 Helmut Schmid
655 David L. Romanoff
656 Hermann Rastorfer
657 Armando Milani
659 Primo Angeli
660 Brian Sadgrove/Lyndon Whaite

ART DIRECTOR / DIRECTEUR ARTISTIQUE:

652 Heimar Doll
653 Heinz Kroehl/Peter Offenberg
655 David L. Romanoff
657 Armando Milani
659 Primo Angeli
660 Brian Sadgrove
661 Alan Franklin

652 Folding boxes for vitamin capsules. Stripes in red and yellow shades. (GER)
653 Folding boxes for a circulation stimulant. (GER)
654 Folding box for 100 ampoules of an anti-inflammatory preparation. Grey and red. (JPN)
655 Folding boxes for vitamin drops and pastilles. (USA)
656 Folding box for a tube of analgesic ointment. (SWI)
657 Folding box for a vitamin preparation. Black and white, name in red. (ITA)
658 Folding box for 100 capsules of an antibiotic. Orange and red. (JPN)
659 Cans and folding box in olive and white for a barium sulphate suspension which is used in X-ray examinations. (USA)
660 Display unit and folding boxes for tubes of a barrier cream for skin protection. (USA)
661 Folding boxes for two types of tracheostomy tubes. (USA)

652 Faltschachteln für einen Energieaktivator. Streifen in Rot- und Gelbtönen. (GER)
653 Faltschachteln für ein Durchblutungspräparat. (GER)
654 Faltschachtel für 100 Ampullen eines entzündungshemmenden Medikaments. Grau, rot. (JPN)
655 Faltschachteln für ein Vitaminpräparat, links für Tropfen, rechts für Tabletten. (USA)
656 Faltschachtel für eine Tube mit einer schmerzstillenden Creme. (SWI)
657 Faltschachtel für ein Vitaminpräparat. Schwarzweiss, Name des Produktes in Rot. (ITA)
658 Faltschachtel für 100 Kapseln eines Antibiotikums. Orange und rot. (JPN)
659 Büchsen und Faltschachtel in Oliv und Weiss für eine Barium-Sulfat-Aufschwemmung zum Gebrauch bei Röntgenaufnahmen. (USA)
660 Display-Verkaufspackung mit Faltschachteln für Tuben einer Hautschutzcreme. (USA)
661 Standardpackungen für Tracheostomie-Röhrchen. (USA)

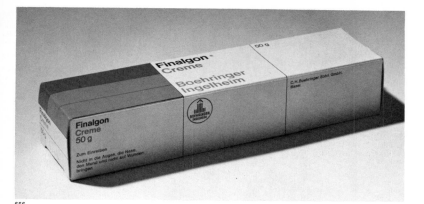

656

Pharmaceutical Products/Pharmazeutische Produkte
Produits pharmaceutiques

AGENCY / AGENTUR / AGENCE – STUDIO:

653 Kroehl Design Gruppe
654, 658 Nippon International Agency
655 USV Pharmaceutical Creative Dept.
656 Visuelles Marketing Rastorfer
657 Studio Grafico Armando Milani
659 Pickerin & Edwards
660 Brian Sadgrove, Inc.
661 Townsend & Russell

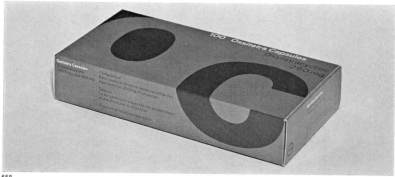

657

658

659

660

CLIENT / AUFTRAGGEBER:

652 Dolorgiet Arzneimittel
653, 656 C. H. Boehringer Sohn
654, 658 Taiho Pharmaceutical
655 U. S. Vitamin Corp.
657 Instituto Vitamine Roche
659 Flow Pharmaceuticals, Inc.
660 F. H. Faulding & Co. Ltd.
661 Shiley Laboratories, Inc.

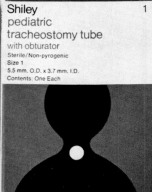

661

652 Boîtes pliantes pour un fortifiant aux vitamines. Bandes en divers tons jaunes, orange. (GER)
653 Boîtes pliantes pour un vasotonique. (GER)
654 Emballage pour 100 ampoules d'une préparation antiphlogistique. Gris et rouge. (JPN)
655 Boîtes pliantes pour un produit vitaminé liquide (à gauche) et en comprimés (à droite.) (USA)
656 Boîte pliante contenant un tube de baume analgésique. (SWI)
657 Boîte pliante pour une préparation vitaminée. Noir et blanc, nom du produit en rouge. (ITA)
658 Boîte pliante pour 100 ampoules d'un antibiotique. Orange et rouge. (JPN)
659 Boîtes métalliques et carton pliant, olive et blanc, pour une suspension de sulfate de baryum utilisée en radioscopie et radiographie. (USA)
660 Présentoir et boîtes pliantes pour des tubes de crème protectrice pour la peau. (USA)
661 Boîtes pliantes standardisées pour deux types de tubes de trachéostomie. (USA)

Promotional Packaging
Werbepackungen
Emballages publicitaires

9

662 Folding box for samples of a medicament against infections of the scalp sent to dermatologists. (USA)
663 Set-up box for samples of a vitamin preparation sent to doctors. Pink, yellow and orange tablets on a grey ground. (ITA)
664 Gift pack containing a coloured paperweight designed to remind doctors of a brand of tranquillizer. (GBR)
665 Set-up box for samples requested by doctors. (CAN)
666 Set-up box for effervescent vitamin tablets. Green and white. (CAN)
667 Set-up box for samples requested by doctors. (CAN)
668 Display pack demonstrating the comparative safety of a sleep-inducing drug. (GBR)
669 Pack for flavours used in health and hygiene products. Fruit in colour. (USA)

662 An Dermatologen versandte Musterpackung für ein neues Medikament zur Behandlung infektiöser Kopfhautreizungen. (USA)
663 An Ärzte versandte Werbepackung für ein Vitaminpräparat. Rosa, gelbe und orange Tabletten auf grauem Hintergrund. (ITA)
664 Geschenkpackung mit einem mehrfarbigen Briefbeschwerer aus Glas, der die Ärzte an das Beruhigungsmittel *Nobrium* erinnern soll. (GBR)
665 Stülpdeckelschachtel für den Versand von Ärztemustern. (CAN)
666 Stülpdeckelschachtel für Brausetabletten. Grün und weiss. (CAN)
667 Stülpdeckelschachtel für den Versand von Ärztemustern. (CAN)
668 Aufstellpackung, die auf die Ungefährlichkeit eines Schlafmittels hinweist. (GBR)
669 Packung für Geruchsessenzen, die für Arzneimittel und Hygieneprodukte verwendet werden. Mehrfarbige Früchte und Blätter auf grauem Grund. (USA)

662 Boîte pliante pour un échantillon d'un médicament des infections du cuir chevelu distribué aux dermatologues. (USA)
663 Boîte montée pour un échantillon médical d'un produit vitaminé. Comprimés roses, jaunes, orange sur fond gris. (ITA)
664 Emballage-cadeau contenant un presse-papiers polychrome en verre rappelant aux médecins les vertus du tranquillisant *Nobrium*. (GBR)
665 Boîte montée pour l'expédition d'échantillons médicaux. (CAN)
666 Boîte montée pour comprimés vitaminés effervescents. Vert et blanc. (CAN)
667 Boîte montée pour échantillons médicaux. (CAN)
668 Elément de présentation faisant ressortir l'innocuité d'un hypnotique. (GBR)
669 Emballage de substances gustatives employées dans la fabrication de produits pharmaceutiques et d'hygiène. Fruits et feuilles polychromes sur fond gris. (USA)

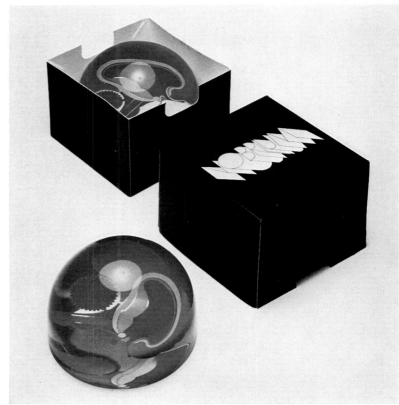

664

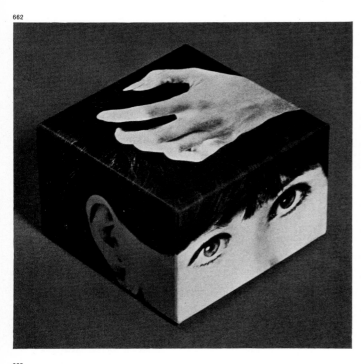

663

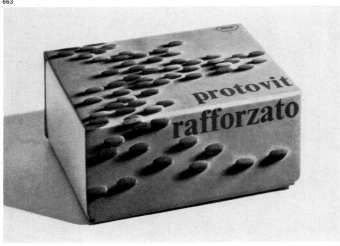

662

665

DESIGNER / GESTALTER / MAQUETTISTE:

662 Ralph Grigg (Photo: Irv Barth)
663 Roche, Ufficio Pubblicità
664 Mervyn Kurlansky
665 Rolf Harder (Photo: G. Hudaff/Rolf Harder)
666, 667 Rolf Harder
668 Graham Evernden
669 Harry & Marion Zelenko

ART DIRECTOR / DIRECTEUR ARTISTIQUE:

662 Dick Jones
664 Mervyn Kurlansky
665 Rolf Harder/Peter Decker
666 Rolf Harder/Leo Schweizer
667 Rolf Harder/John Malough
668 Graham Evernden
669 Harry & Marion Zelenko

666

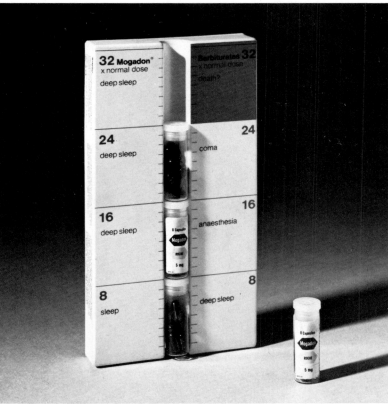

668

667

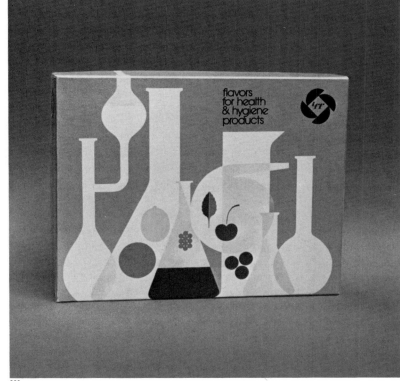

669

AGENCY / AGENTUR / AGENCE – STUDIO:

662 Sudler & Hennessey, Inc.
663 Roche, Ufficio Pubblicità
664 Pentagram
665–667 Design Collaborative
668 Eccleston & Glossop and Assoc.
669 Harry & Marion Zelenko, Inc.

CLIENT / AUFTRAGGEBER:

662 Texas Pharmacal Co.
663 Roche S. p. A.
664, 668 Roche Products Ltd.
665–667 Hoffmann-La Roche Ltd.
669 International Flavors & Fragrances, Inc.

Promotional Packaging
Werbepackungen
Emballages publicitaires

670

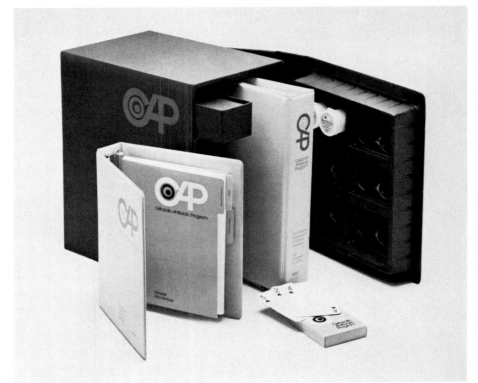

671

670 Tube containing a puzzle, a gift from a manufacturer of printed circuits. Black and white. (GER)
671 Box containing a training programme to introduce a new antibiotic to representatives. The programme includes audiovisual material, tests, question-and-answer cards, a notebook and other study material. (USA)
672 Folding box for quick-germinating clover seed as promotion for a fermentation product. (ITA)
673 Box and prestige gift in the form of a limited-edition game. Box in blue-black and silver, gift in Perspex and aluminium with steel ball bearings. (GBR)
674 Set-up box for pharmaceutical samples sent to doctors on request. (USA)

670 Schachtel für ein Puzzle. Werbegeschenk einer Firma, die gedruckte Schaltungen herstellt. Schwarzweiss. (GER)
671 Zur Einführung von neuen Antibiotika-Produkten zusammengestelltes Studienprogramm mit audiovisuellem Material, Frage- und Antwortkarten, Notizblock, Testmaterial und Studienunterlagen, alles in einer starken Schachtel verpackt. (USA)
672 Faltschachtel für ein schnell keimendes Kleesamen-Präparat als Werbung für ein Fermentprodukt. (ITA)
673 Schachtel und Prestigegeschenk in Form eines Spieles, das in begrenzter Auflage hergestellt wurde. Schachtel in Blauschwarz und Silber, Geschenk in Plexiglas und Aluminium mit Stahlkugellagern. (GBR)
674 Stülpschachtel für den Versand von Ärztemustern. (USA)

670 Emballage cylindrique contenant un puzzle. Cadeau publicitaire d'un fabricant de circuits imprimés. Noir et blanc. (GER)
671 Boîte de carton fort contenant une documentation complète (matériel audio-visuel, tests, cartes avec questions et réponses, bloc-notes, etc.) destinée à l'instruction des visiteurs médicaux chargés d'introduire un nouvel antibiotique. (USA)
672 Boîte pliante pour des graines de trèfle à germination rapide. Publicité pour un adjuvant de fermentation. (ITA)
673 Cadeau de prestige sous forme d'une boîte en plastique Perspex et en aluminium pourvue de roulements à billes en acier contenant un jeu. Carton bleu noir et argent. Edition limitée. (GBR)
674 Boîte montée pour échantillons médicaux. (USA)

Promotional Packaging
Werbepackungen
Emballages publicitaires

673

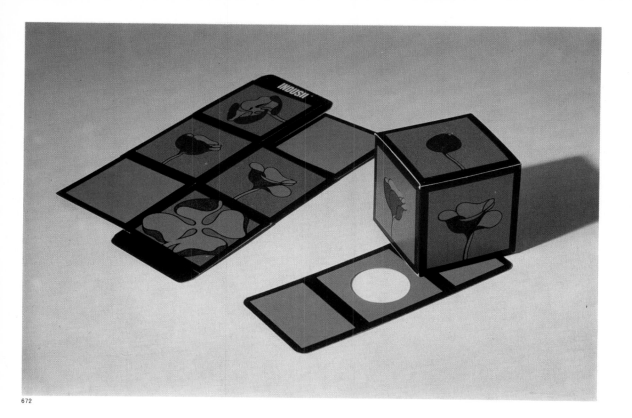

672

DESIGNER / GESTALTER / MAQUETTISTE:

670 Just Reinhold
671 Ford, Byrne & Assoc.
672 Ilio Negri
673 Alan Fletcher
674 Bob Paganucci

ART DIRECTOR / DIRECTEUR ARTISTIQUE:

670 Just Reinhold
671 Ford, Byrne & Assoc.
672 Ilio Negri
673 Alan Fletcher
674 Bob Paganucci

AGENCY / AGENTUR / AGENCE – STUDIO:

670 Schering AG, Atelier für Werbung
671 Ford, Byrne & Associates
672 Studio Negri
673 Pentagram
674 Geigy Pharmaceuticals

CLIENT / AUFTRAGGEBER:

670 Schering AG Galvanotechnik
671 Smith Kline & French Laboratories
672 Recordati Industria Chimica
673 Reuters
674 Geigy Pharmaceuticals

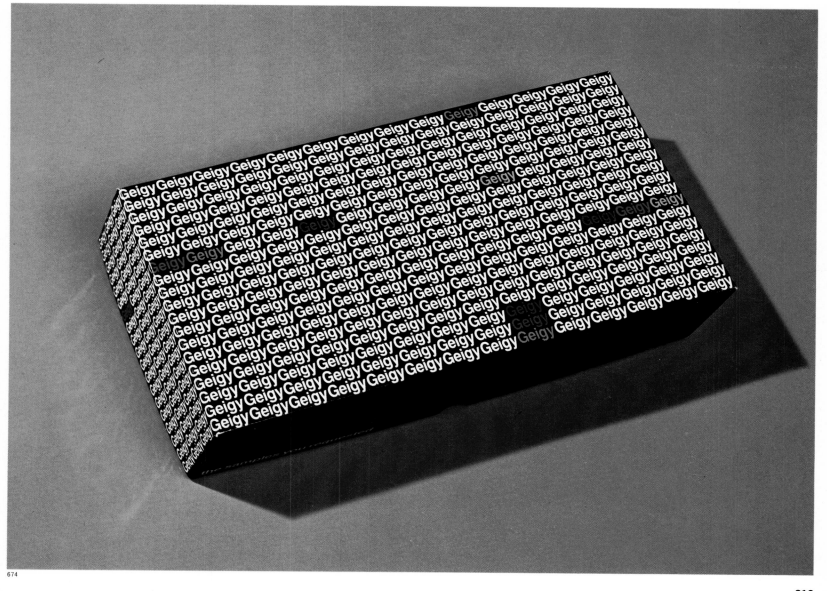

674

675

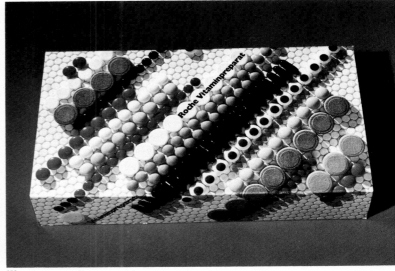

676

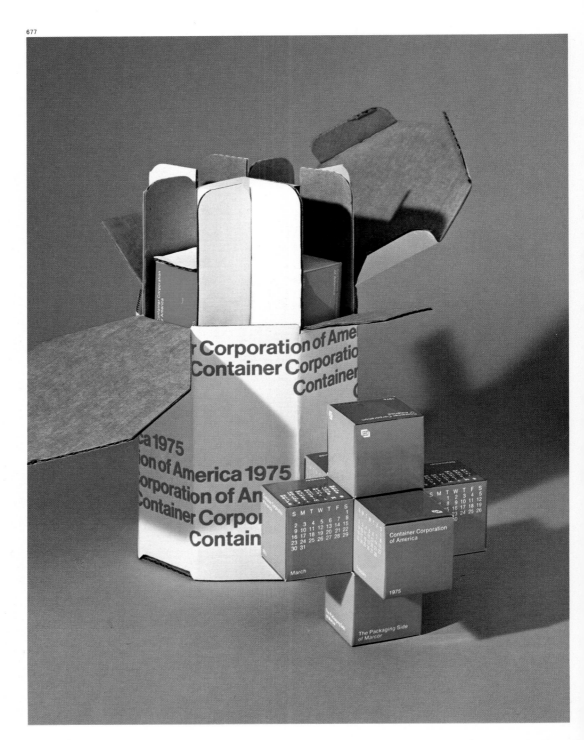

677

675 Set-up box for biophysical products. Light and dark blue on white. (USA)
676 Box containing samples of various vitamin preparations. Photograph in red, yellow and brown. (SWI)
677 Octahedric package for a calendar in the form of cardboard cubes, a New Year's gift from a large packaging company. (USA)
678 Game of darts as a goodwill gift from a French papermaker. (FRA)
679 Small bottles of spices sent as gifts by a magazine to its advertisers. (GER)
680 Set-up box containing samples of a tranquillizer sent to doctors. Shades of grey. (USA)
681 Pack in the form of a doll's house containing two dwarfs, distributed in the practices of pediatricians to advertise pharmaceutical products. (GER)
682 Set-up box for a medicament against complaints of the urinary passages in women and girls. (USA)

675 Stülpdeckelschachtel für biophysikalische Produkte. Hell- und dunkelblau auf Weiss. (USA)
676 Ärzte-Musterpackung für verschiedene Vitaminpräparate. Aufnahme mit roten, gelben und braunen Farbtönen. (SWI)
677 In einem Oktaeder verpackter Würfelkalender. Neujahrsglückwunsch einer Kartonagefirma. (USA)
678 Pfeilwurfspiel als Werbegeschenk eines französischen Papierfabrikanten. (FRA)
679 Kleine Glasflaschen für verschiedene Spezereien, die als Werbegaben einer Zeitschrift an Inserenten verteilt wurden. (GER)
680 Schachtel für Ärztemuster eines Beruhigungsmittels. Mehrere Grautöne. (USA)
681 Als Spielzeughaus aufgemachte Verpackung für zwei Gartenzwerge, die als Werbung für pharmazeutische Präparate an Kinderarztpraxen verteilt wurden. (GER)
682 Packung für ein Medikament gegen Erkrankungen der Harnwege bei Frauen und Mädchen. (USA)

675 Boîte montée pour produits biophysiques. Bleu clair et foncé sur blanc. (USA)
676 Emballage d'échantillons médicaux de diverses préparations vitaminées. Photo aux tons rouges, jaunes, bruns. (SWI)
677 Emballage octaédrique pour un calendrier présenté sous forme de cubes en carton. Cadeau de Noël d'une importante société de cartonnages. (USA)
678 Jeu de fléchettes offert à sa clientèle par un papetier français. (FRA)
679 Petits flacons d'épices. Cadeau publicitaire d'un magazine à ses annonceurs. (GER)
680 Boîte montée pour l'expédition d'échantillons médicaux d'un tranquillisant. Divers gris. (USA)
681 Emballage sous forme de maison de poupée pour deux nains offerts aux pédiatres pour leur salle d'attente. Publicité pharmaceutique. (GER)
682 Boîte montée pour un médicament des infections des voies urinaires chez femmes et fillettes. (USA)

Promotional Packaging
Werbepackungen
Emballages Publicitaires

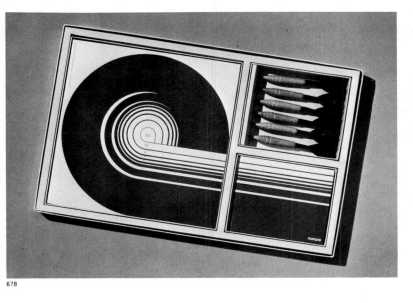

678

681

679

680

DESIGNER / GESTALTER / MAQUETTISTE:

675 Gunter Tschedel/Fred Large
676 Philipp Largiadèr
    (Photo: Heiner Grieder)
677 Bill Bonnell III/Chris Ward
    (Artist: Robert Padgett)
678 Jean Gueillet
679 Robert Hirschberger
680 Bruno Mease (Photo: Len Cohen)
681 Oskar Julius Weiss
682 Frank Wagner

ART DIRECTOR / DIRECTEUR ARTISTIQUE:

675 Fred Large
676 Jacques Hauser
677 Bill Bonnell III
678 Jean Gueillet
679 Wilhelm Bettges
680 I. Robert Parker
681 Oskar Julius Weiss
682 Chris von Wangenheim

AGENCY / AGENTUR / AGENCE – STUDIO:

675 Beaumont Design Group, Inc.
676 Hoffmann-La Roche Werbeabteilung
677 Container Corp. Communications
    Dept.
678 Non Stop
680 Smith Kline & French Laboratories
681 Peter Selinka
682 Sudler & Hennessey, Inc.

CLIENT / AUFTRAGGEBER:

675 International Bio-Physics Corp.
676 Hoffmann-La Roche AG
677 Container Corporation of America
678 Papeteries Navarre
679 Axel Springer Verlag AG
680 Smith Kline & French Laboratories
681 Chemiewerk Homburg
682 Warner-Chilcott Laboratories

682

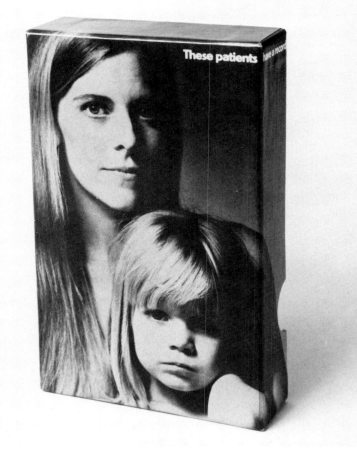

683

DESIGNER / GESTALTER / MAQUETTISTE:

683, 684 Steve Brothers (Artist: Etienne Delessert)
685 Arnold Lutz (Photo: Arnold Lutz)
686 Si Friedman
688, 689 David Stanfield

ART DIRECTOR / DIRECTEUR ARTISTIQUE:

683, 684 Steve Brothers
686 Si Friedman

684

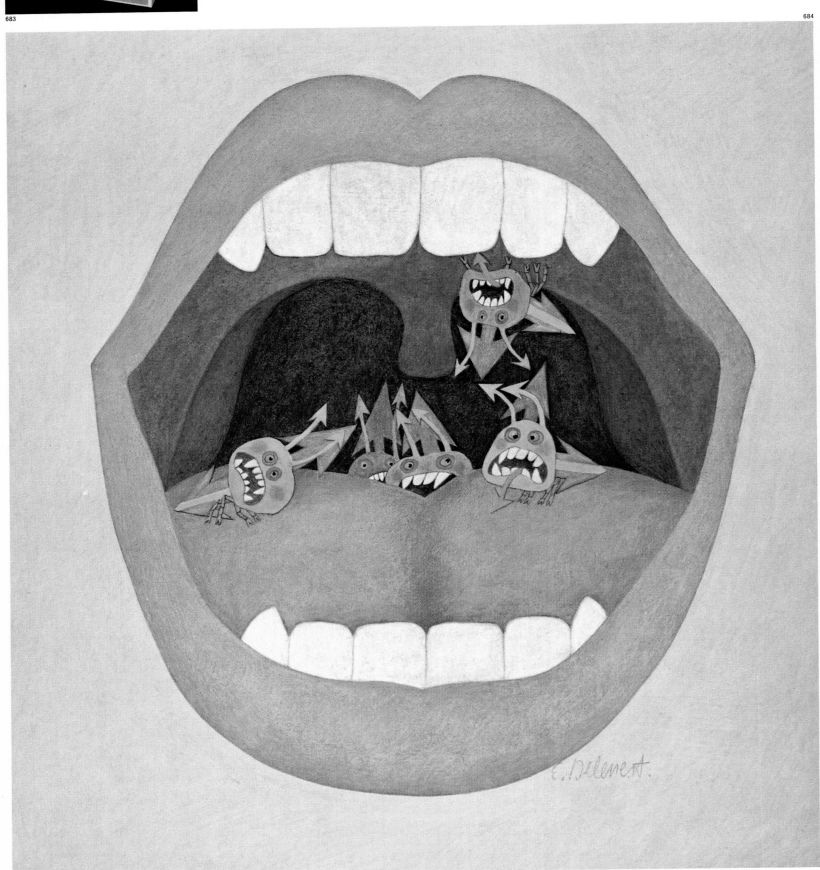

683, 684 Pack for doctor's samples of an antibiotic, with detail of the artwork. (USA)
685 Matchbox as promotion for a photographer. Scenes from Swiss towns appear on the lids. (SWI)
686 Gift and carton from a design studio. (USA)
687 Miniature crate bringing New Year's greetings from a printer. (SWI)
688, 689 Invitation issued by a newspaper to a dinner in honour of a sports journalist who had worked for the paper for forty years. (GBR)

683, 684 Werbepackung für ein neues Antibiotikum, zum Versand als Ärztemuster bestimmt. (USA)
685 Streichholzschachtel als Werbung eines Photographen. Auf dem Deckel sind verschiedene Motive aus Schweizer Städten in Schwarzweiss wiedergegeben. (SWI)
686 Werbegeschenk und Packung eines Graphikstudios. (USA)
687 Miniaturpalette als Glückwunsch einer Druckerei. (SWI)
688, 689 Einladung zu einem Nachtessen, das zu Ehren eines Sportjournalisten anlässlich seines 40jährigen Jubiläums bei einer Tageszeitung gegeben wurde. (GBR)

685

687

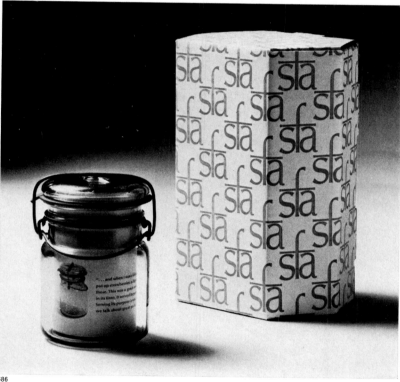

686

688

683, 684 Emballage d'échantillons médicaux d'un nouvel antibiotique. (USA)
685 Boîte d'allumettes utilisée pour la publicité d'un photographe. Les couvercles sont décorés de diverses scènes de villes suisses. Noir et blanc. (SWI)
686 Cadeau publicitaire et emballage réalisés pour un atelier d'art graphique. (USA)
687 Caisse miniature distribuée par une imprimerie en guise de vœux de Nouvel An. (SWI)
688, 689 Invitation par laquelle un journal désireux d'honorer un journaliste sportif pour ses 40 ans d'activité professionnelle convie à un dîner d'apparat. (GBR)

AGENCY / AGENTUR / AGENCE – STUDIO:

683, 684 Sudler & Hennessey, Inc.
686 Si Friedman Associates
688, 689 Daily Mirror Design Group

CLIENT / AUFTRAGGEBER:

683, 684 Bristol Laboratories
685 Arnold Lutz
686 Si Friedman Associates
687 Graphische Anstalt Schüler AG
688, 689 Daily Mirror Design Group

689

Promotional Packaging
Werbepackungen
Emballages publicitaires

690

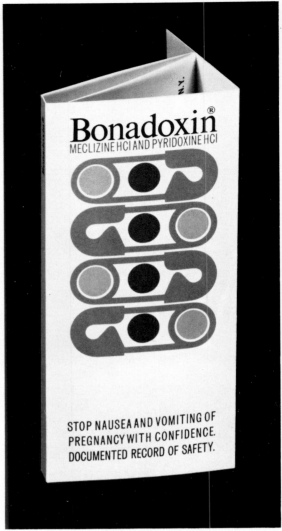

692

Promotional Packaging/Werbepackungen
Emballages publicitaires

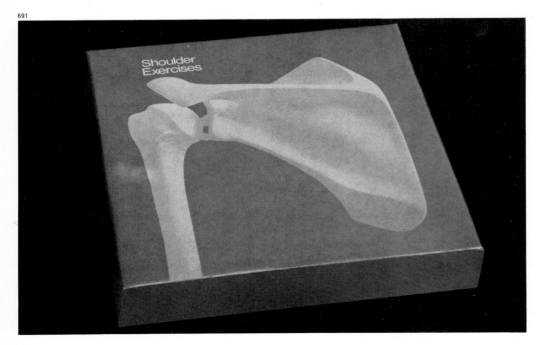

691

DESIGNER / GESTALTER / MAQUETTISTE:

690 Herbert Auchli
691 Ken Jordan/Ron Vareltzis (Artist: Bob Havell)
692, 696 Charles Goslin
693, 694 H. D. Haren
695 Roland Aeschlimann (Photo: Rudolf Lichtsteiner)
697 Friedel Ernst Maischein

690 Promotional gift pack for Swiss Federal Railways. Tubes of chocolates as "passengers" in a box in the form of a railway carriage with cellophane windows. (SWI)
691 Carton for a folding toy on which diagrams of various shoulder exercises are shown. (USA)
692 Folding pack of doctor's samples of a drug to prevent nausea and vomiting during pregnancy. (USA)
693, 694 Two sides of a box for a pharmaceutical to relieve difficult breathing. Ochre, purple and black on white. (AUS)
695 Folding box for doctor's samples of an iron tonic. (SWI)
696 Decorative cups containing doctor's samples of a wide-spectrum tranquillizer. (USA)
697 Carton in the form of a brick containing printed matter between the plastic slabs. It provides information on the organic intermediate products of a chemical company. (GER)

690 Werbegeschenk der Schweizerischen Bundesbahnen. «Passagiere» aus Schokolade in einer Eisenbahnwagen-Schachtel mit Cellophan-Fenstern. (SWI)
691 Versandkarton für ein faltbares Spielzeug, auf dem verschiedene Schultergymnastik-Übungen abgebildet sind. (USA)
692 Faltpackung für eine Ärzte-Mustersendung mit einem Medikament gegen Übelkeit und Erbrechen während der Schwangerschaft. (USA)
693, 694 Faltschachtel mit Bild- und Schriftseite für ein pharmazeutisches Produkt gegen Atembeschwerden. Ocker, violett und schwarz auf weissem Grund. (AUS)
695 Faltschachtel für Ärztemuster eines Eisenpräparates. (SWI)
696 Pappdose für Ärztemuster eines Beruhigungsmittels. (USA)
697 Packung in Form und Farbe eines Ziegelsteines. Zwischen den beiden Schaumstoffeinlagen befinden sich Prospekte, die über die organischen Zwischenprodukte eines grossen Chemiekonzerns Auskunft geben. (GER)

693

694

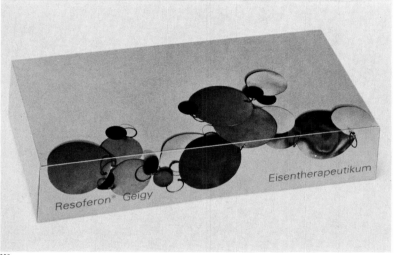

695

696

ART DIRECTOR / DIRECTEUR ARTISTIQUE:

690 Werner Belmont
691 Joe Fazio
692, 696 Charles Goslin
693, 694 H. D. Haren
695 Max Schmid
697 Friedel Ernst Maischein

697

690 Cadeau publicitaire des Chemins de Fer Fédéraux suisses. Tubes de pastilles de chocolat déguisés en passagers, emballage sous forme de voiture de chemin de fer, fenêtres en cellophane. (SWI)
691 Carton d'expédition pour un jouet pliable, avec reproduction de différents exercices de gymnastique mobilisant les épaules. (USA)
692 Emballage pliant pour un échantillon médical d'un médicament des nausées et vomissements de la grossesse. (USA)
693, 694 Boîte pliante, côté texte et illustration, pour un remède asthmolytique. Ocre, mauve et noir sur fond blanc. (AUS)
695 Boîte pliante pour un échantillon de fer thérapeutique. (SWI)
696 Etuis décoratifs contenant un échantillon médical d'un tranquillisant à large spectre. (USA)
697 Emballage carton affectant la forme et la couleur d'une brique. Entre deux couches de plastique, une documentation sur les produits intermédiaires d'une importante société de chimie organique. (GER)

AGENCY / AGENTUR / AGENCE – STUDIO:

690 SBB Publizitätsdienst
691 Geigy Pharmaceuticals
692, 696 Barnett/Goslin/Barnett
693, 694 H. D. Haren, Fotografik
695 Ciba-Geigy Werbeabteilung

CLIENT / AUFTRAGGEBER:

690 Schweizerische Bundesbahnen
691 Geigy Pharmaceuticals
692, 696 Pfizer, Inc.
693, 694 Chemiewerk Homburg
695 Ciba-Geigy AG
697 BASF AG

AGENCY / AGENTUR / AGENCE – STUDIO:

698 Institut Dr. Friesewinkel
699 Sudler & Hennessey, Inc.
700 Erwin Halpern
701 Cook & Shanosky Associates, Inc.
704 CBS Broadcast Group
705 Lubalin Smith Carnase

CLIENT / AUFTRAGGEBER:

698 Laboratorien Hausmann AG
699 Lever Bros.
700 Foto Transport AG
701 Smith Kline & French Laboratories
702 Comalco Aluminium Ltd.
703 Dewar-Mills Associates Ltd.
704 CBS News
705 Lubalin Smith Carnase

698

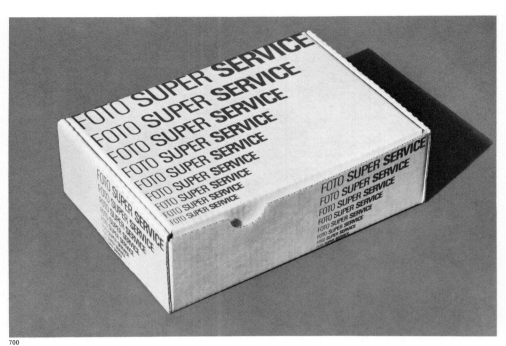

700

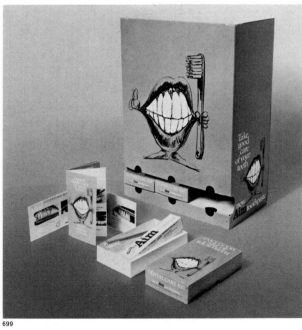

699

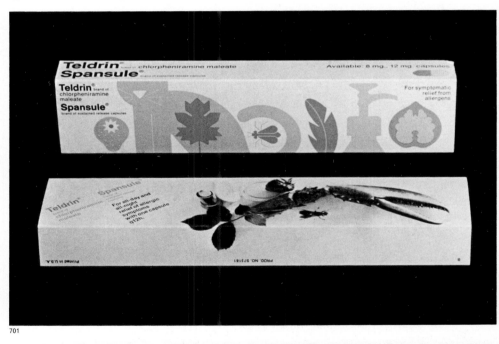

701

DESIGNER / GESTALTER / MAQUETTISTE:

698 Maya Stange
699 Dick Russinko (Artist: Wally Neibart)
700 Dario Zutto
701 Roger Cook/Don Shanosky
702 Les Mason
703 John Nash
704 David November/Akihiko Seki (Artist: Akihiko Seki)
705 Herb Lubalin (Artist: Tom Carnase)

ART DIRECTOR./ DIRECTEUR ARTISTIQUE:

699 Dick Russinko
701 Alan J. Klawans
702 Les Mason
703 Joh Nash
704 Lou Dorfsman
705 Herb Lubalin

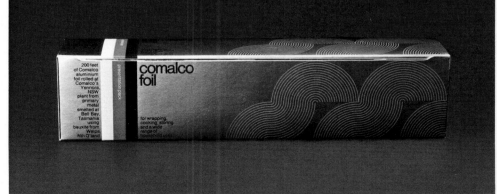

702

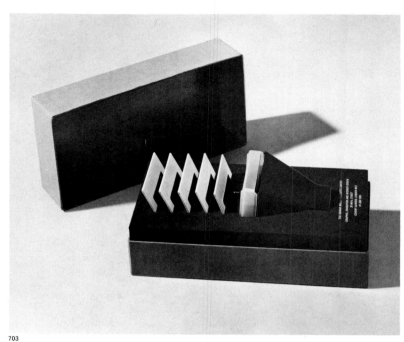

705

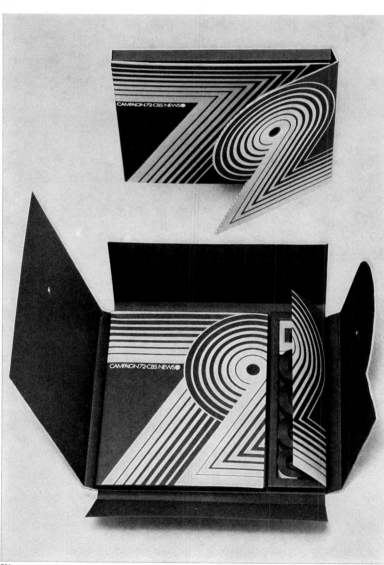

703

704

698 Set-up box containing a bottle of iron syrup as a tonic for children. Doctor's sample. Green and red on white. (SWI)
699 Dental care kit as a promotional aid in introducing a new brand of toothpaste. Light blue and black. (USA)
700 Promotional pack containing a toy car for a photographic service. Red-brown text on white board. (SWI)
701 Carton for doctor's samples of capsules against allergies. (USA)
702 Presentation pack of aluminium foil used for overseas promotion by an aluminium company. Silk-screened in silver on silver matt board, stripes in yellow, red and blue. (AUL)
703 Promotion kit for a design studio. The red box contains a viewer for the slides showing examples of the studio's work. (GBR)
704 Kit issued by a television company with film material on the 1972 elections. Graphics in blue and red on black. (USA)
705 Bottle and label for a Christmas drink distributed as a gift to clients by a design studio. (USA)

698 Stülpdeckelschachtel für eine Flasche Eisensirup als Aufbaumittel für Kinder. Ärztemuster. Grün und rot auf Weiss. (SWI)
699 Werbebox, die zur Einführung einer neuen Zahnpasta gleichzeitig eine Zahnbürste und einen Prospekt mitliefert. Hellblau, schwarz. (USA)
700 Werbepackung mit Spielzeugauto für einen photographischen Dienst. Rotbrauner Text auf weissem Karton. (SWI)
701 Packung für Kapseln gegen verschiedene Allergien. (USA)
702 Geschenkpackung für eine Aluminiumfolie zum Gebrauch in Küche, Haushalt und Geschäft. Linienmuster: Siebdruck in Silber auf mattsilbernem Hintergrund, Streifen gelb, rot und blau, Schrift schwarz. (AUL)
703 Werbepackung für ein Gestaltungsstudio. Die rote Schachtel enthält einen Diabetrachter und Lichtbilder von Arbeiten des Studios. (GBR)
704 Faltschachtel einer Fernsehgesellschaft mit Filmmaterial über die Wahlkampagne 1972. Graphik blau und rot auf Schwarz. (USA)
705 Flasche und Etikett für einen Weihnachtstrunk, der als Geschenk eines Graphikstudios an die Kunden verteilt wurde. (USA)

698 Boîte montée pour une bouteille-échantillon de sirop ferrique recommandé comme fortifiant pour les enfants. Vert, rouge sur blanc. (SWI)
699 Emballage publicitaire pour un nouveau dentifrice, livré avec une brosse à dents et une notice explicative. Bleu clair et noir. (USA)
700 Emballage publicitaire d'un service photo, contenant un modèle réduit d'auto. Texte brun rouge sur carton blanc. (SWI)
701 Emballage de capsules antiallergiques. Echantillon médical. (USA)
702 Emballage promotionnel d'un rouleau de feuilles alu pour la publicité d'outre-mer d'un producteur d'aluminium. Sérigraphie argent sur carton argent mat, bandes jaunes, rouges, bleues, texte noir. (AUL)
703 Emballage promotionnel d'un atelier de design. Dans la boîte rouge, une visionneuse pour les dias montrant les travaux du studio. (GBR)
704 Boîte de présentation d'extraits de films consacrés aux élections de 1972 par une société de TV. Graphisme bleu et rouge sur noir. (USA)
705 Bouteille et étiquette pour une boisson de Noël distribuée à sa clientèle par un studio d'art graphique. (USA)

Promotional Packaging

Promotional Packaging/Werbepackungen
Emballages publicitaires

DESIGNER / GESTALTER / MAQUETTISTE:

706 Bill Bonnell III
707 Ken Ayres/Michael Carr (Artist: Michael Carr)
708, 709 Eckhard Kruse/Hans-Georg Oehring
710, 712 Fred Jordan
711 Robert Lipman
713 Maya Stange

706

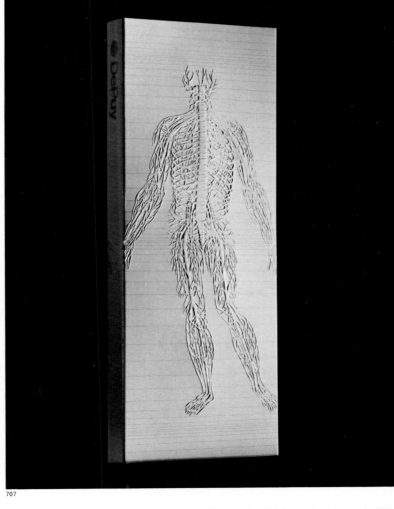

707

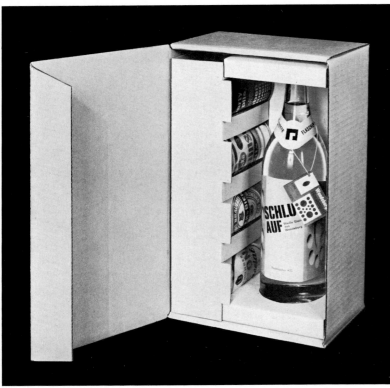

708

709

ART DIRECTOR / DIRECTEUR ARTISTIQUE:

706 Bill Bonnell III
707 Ken Ayres
708, 709 Klaus Grözinger
710, 712 Fred Jordan

CLIENT / AUFTRAGGEBER:

706 Container Corporation of America
707 Depuy Orthopedic & Surgical Co.
708, 709 Radmacher KG, Kalksandsteinwerk Wendeburg
710, 712 L. Niccolini SA
711 Abbott Laboratories
713 Laboratorien Hausmann AG

AGENCY / AGENTUR / AGENCE – STUDIO:

706 Container Corporation, Communications Dept.
707 The Design Group, Inc
713 Institut Dr. Friesewinkel

710

712

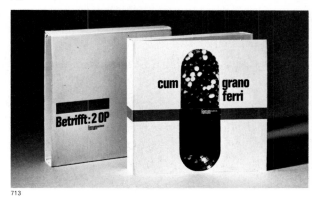

713

711

706 Sleeve-and-tray pack containing a metal rule as a promotional gift from a packaging company. (USA)
707 Promotional package containing a neurological examining hammer mailed to neurosurgeons by a company making surgical instruments. (USA)
708, 709 Promotional gift package from a limestone brick manufacturer. The package is in the form of a brick and contains four cans of beer and a bottle of spirits. (GER)
710 Christmas gift package with a diaphragm closure distributed by a São Paulo printing firm to clients and friends. (BRA)
711 Open box to take brochures about the diet plan of a manufacturer of pharmaceuticals. (USA)
712 Gift package with which a Brazilian printer announced the introduction of hot process embossing into his programme. (BRA)
713 Package for doctor's samples of capsules for the treatment of iron deficiency disorders. Black and white with red-brown stripe. (SWI)

706 Schiebeschachtel mit einem ausziehbaren Bandmass aus Metall. Werbegeschenk einer Verpackungsgesellschaft. (USA)
707 Werbepackung mit einem Perkussionshammer, der von einer Firma für chirurgische Instrumente und orthopädische Geräte verteilt wurde. (USA)
708, 709 Packung mit Ausstattung für eine Werbegabe eines Kalksteinwerkes. Das Format der Packung entspricht den weissen Bausteinen der Firma. Inhalt: vier Dosen Bier und eine Flasche «Korn». (GER)
710 Weihnachtsgeschenkpackung für die Kunden einer Druckerei in São Paulo. Rosettenverschluss. (BRA)
711 Offene Schachtel zur Aufbewahrung von Prospekten mit dem Diätplan einer pharmazeutischen Firma. (USA)
712 Packung, mit der eine brasilianische Druckerei die Heissprägung als Neuheit in ihrem Fertigungsprogramm ankündigt. (BRA)
713 Werbepackung als Ärztemuster für Kapseln zur Behandlung von Eisenmangelanämie. Schwarzweiss mit rotbraunem Streifen. (SWI)

706 Boîte coulissante contenant un mètre métallique. Cadeau publicitaire d'une société de cartonnages. (USA)
707 Emballage publicitaire pour un marteau de percussion offert aux neurochirurgiens par un fabricant d'équipements chirurgicaux. (USA)
708, 709 Emballage-cadeau pour la promotion d'une briqueterie, exécuté sous forme d'une brique silico-calcaire et contenant quatre boîtes de bière et une bouteille d'eau-de-vie de grain. (GER)
710 Emballage-cadeau de Noël, avec fermeture à soufflet, pour les clients et les amis d'un imprimeur de São Paulo. (BRA)
711 Boîte d'archives pour les brochures de régime d'un fabricant de produits pharmaceutiques. (USA)
712 Emballage-cadeau d'une imprimerie brésilienne annonçant l'introduction de la technique de l'estampage à chaud. (BRA)
713 Emballage d'un échantillon médical de capsules combattant l'anémie ferriprive. Noir et blanc, bande brun rouge. (SWI)

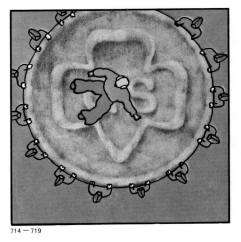

714 — 719

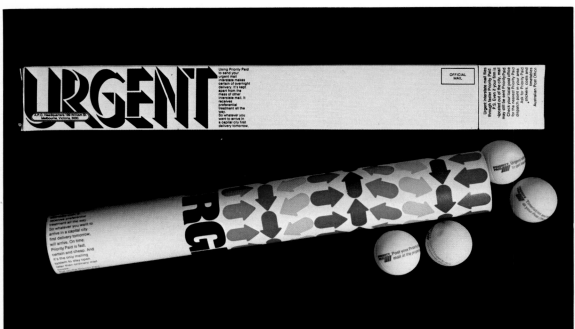

720

721

**Promotional Packaging/Werbepackungen
Emballages publicitaires**

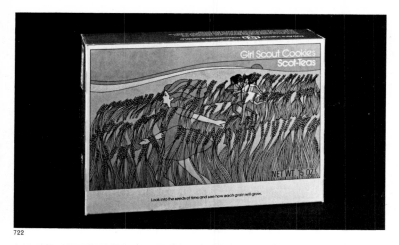

722

723

724

714–719, 722, 724 Bilder in Originalgrösse und vollständige Packung (Vorder- und Rückseite) für Biskuits, die von einem Pfadfinderinnenverband verkauft wurden. (Schwer zu schlagen / Gut aussehend / Lebenslänglich gut / Für unerwarteten Besuch / Gut zu Milch / Gut für Tiefschläge). (USA)
720 Packung mit Tischtennisbällen, deren Text darauf hinweist, dass die australische Postverwaltung für dringende Sendungen eine Nachtzustellung eingeführt hat. (AUL)
721 Werbedose, deren Signet die Getränkeindustrie auf einen neuen Dosenverschluss hinweist. (USA)
723 Musterpackung für ein Mittel, mit dem urologische Bakterien bekämpft werden können. (USA)
725 Etikett und Einwickelpapier für eine Flasche 25 Jahre alten Portweins als Geschenk anlässlich des 25jährigen Jubiläums einer Werbeagentur. (AUL)
726 Einladung mit Miniatur-Kopfkissen, zur Vorführung einer neuen Bettücher-Kollektion. (FRA)

714–719, 722, 724 Vignettes grandeur nature et les deux faces illustrées d'un paquet de biscuits vendu au profit d'une association de jeunes filles scoutes; biscuits «imbattables — présentant bien — de qualité perpétuelle — bons pour les visites inattendues — avec du lait — pour les grands jours». (USA)
720 Emballage de balles de ping-pong utilisé comme élément de publicité directe par les P & T australiennes pour annoncer un nouveau service de nuit pour colis urgents. (AUL)
721 Boîte publicitaire annonçant à l'industrie des boissons sans alcool l'existence d'un nouveau système de fermeture par soudage. (USA)
723 Emballage d'échantillon distribué au corps médical: médicament combattant les bactéries des voies urinaires. (USA)
725 Cadeau publicitaire pour les 25 ans d'une agence de publicité. Le porto a aussi 25 ans. (AUL)
726 Invitation assortie d'un mini-oreiller, pour la présentation d'une collection de literie. (FRA)

725

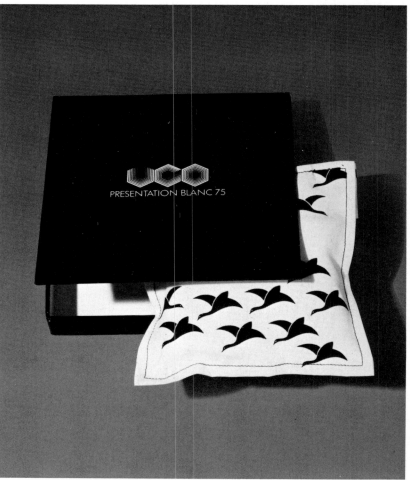

726

727

728

Promotional Packaging
Werbepackungen
Emballages publicitaires

731

732

727, 728 Calendar consisting of a Perspex cube into which fit six differently coloured folding boxes, each bearing a calendar for two months. (USA)
729 Promotional pack sent to tyre dealers with an aerosol container for the production of artificial snow. Black and white. (SWI)
730 Miniature crate just large enough to take an apple. Its label bears an invitation to a play, *The Ugly Apple*. (USA)
731 Gift pack with three cups bearing the initials of a Hamburg blockmaker. Cups black and white, pack grey, brown and purple. (GER)
732 Promotional pack for soft leather shoes; real shoelace. (ITA)
733 Building blocks of various qualities of board as promotion material for a papermaker. (SPA)

727, 728 Kalender in Form eines zweiteiligen Würfels aus Karton und Plexiglas mit Kalendarien, die auf verschiedenfarbigen Schachteln gedruckt sind. (USA)
729 Werbepackung für Händler einer Pneumarke mit einer Spraydose zur Erzeugung von künstlichem Schnee. Schwarzweiss. (SWI)
730 Miniatur-Holzkiste, nicht grösser als zum Transport eines Apfels nötig. Auf dem Schild wird zum Besuch eines Theaterstückes («Der hässliche Apfel») eingeladen. (USA)
731 Geschenkpackung mit drei kleinen Trinkbechern, auf denen die Initialen der Cliché-Anstalt ABC in Hamburg stehen. Becher schwarzweiss, Packung grau, violett, braun. (GER)
732 Werbepackung für Schuhe aus weichem Leder mit einem echten Schnürsenkel. (ITA)
733 Kinder-Bauklötze aus verschiedenen Kartonsorten als Werbung für einen Papierhersteller. (SPA)

727, 728 Calendrier sous forme d'un cube de plastique Perspex recevant six boîtes pliantes de coloris divers, dont chacune porte un calendrier pour deux mois de l'année. (USA)
729 Emballage publicitaire destiné aux marchands de pneus et comprenant une bombe aérosol pour la production de neige artificielle. Noir et blanc. (SWI)
730 Cageot miniature pour une seule pomme. L'étiquette invite le destinataire à assister à une représentation de la pièce intitulée *The Ugly Apple* (La Vilaine Pomme). (USA)
731 Emballage-cadeau avec trois petites chopes aux initiales de l'atelier de clichage ABC de Hambourg. Chopes noir et blanc, emballage gris, brun, mauve. (GER)
732 Emballage publicitaire pour des souliers en cuir souple; lacet véritable. (ITA)
733 Cubes réalisés en diverses sortes de carton. Publicité d'un papetier. (SPA)

DESIGNER / GESTALTER / MAQUETTISTE:

727, 728 Bill Bonnell III
729 Atelier Wiener & Deville
730 Karen Bunde
731 Gerd F. Setzke
732 Aurelio Sangalli
733 Joe Romero

ART DIRECTOR / DIRECTEUR ARTISTIQUE:

727, 728 Bill Bonnell III
730 Karen Bunde
731 Gerd F. Setzke
732 Aurelio Sangalli
733 Daniel Panicello

729

730

AGENCY / AGENTUR / AGENCE – STUDIO:

727, 728 Container Corporation Communications Dept.
729 Wiener, Deville & Wälchli
731 Atelier Setzke
732 Publinter
733 Costa SA

CLIENT / AUFTRAGGEBER:

727, 728 Container Corporation of America
729 Tebak AG/Continental Pneus
731 Albert Bauer KG
732 Hush Puppies, Shoe Mart S. p. A.
733 Papelera Española SA

733

Industrial Packaging
Shipping Containers

Industriepackungen
Versandpackungen

Emballages industriels
Emballages d'expédition

10

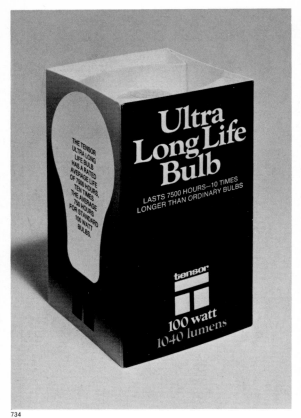

734

735

DESIGNER / GESTALTER / MAQUETTISTE:

734 Harry & Marion Zelenko
735 Jonathan Milne (Photo: Latrobe Studios)
736 Zofia Bialas
737 Creative Team Nacke & Flink
738 Takeshi Ikeda/Nakayuki Okamoto
739 John S. Blyth/Paul S. Hastings/Joe Lombardo
740 Martin Stringer
741 Quadragono

ART DIRECTOR / DIRECTEUR ARTISTIQUE:

734 Harry & Marion Zelenko
735 Jonathan Milne
736 Jerzy Warchal
738 Takeshi Ikeda
739 John S. Blyth
740 Martin Stringer/Lloyds Cartons Ltd.
741 Rino Maturi

AGENCY / AGENTUR / AGENCE – STUDIO:

734 Harry & Marion Zelenko, Inc.
735 Taylor O'Brian Advertising
736 Atelier des Arts Plastiques
737 Slesina Bates Werbegesellschaft
738 Ai Kobo
739 Peterson & Blyth Associates, Inc.
741 Quadragono

CLIENT / AUFTRAGGEBER:

734 Tensor Corporation
735 Imperial Chemical Industries of Australia & New Zealand
736 Erdal
737 Mobil AG Deutschland
738 Nisshin Denki Co.
739 E. I. DuPont de Nemours & Co.
740 Ronson Products Ltd.
741 S. I. C. A. R. T.

736

737

Industrial Packaging, Shipping Container
Industriepackungen, Versandpackungen
Emballages industriels, Emballages d'expédition

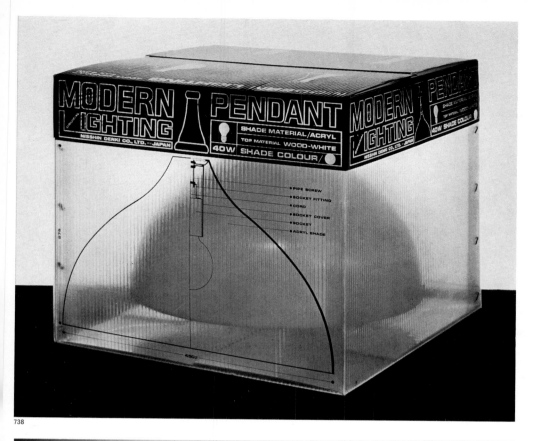

738

739

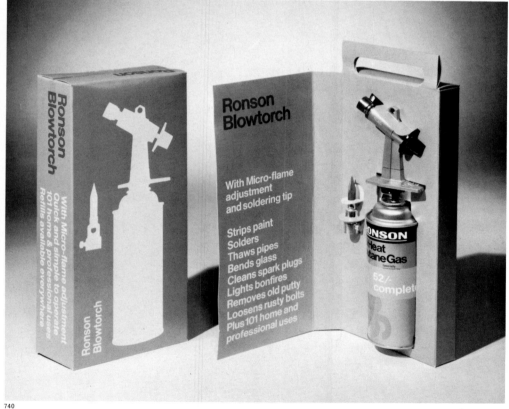

740

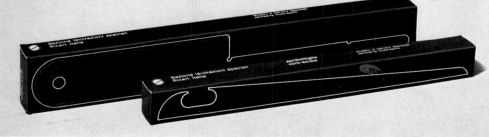

741

734 Box for an electric bulb for ultra long life. Left-hand side red, blue and green, front black and white. (USA)

735 Folding box for products of the organic chemistry department of a large chemical company. Black and white. (AUL)

736 Tin for enamel paint. The colour of the contents is shown in a darker and lighter shade between the text areas. (POL)

737 Metal container with a black plastic cap for a synthetic motor lubricant. (GER)

738 Package for a plastic lampshade. Transparent polypropylene box with a drawing of the shade, black lid. (JPN)

739 Aerosol container for a windscreen de-icer. Printed red, black and blue. The lid can be used for breaking thin films of ice. (USA)

740 Carrier pack for a blowtorch. The open carton can be used for display as shown. (USA)

741 Folding boxes for a paper knife and a bottle opener, from a range of household utensils of stainless steel. (ITA)

734 Verpackung einer Glühbirne mit extrem langer Brenndauer. Linke Seite in Irisdruck (rot, blau, grün), Vorderseite schwarzweiss. (USA)

735 Faltschachtel für Produkte der Abteilung für organische Chemie eines Chemiekonzerns. Schwarzweiss, Signet rot und gelb. (AUL)

736 Dose für Emailfarben. Zwischen den Schriftbändern erscheint die Farbe des Doseninhaltes in heller und dunkler Tönung. (POL)

737 Metallbehälter mit schwarzem Kunststoff-Verschluss für ein synthetisches Motorenschmieröl. (GER)

738 Verpackung für einen Lampenschirm. Durchsichtige Polypropylen-Schachtel mit Konstruktionszeichnung der Lampe. Deckel schwarz. (JPN)

739 Aerosoldose für einen Windschutzscheiben-Entfroster. Rot, schwarz und blau auf weissem Grund. (USA)

740 Verpackung für eine Lötlampe. Die geöffnete Packung kann gleichzeitig als Aussteller verwendet werden. (USA)

741 Faltschachteln für ein Papiermesser und einen Flaschenöffner aus einer Reihe von Haushaltsartikeln aus rostfreiem Stahl. (ITA)

734 Emballage d'une ampoule à longue durée de vie. Face gauche rouge, bleu, vert; la face de droite est en noir et blanc. (USA)

735 Boîte pliante pour les produits du département de chimie organique d'un important groupe chimique. En noir et blanc, emblème en rouge et jaune. (AUL)

736 Boîte de peinture émail, dont la couleur apparaît en tons clairs et foncés dans l'intervalle du texte. (POL)

737 Conditionnement métallique pour une huile synthétique pour le graissage des moteurs. Capuchon plastique noir. (GER)

738 Emballage pour un abat-jour plastique. Boîte en polypropylène transparent, avec schéma de construction de l'abat-jour. Couvercle noir. (JPN)

739 Flacon atomiseur pour un dégivreur pour pare-brise. Impression en rouge, noir, bleu sur blanc. Couvercle dentelé pour enlever la glace. (USA)

740 Emballage de lampe à souder. Une fois ouvert, le carton peut servir de présentoir en magasin. (USA)

741 Boîtes pliantes pour un coupe-papier et un ouvre-bouteilles. Eléments d'une gamme d'ustensiles de ménage en acier inox. (ITA)

DESIGNER / GESTALTER / MAQUETTISTE:

742, 743 Jonathan Milne
744 Burton Kramer
745–750 E + U Hiestand/H. Eggmann
751 Paul Hauge/Hal Frazier
752 Howard Gerrard
753 E + U Hiestand

ART DIRECTOR / DIRECTEUR ARTISTIQUE:

742, 743 Jonathan Milne
744 Burton Kramer
745–750 E + U Hiestand/H. Eggmann
751 Paul Hauge/Hal Frazier
752 Raymond French
753 E + U Hiestand

AGENCY / AGENTUR / AGENCE – STUDIO:

742, 743 Taylor O'Brian Advertising
744 Burton Kramer Associates Ltd.
745–750 E + U Hiestand/H. Eggmann
751 Neumarket Design Associates
752 Matthew Finch Associates Ltd.
753 E + U Hiestand

CLIENT / AUFTRAGGEBER:

742, 743 W. R. Grace Australia Ltd.
744 Noma Lites Canada Ltd.
745–750 Maus Frères SA
751 Paramount
752 Jet Petrol (Conoco Ltd.)
753 ABM Au Bon Marché

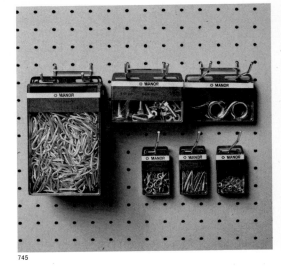

745

742

743

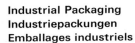

749

Industrial Packaging
Industriepackungen
Emballages industriels

744

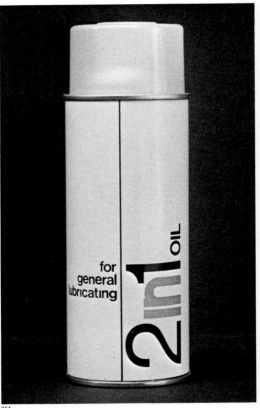

751

238

746

747

748

750

742, 743 Tins for a range of adhesives and powders. The family image is based on the notched trowel with which they are applied but can be modified to suit the contents. (AUL)
744 Cubic and oblong folding boxes in various colours for a range of projector kits and bulbs. (CAN)
745, 749 Unit packs for do-it-yourself articles and electric fittings. Rational and economical packaging done by the manufacturer to the store's basic designs. (SWI)
746–748, 750 From the packaging programme of a department store: folding box for a bulb (shape shown at top left), range of batteries, cans for synthetic paints, plastic and metal containers for car washing and maintenance products (with racing strip as standard design element). (SWI)
751 Aerosol container for a general lubricant. (USA)
752 Tin and canister for a multigrade oil. (USA)
753 Family of packs for radio and stereo equipment from a department store's range. (SWI)

742, 743 Dosen für technische Kleber, Pulver und Pasten mit einem einheitlichen Gestaltungselement, das lediglich durch veränderte Farben und Anzahl der Linien variiert wird. (AUL)
744 Auswahl kubischer und länglicher Faltschachteln in verschiedenen Farben für Flutlichtbirnen und Projektionslampen. (CAN)
745, 749 Packungen für das Elektro- und Do-it-yourself-Programm eines Warenhauses. Rationelle und ökonomische Verpackung. (SWI)

746–748, 750 Aus dem Verpackungsprogramm eines Warenhauses. Glühbirnenpackung (Birnenform links oben sichtbar), Batteriensortiment, Dosensortiment für Dispersions- und Kunstharzfarben, sowie Dosen, Flaschen und Kanister für Autopflegemittel mit Racing-Streifen als durchgehendes Gestaltungselement. (SWI)
751 Aerosoldose für ein Autoschmiermittel. (USA)
752 Dose und Kanister für ein Mehrzweck-Autoöl. (USA)
753 Packungsfamilie für Radio- und Stereogeräte. (SWI)

742, 743 Boîtes pour colles et mastics industriels. Le motif uniforme, inspiré de la taloche, est adapté au contenu par variation des lignes stylisées et des couleurs. (AUL)
744 Boîtes pliantes cubiques et oblongues de différentes couleurs pour des ampoules de spots et les spots eux-mêmes. (CAN)
745, 749 Emballages standardisés, à la fois rationnels et économiques, pour le département outillage et électricité libre-service d'un grand magasin. Conception graphique unifiée. (SWI)
746–748, 750 Eléments du programme d'emballages d'un grand magasin: pour une ampoule électrique (la forme apparaît en haut, à gauche), des piles, des dispersions et peintures synthétiques; boîtes, flacons, bidons, plastique et métal, pour des produits d'entretien pour l'auto, avec bande évoquant les bolides. (SWI)
751 Bombe aérosol pour un lubrifiant d'emploi général. (USA)
752 Boîte et bidon pour une huile multigrade. (USA)
753 Ligne d'emballages pour équipements radio et stéréo. (SWI)

752

753

754

755

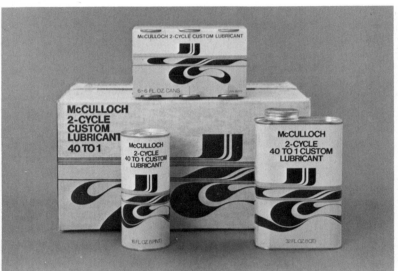

756

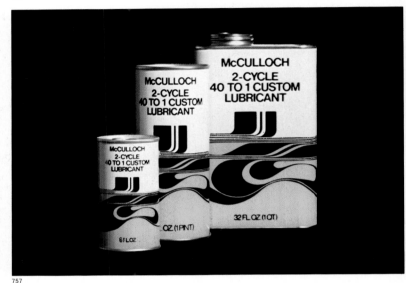

757

Industrial Packaging/Industriepackungen
Emballages industriels

758

759

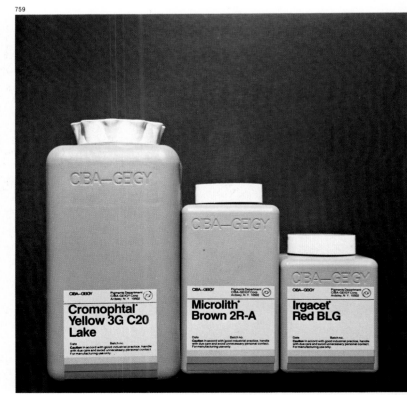

240

754 Cartons for automotive parts. Black and white with orange-brown arrows. (USA)
755 Space-saving canister for synthetic oil. (FRA)
756, 757 Cartons, tins and canisters for oil to be mixed with petrol for two-stroke engines. (USA)
758 Range of aerosol containers for spraying paints. (SWI)
759 Labels for plastic containers of industrial pigments. (USA)
760 Fibreboard container and label for bulk shipment of pigments. (USA)
761 Carton taking the catalogue of a manufacturer of ceramic tiles. (ITA)
762, 763 Carrier carton for a colour television set. The open carton can also be used for display. Lettering in blue, white and orange on blue. (GBR)

754 Verpackungen für Autozubehör. Schwarzweiss mit orange-braunen Pfeilen. (USA)
755 Ölkanister mit raumsparender Form. (FRA)
756, 757 Dosen, Kanister und Verpackungskartons für Zweitakt-Motorenöle. (USA)
758 Aerosoldosen-Sortiment für Farben im graphischen Anwendungsbereich. (SWI)
759 Kunststoffbehälter für Farbpulver. (USA)
760 Kartondosen mit Metalldeckel und -boden für Farbpulver technischer Anwendungsbereiche. (USA)
761 Katalog-Verpackungsschachtel für einen Fabrikanten von Keramikplatten. (ITA)
762, 763 Versandkarton für ein Farbfernsehgerät. Mit aufgeklapptem Deckel dient er gleichzeitig als Aussteller. Schrift in Blau, Weiss und Orange auf blauem Grund. (GBR)

754 Emballages d'accessoires automobiles. Noir, blanc; flèches brun orangé. (USA)
755 Bidon d'huile synthétique étudié de manière à réduire l'encombrement. (FRA)
756, 757 Cartons, boîtes et bidons. Huile destinée aux mélanges pour moteurs à deux temps. (USA)
758 Gamme de bombes aérosols pour la pulvérisation de peintures à l'atelier graphique. (SWI)
759 Etiquettes pour conditionnements plastiques de pigments industriels. (USA)
760 Boîte en carton comprimé, à couvercle et fond métalliques, pour pigments en vrac. (USA)
761 Carton d'expédition du catalogue d'un fabricant de carreaux de faïence. (ITA)
762, 763 Carton portatif pour un téléviseur couleur. Le couvercle rabattu, il sert à la présentation de l'article en magasin. Texte blanc et orange sur fond bleu. (GBR)

762, 763

DESIGNER / GESTALTER / MAQUETTISTE:

754 Larry Profancik/Frank Ross
755 Roger Tallon
756, 757 Don Weller/Jim van Noy
758 Nikolaus Müller-Behrendt
759, 760 Stan Baker
761 Silvio Coppola
762, 763 Martin Finch

AGENCY / AGENTUR / AGENCE – STUDIO:

754 PW, Inc. Swearingen Graphics, Inc.
755 Design Programmes SA
756, 757 Weller & Juett, Inc.
758 Marktwerbung
759, 760 Ciba-Geigy Corp.
761 Studio Coppola
762, 763 Matthew Finch Associates Ltd.

ART DIRECTOR / DIRECTEUR ARTISTIQUE:

754 Frank Ross/Larry Profancik
755 Roger Tallon
756, 757 Don Weller/Dennis S. Juett
758 Hans Demuth
759, 760 Markus J. Low
761 Silvio Coppola
762, 763 Martin Finch

CLIENT / AUFTRAGGEBER:

754 ITT Corp., Automotive Distributor Division
755 Elf/France
756, 757 McCulloch Corp.
758 Jet Color AG
759, 760 Ciba-Geigy Corp.
761 Cilsa S.r.l.
762, 763 ITT Consumer Products (U.K.) Ltd.

760

761

764

Industrial Packaging / Industriepackungen / Emballages industriels

764 Range of cartons for locks, keys and fittings. Black and white on blue. (GBR)
765 Folding box for an automatic light regulator, part of a range of electric equipment sold by a department store. The unit is visible through the die-cut windows. (SWI)
766 Cartons for carpet tiles. Standard graphic treatment with the various types distinguished by names and colours. (USA)
767 Paper bags for moulding granules. Trade mark and logo in red and black. (GBR)
768 Can label design for a motor oil. (USA)
769 Plastic bottle for a windscreen cleaning fluid and metal canister for a liquid car wax. Bottle red and black on yellow, canister blue, black and red on white. (SWI)

764 Packungsfamilie für Schlösser, Beschläge und Schlüssel. Schwarz und weiss auf Blau. (GBR)
765 Faltschachtel für einen automatischen Lichtregler, aus dem Sortiment eines Warenhauses. Das Gerät ist im ausgestanzten Fenster sichtbar. (SWI)
766 Unter Verwendung eines graphischen Elementes einheitlich gestaltete, nur durch veränderte Farben und Fabrikatsbezeichnungen variierte Verpackungen für Teppichfliesen. (USA)
767 Kombination von Schutzmarke und Logo als Teil eines einheitlichen Hausstils auf den Papiersäcken für ein gekörntes Modelliermaterial. (GBR)
768 Dosengestaltung für ein Motorenöl. (USA)
769 Kunststoff-Flasche für ein Autoscheiben-Reinigungsmittel und Blechkanister für ein flüssiges Autowachs. Links, rot und schwarz auf Gelb; rechts, blau, schwarz und rot auf Weiss. (SWI)

764 Famille d'emballages de serrures, clés et ferrures. Noir et blanc sur bleu. (GBR)
765 Boîte pliante pour un régulateur automatique de la luminosité figurant dans l'assortiment électrique d'un grand magasin. L'appareil est visible dans la découpe. (SWI)
766 Cartons de plaques de tapis. Motif graphique uniforme. Les différents emballages se distinguent par leurs couleurs et les noms des produits. (USA)
767 Cornets de matériau à modeler, en granules. Marque et logo en rouge et noir. (GBR)
768 Etiquette d'un bidon d'huile à moteurs. (USA)
769 Flacon plastique pour un produit de nettoyage pour glaces de voitures (rouge, noir sur jaune) et bidon métallique de cire liquide pour la voiture (bleu, rouge, noir sur blanc). (SWI)

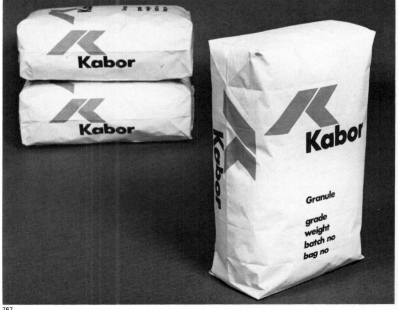

767

DESIGNER / GESTALTER / MAQUETTISTE:

764 Michael Tucker
765 E + U Hiestand
766 Tom Wood
767 David Dathan/Gillian Dathan/Peter Cockburn
768 Willi Kunz
769 Migros Genossenschaftsbund, Abt. Verpackung

ART DIRECTOR / DIRECTEUR ARTISTIQUE:

766 Dick Henderson
767 Christopher Timings
768 Eugene J. Grossman
769 H. Uster

AGENCY / AGENTUR / AGENCE – STUDIO:

764 Michael Tucker & Associates
765 E + U Hiestand
766 Cole Henderson Drake, Inc.
767 Design Research Unit
768 Anspach Grossman Portugal, Inc.
769 Migros Genossenschaftsbund, Abt. Verpackung

CLIENT / AUFTRAGGEBER:

764 Chubb & Son's Lock & Safe Co. Ltd.
765 ABM Au Bon Marché
766 Tile Company of America, Inc.
767 Kabor Ltd.
768 Meadville Corp.
769 Migros Genossenschaftsbund

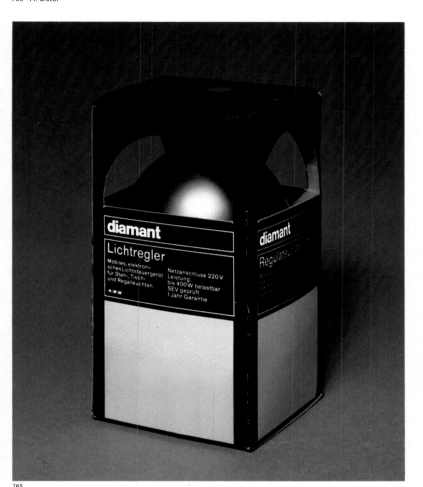

765

766

768

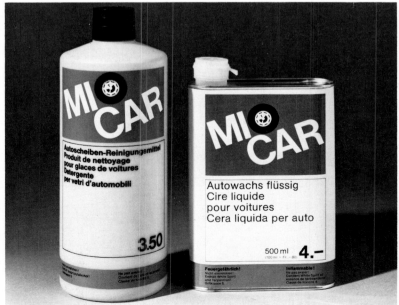

769

243

770 Folding box for ear muffs to attenuate dangerous noise. (AUL)
771 Can and pail for paint. Rainbow in full colour. (USA)
772 Plastic bottles for a motor oil sold by a department store. Blue and red on white. (SWI)
773, 774 Metal bottle and can from a range for car cleaning and maintenance products. (AUL)
775 Tins for various grades of calcium carbonate, with circles used for colour coding. (SWI)
776 Pail and cans for a gunstock oil. (USA)
777 Cartons for commercial automotive parts. Identification by drawings and numbers. (GBR)
778 Packs for small plastic seals, which are visible through the windows. The colours of the boxes are yellow and silver. (USA)
779 Carrier packs for samples of parquet flooring. (AUL)
780 Folding box for a fluorescent lamp. Lid with tuck-in closure. (GER)

770 Faltschachtel für Ohrenschützer, die gehörschädigenden Lärm dämpfen. (AUL)
771 Dose und Kübel mit Henkel für Farben. Das mehrfarbige Regenbogenmotiv wurde zur Einführung der Farben entworfen und dient seitdem zur Werbung für diese Marke. (USA)
772 Kunststoff-Flaschen für ein Motorenöl. Blau und rot auf weissem Grund. (SWI)
773, 774 Flasche und Dose aus einer Serie von Behältern für Auto-Pflegemittel. (AUL)
775 Dosen für verschiedene Qualitäten von Kalziumkarbonat. Farbige Kreise. (SWI)
776 Kübel und Dosen für ein Öl, das zur Pflege von Gewehrschäften bestimmt ist. (USA)
777 Verpackungen für Auto-Ersatzteile. (GBR)
778 Packungen für kleine Plastikverschlüsse, die durch ein Sichtfenster deutlich zu erkennen sind. Schachteln in Gelb und Silber. (USA)
779 Tragschachtel für Muster verschiedener Parkettboden-Hölzer. (AUL)
780 Faltschachtel für eine Leuchtröhre. Deckel mit Einsteck- und Klebeverschluss. (GER)

770 Boîte pliante pour une paire de protège-oreilles préservant des risques de surdité. (AUL)
771 Bidon et seau de peinture. L'arc-en-ciel a été étendu à tous les produits de la marque. (USA)
772 Bouteilles en plastique pour une huile à moteurs. Bleu et rouge sur fond blanc. (SWI)
773, 774 Bouteille et bidon métalliques. Gamme de produits pour l'entretien de la voiture. (AUL)
775 Boîtes pour diverses qualités de carbonate de chaux identifiées par cercles couleurs. (SWI)
776 Seau et boîtes d'huile à monture de fusil. (USA)
777 Emballages d'accessoires automobiles, identifiés par les dessins et les numéros. (GBR)
778 Emballages de petites fermetures en matière plastique, visibles à travers les fenêtres ménagées dans les boîtes. Ces dernières sont en jaune et argent. (USA)
779 Boîtes portatives pour des échantillons de lames de parquet. (AUL)
780 Boîte pliante pour une lampe fluorescente. Couvercle à languettes. (GER)

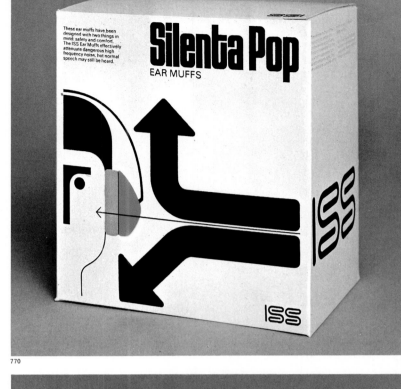

770

773

774

775

DESIGNER / GESTALTER / MAQUETTISTE:

770 Emery, Fowler-Brown Pty Ltd.
771 James Hight/Nicholas DiGiuseppe
772 E + U Hiestand
773, 774 Cato Hibberd Hawksby Pty Ltd.
775 B. Kopczinski
776 Stephen Frykholm/Philip Mitchell
777 Raymond French (Artist: Christopher Gillings)
778 John Rieben
779 Wolfram Hörschinger/Freund Werbung

ART DIRECTOR / DIRECTEUR ARTISTIQUE:

773, 774 Cato Hibberd Hawksby Pty Ltd.
777 Martin Finch
778 James Fogleman

AGENCY / AGENTUR / AGENCE – STUDIO:

770 Emery, Fowler-Brown Pty Ltd.
771 Creative Design/American Can Co.
772 E + U Hiestand
773, 774 Brainsell
775 Werberei Woodtli
777 Matthew Finch Associates Ltd.
778 Raychem Communications & Design Division

CLIENT / AUFTRAGGEBER:

770 International Safety Services
771 American Can Co.
772 ABM Au Bon Marché
773, 774 Sample Chemicals Pty Ltd.
775 Plüss Staufer AG
776 Hermann Miller, Inc.
777 Intertruck Ltd.
778 Raychem Devices Division
779 Michael Lattner & Söhne
780 Osram

778

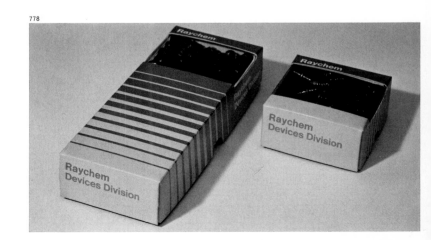

771

772

776

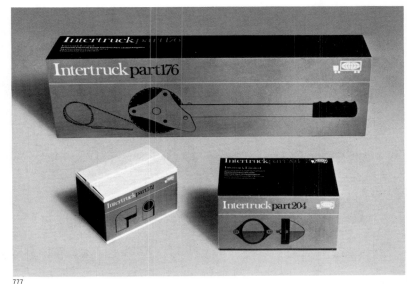

777

Industrial Packaging
Industriepackungen
Emballages industriels

779

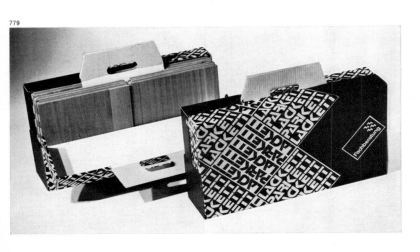

780

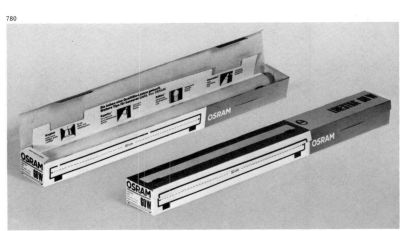

781

782

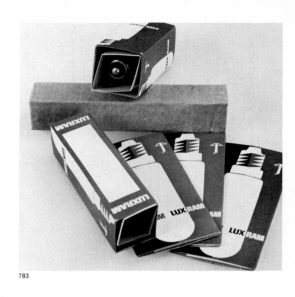

783

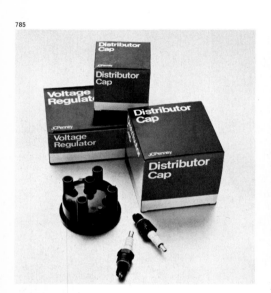

785

786

DESIGNER / GESTALTER:

784 Paul Rand
785, 791, 792 R. G. Smith/
C. C. Woodring
786 Art Goodman/Mamóru
Shimokochi
787, 788 Colin Forbes/Georg
Staehelin (Photo: Heini
Schneebeli)
790 Albert Kastelec/Martin
Gruden/Marjan Loborec

ART DIRECTOR:

784 Paul Rand
785, 791, 792 Harry Beatty
786 Saul Bass
787, 788 Colin Forbes/Georg
Staehelin

AGENCY / AGENTUR:

786 Saul Bass & Associates
787, 788 Pentagram
790 Design Iskra

CLIENT / AUFTRAGGEBER:

782 Dold AG, Lack- und
Farbenfabrik
783 Luxram-Licht AG
784 Westinghouse Electric Corp.
785, 791, 792 J. C. Penney Co.
786 American Telephone &
Telegraph, Inc.
787, 788 British Petroleum Co. Ltd.
789 Saar Gummiwerke GmbH
790 Iskra Electromecanics

787

788

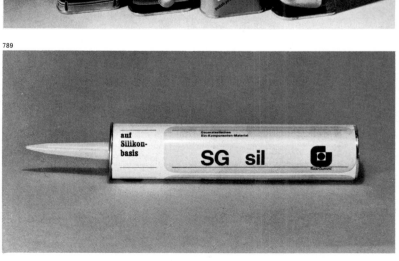

789

781 Stackable canisters of high-density polyethylene. A stack can also be used as a man-at-work sign. (SWI)
782 Oval pails of paint for indoor use. (SWI)
783 Folding boxes with liners for electric bulbs. (SWI)
784 Packs for light bulbs, with clear wattage indication. (USA)
785 Folding boxes for electric fittings sold by a department store. White lettering on black, grey or red. (USA)
786 Carton for a decorative telephone. Reds and yellows. (USA)
787, 788 Metal containers with plastic lids for a range of car cleaning products sold at petrol stations. (USA)
789 Tube with plastic nozzle for an elastic sealant. (GER)
790 Family of packs for electric power tools. (YUG)
791 Packaging system for paintbrushes. The nylon bristles are visible through the blue sleeve. (USA)
792 Carrier carton for an electric drill. Black, blue, white. (USA)

781 Stapelkanister aus Niederdruck-Polyäthylen. (SWI)
782 Ovale Malerkübel für Innenanstriche. (SWI)
783 Faltschachteln mit einfachem Einsatz für Glühbirnen. (SWI)
784 Glühbirnenpackung mit klarer Angabe der Wattzahl. (USA)
785 Packungen für kleine Zubehörteile elektrischer Geräte. Weisse Schrift auf einfarbigem Grund. Schwarz, grau oder rot. (USA)
786 Karton für dekorative Telephonapparate. Rot, gelb. (USA)
787, 788 Blechdosen mit Plastikdeckeln. Aus einem Sortiment von Autopflegemitteln, die an Tankstellen verkauft werden. (USA)

789 Metalltube mit Plastikdüse für ein elastisches Ein-Komponenten-Dichtungsmaterial. (GER)
790 Packungsfamilie für Elektrogeräte. (YUG)
791 Verpackung für Pinsel. Die Nylonborsten sind teilweise durch das blaue Etui sichtbar. (USA)
792 Tragkarton für einen elektrischen Bohrer. Graphische Darstellung schwarz auf blauem Grund, Schrift weiss. (USA)

781 Bidons empilables en polyéthylène basse pression. Une pile de ces bidons peut s'employer comme signal de travaux. (SWI)
782 Seaux de peinture ovales pour revêtements intérieurs. (SWI)
783 Boîtes pliantes, avec doublage intérieur, pour ampoules. (SWI)
784 Emballages d'ampoules. La présentation graphique en est axée sur le chiffre indiquant la puissance en watts. (USA)
785 Boîtes pliantes pour les petites fournitures électriques d'un grand magasin. Texte blanc sur noir, gris ou rouge. (USA)
786 Carton pour un téléphone décoratif. Impression en tons jaunes et rouges. (USA)
787, 788 Bidons métalliques, couvercles plastiques. Produits pour l'entretien de la voiture vendus dans les stations-service. (USA)
789 Tube métallique à gicleur plastique pour une masse de jointoyage à un composant. (GER)
790 Famille d'emballages pour appareillages électriques. (YUG)
791 Emballages bleus pour pinceaux à poils de nylon. (USA)
792 Carton pour perceuse. Noir sur bleu, texte blanc. (USA)

784

790

791

792

Industrial Packaging
Industriepackungen
Emballages industriels

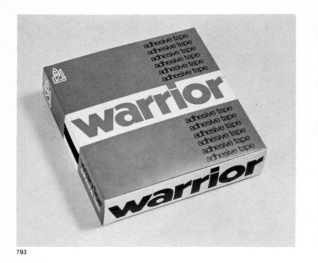

793

794

DESIGNER / GESTALTER / MAQUETTISTE:

793 Ivor Kaplin
794 Richard Nava
795 Michael Baviera
796 David Goodman/Frank Cheatham/Roy Ritola
797 Patrick Maddux (Photo: Michael Lawton)
798 Bruce Beck
799 Ken Macey
800 Connie Beck/Wayne Hunt
     (Photo: Scott Slobodian)
801 Chuck Carlberg/Larry Keith

ART DIRECTOR / DIRECTEUR ARTISTIQUE:

793 Ivor Kaplin
794 Richard Nava
795 Michael Baviera
796 Gary Familian
797 Patrick Maddux
798 Bruce Beck
799 Ed DeMartin
800 John Follis
801 Chuck Carlberg

795

796

793 From a range of packages for adhesive tape. (JPN)
794 Shipping carton for rubber products. White on orange. (USA)
795 Packs of various sizes from a large range for screws and fittings. Black and white on red. (SWI)
796 Cartons for plumbing supplies. Blue, black and white. (USA)
797 Folding boxes for cam components. Black and white. (USA)
798 Package for sparking plugs. Red and black on white. (USA)
799 Shipping cartons for a papermaker. Green on white. (USA)
800 Packaging range for car spares from a garage. (USA)
801 Promotion package for an office lighting supplier. (CAN)

793 Aus einer Serie von Packungen für Klebebänder. (JPN)
794 Versandkarton für Gummiprodukte. Weiss, orange. (USA)
795 Packungen in verschiedenen Grössen zum Verpacken von Schrauben, Beschlägen usw. Rot, weiss und schwarz. (SWI)
796 Karton für Spenglereiartikel. Blau, weiss, schwarz. (USA)
797 Faltschachtel für Nockenteile. Schwarzweiss. (USA)
798 Packung für Zündkerzen. Rot, weiss und schwarz. (USA)
799 Versandkarton für Papier. Grün auf Weiss. (USA)
800 Packungen für Autozubehör von einer Garage. (USA)
801 Werbepackung einer Bürobeleuchtungsfirma. (CAN)

793 Exemple d'emballages de rubans adhésifs. (JPN)
794 Carton pour produits de caoutchouc. Blanc, orange. (USA)
795 Emballages de dimensions variables pour une gamme étendue de vis, ferrures, etc. Noir, blanc sur rouge. (SWI)
796 Cartons de ferblanterie. Bleu, noir, blanc. (USA)
797 Boîtes pliantes pour cames. Noir et blanc. (USA)
798 Emballage de bougies d'allumage. Rouge, blanc, noir. (USA)
799 Cartons d'expédition d'un papetier. Vert sur blanc. (USA)
800 Gamme d'accessoires auto vendus par un garage. (USA)
801 Emballage pub pour une maison d'éclairage bureaux. (CAN)

CLIENT / AUFTRAGGEBER:

793 Gluewell Tape Co.
794 Pirelli Tire Corp.
795 OPO, Paul Oeschger & Cie.
796 Price Pfister Brass Manufacturing Co.
797 Crower Cames & Equipment Co.
798 National Automotive Parts Association
799 Boise Cascade Corp.
800 At-Ease (Al's Garage)
801 Gerald D. Hines Interests

AGENCY / AGENTUR / AGENCE – STUDIO:

793 Nakamoto International Agency
794 Image Communications
795 M & M Baviera
796 Porter, Goodman & Cheatham
797 Patrick Maddux & Associates
798 The Design Partnership, Inc.
799 DeMartin, Marona, Cranstoun, Downes
800 John Follis & Associates
801 Smith, Smith. Baldwin & Carlberg

797

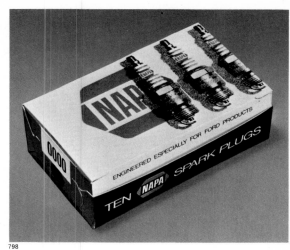

798

799

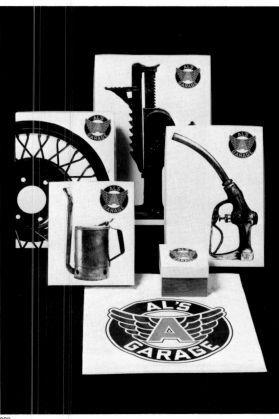

800

801

249

Packaging Competitions

Packungs-Wettbewerbe

Concours d'emballages

	English	Deutsch	Français
International	"Worldstar." Since 1970. Worldwide contest organized by the World Packaging Organization (WPO). Open to winners of an "Asiastar", "Eurostar" or "Northstar". Categories: transport containers, consumer packaging, packaging materials. World Packaging Organization, Eldex Industrial Building, 12th Floor, Unit A, 21 Ma Tau Wei Rd., Hunghom / Hong Kong.	«Worldstar.» Seit 1970. Organisiert von der World Packaging Organization (WPO). Teilnahmeberechtigt sind Gewinner der Wettbewerbe «Asiastar», «Eurostar» oder «Northstar». Kategorien: Versandpackungen, Verkaufspackungen, Verpackungsmaterialien. World Packaging Organization, Eldex Industrial Building, 12th Floor, Unit A, 21 Ma Tau Wei Rd., Hunghom / Hongkong.	«Worldstar.» Concours international, organisé depuis 1970 par la World Packaging Organization (WPO). Participation réservée aux gagnants de «L'Asiastar», «L'Eurostar» et du «North Star». Catégories: emballages d'expédition, de vente, matériaux. World Packaging Organization, Eldex Industrial Bldg., 12th Floor, Unit A, 21 Ma Tau Wei Rd., Hunghom, Hongkong.
Continental	"Asiastar." Organized bi-annually by the Asian Packaging Federation, to which belong packaging organizations from India, Japan, Korea, Australia, the Philippines, Thailand and Hongkong. Asian Packaging Federation, Honshu Bldg., 12-8, 5 Ginza, Chuo-ku, Tokyo.	«Asiastar.» Veranstaltet alle zwei Jahre von der Asian Packaging Federation, der Verpackungsorganisationen in Indien, Japan, Korea, Australien, den Philippinen, Thailand und Hongkong angehören. Asian Packaging Federation, Honshu Bldg., 12-8, 5 Ginza, Chuo-ku, Tokio.	«Asiastar.» Concours bi-annuel de l'Asian Packaging Federation qui réuni les organisations nationaux de l'Inde, du Japon, de la Corée, de l'Australie, des Philippines, de Thaïlande et de Hongkong. Asian Packaging Federation, Honshu Bldg., 12-8 5 Ginza, Chuo-ku, Tokyo.
	"Eurostar." Since 1958, annually. Organized by the European Packaging Federation. Open to winners of national awards. European Packaging Federation, Van Alkemadelaan 700, The Hague / Netherlands.	«Eurostar.» Seit 1958. Jährlich veranstaltet von der European Packaging Federation. Teilnahmeberechtigt sind Gewinner nationaler Wettbewerbe. European Packaging Federation, Van Alkemadelaan 700, Den Haag / Niederlande.	«Eurostar.» Concours annuel depuis 1958, organisé par la European Packaging Federation. Participation réservée aux gagnants de concours nationaux. European Packaging Federation, Van Alkemadelaan 700, La Haie, Pays-Bas.
	"North Star." Organized by the North American Packaging Federation, c/o Packaging Institute, 342 Madison Avenue, New York, N.Y. 10017.	«Northstar.» Veranstaltet von der North American Packaging Federation, c/o Packaging Institute, 342 Madison Avenue, New York, N.Y. 10017.	«North Star.» Concours organisé par la North American Packaging Federation, c/o Packaging Institute, 342 Madison Avenue, New York, N.Y. 10017.
Australia/Australien Australie	Anpac Pack Competition. Since 1958, annually organized by the National Packaging Association of Australia, 370 St. Kilda Road, Melbourne, 3004 Victoria.	«Anpac Pack Competition.» Seit 1958. Jährlich veranstaltet von der National Packaging Assoc. of Australia, 370 St. Kilda Road, Melbourne, 3004 Victoria.	Anpac Pack Competition. Organisé annuellement depuis 1958 par la National Packaging Assoc. of Australia, 370 St. Kilda Road, Melbourne, 3004 Victoria.
Austria Österreich Autriche	Austrian Packaging Competition. State Prize for excellence in packaging. Organized annually by the Bundesministerium für Handel, Gewerbe und Industrie and the Österreichisches Institut für Verpackungswesen. Categories: transport packages, consumer packages, packaging materials and accessories, packaging as sales promotion. Österreichisches Verpackungszentrum im Wirtschaftsförderungsinstitut der Bundeskammer der Gewerblichen Wirtschaft, Hoher Markt 3, A-1011 Vienna. Österreichisches Institut für Verpackungswesen, Franz-Klein-Gasse 1, A-1190 Vienna.	Österreichischer Verpackungswettbewerb. Staatspreis für vorbildliche Verpackung. Jährlich, seit 1957. Veranstaltet vom Bundesministerium für Handel, Gewerbe und Industrie und dem Österreichischen Institut für Verpackungswesen. Kategorien: Versandpackungen, Verkaufspackungen, Verpackungsmaterialien und Hilfsmittel, verkaufsfördernde Verpackungen. Österreichisches Verpackungszentrum im Wirtschaftsförderungs-Institut der Bundeskammer der Gewerblichen Wirtschaft, Hoher Markt 3, A-1011 Wien. Österreichisches Institut für Verpackungswesen, Franz-Klein-Gasse 1, A-1190 Wien.	Prix national pour d'excellents emballages. Concours annuel, organisé depuis 1957 par le Bundesministerium für Handel, Gewerbe und Industrie et par l'Österreichischen Institut für Verpackungswesen. Catégories: emballages d'expédition, emballages de vente, matériaux et accessoires d'emballage, emballages incitant à l'achat. Österreichisches Verpackungszentrum im Wirtschaftsförderungsinstitut der Bundeskammer der Gewerblichen Wirtschaft, Hoher Markt 3, A-1011 Vienne. Österreichisches Institut für Verpackungswesen, Franz-Klein-Gasse 1, A-1190 Vienne.
Belgium Belgien Belgique	"Oscars Belges de l'Emballage." Since 1956, organized annually by the Institut Belge de l'Emballage. Categories: shipping containers, consumer packaging, packaging materials. Institut Belge de l'Emballage, Rue Picard 15, B-1020 Bruxelles.	«Oscars Belges de l'Emballage.» Seit 1956. Jährliche Veranstaltung des Institut Belge de l'Emballage. Kategorien: Versandverpackungen, Verkaufsverpackungen, Verpackungsmaterialien. Institut Belge de l'Emballage, rue Picard 15, B-1020 Bruxelles.	«Oscars Belges de l'Emballage.» Concours annuel, organisé depuis 1956 par l'Institut Belge de l'Emballage. Catégories: emballage d'expédition, emballages de distribution, matériaux. Institut Belge de l'Emballage, Rue Picard 15, B-1020 Bruxelles.
Canada Kanada	Packaging Association of Canada. Gold, silver and bronze awards. Folding and Set-up Paper Box Competition, since 1964. Flexible Packaging Competition, since 1965. Rigid Containers Competition, since 1966. Corrugated Packaging Competition, since 1965. Packaging Association of Canada, 45 Charles Str. E., Toronto 5, Ontario.	Gold-, Silber- und Bronzeauszeichnungen verliehen von der Packaging Association of Canada. Falt- und Festkartonpackungswettbewerb seit 1964. Wettbewerb für flexible Packungen seit 1965. Wettbewerb für feste Behälter seit 1966. Wettbewerb für Wellkartonpackungen seit 1965. Packaging Association of Canada, 45 Charles Str. E., Toronto 5, Ontario.	Concours organisés par la Packaging Association of Canada. Médailles d'or, d'argent et de bronze: pour des boîtes pliantes et des boîtes en carton monté – depuis 1964; pour des emballages flexibles – depuis 1965; pour des récipients solides – depuis 1966; pour des emballages en carton ondulé – depuis 1965. Packaging Association of Canada, 45 Charles Str. E., Toronto 5, Ontario.
Czechoslovakia Tschechoslowakei Tchécoslovaquie	Package of the Year. Since 1965. Organized by the Institute of Handling, Transport, Packaging and Storage Systems (IMADOS). Categories: consumer packages, transport packages, partial elements for increasing packaging level. IMADOS – Institute of Handling, Transport, Packaging and Storage Systems, U Michelského Lesa 366, Prague 4.	Beste Verpackung des Jahres. Seit 1965. Veranstaltet von IMADOS, Institut für Fördertechnik, Versand, Verpackung und Lagerung. Kategorien: Verkaufs- und Versandpackungen, Einzelelemente für bessere Verpackung. IMADOS – Institute of Handling, Transport, Packaging and Storage-Systems, U Michelského Lesa 366, Prag 4.	Concours pour le meilleur emballage commercial. Organisé annuellement par l'Institut de Manutention, de Transport, de l'Emballage et de Systèmes d'entreposage (IMADOS). Catégories: emballages de distribution, d'expédition, éléments et matériaux. IMADOS – Institut de Manutention, de Transport, de l'Emballage et de Systèmes d'entreposage, U Michelského Lesa 366, Prague 4.
France Frankreich	"Oscar de l'Emballage." Annual contest since 1955, organized by the Institut Français de l'Emballage et du Conditionnement. Judged by two separate juries for technical, sales-promotional merits. Two categories for entries: from manufacturers of goods, from manufacturers of packaging and materials. Institut Français de l'Emballage et du Conditionnement, 40, Rue du Colisée, F-75008 Paris.	«Oscar de l'Emballage», seit 1955. Jährlich verliehen vom Institut Français de l'Emballage et du Conditionnement. Je eine Jury für die Beurteilung nach technischen oder verkaufsfördernden Kriterien. Zwei Teilnehmerkategorien: Produzenten von Gütern, Produzenten von Packungen und Verpackungsmaterial. Institut Français de l'Emballage et du Conditionnement, 40, rue du Colisée, F-75008 Paris.	«Oscar de l'Emballage.» Concours annuel de l'Institut Français de l'Emballage et du Conditionnement. Deux jurys différents pour le jugement de la conception technique et de l'attrait pour la vente. Deux catégories: fabricants de produits, fabricants d'emballages et de matériaux. Institut Français de l'Emballage et du Conditionnement, 40, Rue du Colisée, F-75008 Paris.
Germany Deutschland Allemagne	German Packaging Competition. Since 1963, organized annually by the Rationalisierungs-Gemeinschaft Verpackung im RKW. Two judging classifications: transport packages and consumer packages. Rationalisierungs-Gemeinschaft Verpackung im RKW, Postfach 11 91 93, D-6000 Frankfurt/M 11.	Deutscher Verpackungswettbewerb, seit 1963. Jährlich veranstaltet von der Rationalisierungs-Gemeinschaft Verpackung im RKW. Einsendungen unterteilt in Versand- und Verkaufspackungen. Rationalisierungs-Gemeinschaft Verpackung im RKW, Postfach 11/91/93, D-6000 Frankfurt/M.	Concours national, organisé annuellement par la Rationalisierungs-Gemeinschaft Verpackung im RKW. Deux classifications: conception graphique/ publicitaire ou conception technique/économique. Rationalisierungs-Gemeinschaft Verpackung im RKW, Case postale 11 91 93, D-6000 Francfort/M.
Great Britain Grossbritannien Grande Bretagne	"Starpacks." The British Packaging Contest, since 1960, organized annually by the Institute of Packaging. Two sections: consumer packages, transit packages.	«Starpacks», Wettbewerb für Packungen aus Grossbritannien, seit 1960. Jährlich ausgeschrieben vom Institute of Packaging, für zwei Kategorien: Versand- und Verkaufspackungen.	«Starpacks.» Concours anglais, organisé annuellement depuis 1960 par l'Institute of Packaging. Deux catégories: emballages de vente, emballages d'expédition.

	The Institute of Packaging, Fountain House, 1A Elm Park, Stanmore, Middlesex HA7 4BZ.	The Institute of Packaging, Fountain House, 1A Elm Park, Stanmore, Middlesex HA7 4BZ.	Institute of Packaging, Fountain House, 1A Elm Park, Stanmore, Middlesex HA7 4BZ.

Ireland / Irland / Irlande

Irish Packaging Awards. Since 1960. Organized by the Irish Packaging Institute, usually in conjunction with the Irish Packaging Exhibition. Categories: Consumer packages, transport packages, family ranges, family groups.
Irish Packaging Institute, 28 Fitzwilliam Place, Dublin 2.

Irischer Packungspreis. Veranstaltet seit 1960 vom Irish Packaging Institute, meist in Zusammenarbeit mit der Irish Packaging Exhibition. Kategorien: Verkaufspackungen, Versandpackungen, Packungsreihen, Packungsgruppen.
Irish Packaging Institute, 28 Fitzwilliam Place, Ei-Dublin 2.

Distinction irlandaise pour l'emballage. Concours organisé par l'Irish Packaging Institute en collaboration avec la Irish Packaging Exhibition. Catégories: emballages de vente, emballages d'expédition, familles d'emballages, groupes d'emballages.
Irish Packaging Institute, 28 Fitzwilliam Place, Dublin 2.

Italy / Italien / Italie

"Oscar dell'Imballagio." Since 1957 annually organized by the Istituto Italiano Imballagio. Categories: transport containers, consumer packaging, packaging materials and adjuncts.
Istituto Italiano Imballagio, Via Carlo Cassan, 34, I-35100 Padova.

«Oscar dell'Imballagio», seit 1957. Jährlich veranstaltet vom Istituto Italiano Imballagio. Kategorien: Versand-, Verkaufspackungen, Verpackungsmaterial und -hilfsmaterial.
Istituto Italiano Imballagio, Via Carlo Cassan 34, I-35100 Padua.

«Oscar dell'Imballagio.» Concours annuel, organisé depuis 1957 par l'Istituto Italiano Imballagio. Catégories: emballages d'expédition, emballages de vente, matériaux et accessoires d'emballage.
Istituto Italiano Imballagio, Via Carlo Cassan, 34, I-35100 Padoue.

Japan / Japon

"Japanstar." Annual contest organized by the Japan Packaging Institute, Honshu Bldg., 12-8, 5 Ginza, Chuo-ku, Tokyo.

«Japanstar», jährlich veranstalteter Packungswettbewerb des Japan Packaging Institute, Honshu Bldg., 12-8, 5 Ginza, Chuo-ku, Tokio.

«Japanstar.» Concours annuel organisé par l'Institut Japonais de l'Emballage, Honshu Bldg., 12-8, 5 Ginza, Chuo-ku, Tokyo.

Netherlands / Niederlande / Pays-Bas

"The Golden Walnut." Packaging Contest. Since 1958, bi-annual. Organized jointly by Nederlands Verpakkingscentrum and Koninklijke Nederlandse Jaarbeurs (Royal Netherlands Industries Fair). Categories: retail packages, transport packages, packaging materials, new packages and materials not yet in use. Nederlands Verpakkingscentrum, Van Alkemadelaan 700, The Hague/Netherlands.

«Die goldene Nuss», seit 1958 alle zwei Jahre veranstaltet vom Nederlands Verpakkingscentrum, gemeinsam mit der Koninklijke Nederlandse Jaarbeurs (Königlich Niederländische Industriemesse). Kategorien: Detailverkaufs- und Transportpackungen, Verpackungsmaterial, neue Verpackungsarten.
Nederlands Verpakkingscentrum, van Alkemadelaan 700, Den Haag / Niederlande.

«Le Gland d'or.» Concours bi-annuel, organisé par Nederlands Verpakkingscentrum et Koninklijke Nederlandse Jaarbeurs (Foire Royale d'Industrie Néerlandaise). Catégories: emballages de vente, d'expédition, matériaux, emballages et matériaux nouveaux qui ne sont pas encore sur le marché.
Nederlands Verpakkingscentrum, Van Alkemadelaan 700, La Haie.

Portugal

National Packaging Competition: Concurso Nacional de Embalagem, "EMBA", annually organized by the Instituto Português de Embalagem.
Centro Nacional de Embalagem, Praca das Industrias, Lisbon 3.

«Concurso Nacional de Embalagem, EMBA». Portugiesischer Packungswettbewerb, jährlich veranstaltet vom Instituto Português de Embalagem.
Centro Nacional de Embalagem, Praca das Industrias, Lissabon 3.

Concurso Nacional de Embalagem «EMBA». Concours national, organisé annuellement par l'Instituto Português de Embalagem.
Centro Nacional de Embalagem, Praca das Industrias, Lisbonne 3.

Scandinavia / Skandinavien / Scandinavie

"Scanstar." Scandinavian Packaging Competition. Since 1969. Organized bi-annually by the Danish, Finnish and Norwegian Packaging Associations and the Swedish Packaging Federation, the administration alternating between these four.
Emballageinstituttet, Jemtelandsgade 1, DK-2300 Copenhagen.
Finnish Packaging Association, Ritarikatu 3b, Helsinki 17.
Den Norske Emballasjeforening, Postboks 1754 — Vika, Klingenberg gt. 7, Oslo 1.
Svenska Förpackningsföreningen, Box 9038, Drakenbergsgatan 61, S-102 71 Stockholm 9.

«Scanstar.» Skandinavischer Packungswettbewerb, seit 1969, alle zwei Jahre. Veranstaltet und abwechslungsweise geleitet vom Dänischen, Finnischen und Norwegischen Packungsverband und der Schwedischen Packungsvereinigung.
Emballageinstituttet, Jemtelandsgade 1, DK-2300 Kopenhagen.
Finnish Packaging Association, Ritarikatu 3b, Helsinki 17.
Den Norske Emballasjeforening, Postboks 1754 — Vika, Klingenberg gt. 7, Oslo 1.
Svenska Förpackningsföreningen, Box 9038, Drakenbergsgatan 61, S-102 71 Stockholm 9.

«Scanstar.» Concours scandinave bi-annuel, organisé depuis 1969 par les Associations Danoise, Finlandaise et Norvégienne de l'Emballage et la Fédération Suédoise de l'Emballage. Ces associations se relaient quant à l'administration.
Emballageinstituttet, Jemtelandsgade 1, DK-2300 Copenhague.
Association Finlandaise de l'Emballage, Ritarikatu 3b, Helsinki 17.
Den Norske Emballasjeforening, Case postale 1754 — Vika, Klingenberg gt. 7, Oslo 1.
Svenska Förpackningsföreningen, Case postale 9038, Drakenbergsgatan 61, S-102 71 Stockholm 9.

Spain/Spanien / Espagne

"Span-Pack." Annual awards organized by the Instituto Español de Envase y Embalaje, S.A., Breton de los Herreros, 57, Madrid 3.

«Spanpack.» Jährliche Preise verliehen vom Istituto Espagnol de Envase y Embalaje, S.A., Breton de los Herreros 57, Madrid 3.

«Span-Pack.» Concours annuel, organisé par l'Istituto Español de Envase y Embalaje, S.A., Breton de los Herreros, 57, Madrid 3.

Switzerland / Schweiz / Suisse

Swiss Packaging Awards. National packaging competition. Since 1957. Annually organized by the Vereinigung Schweizerisches Verpackungsinstitut. Judged by two separate juries for graphic, technical-economic merits.
Vereinigung Schweizerisches Verpackungsinstitut, Verlag Max Binkert & Co., CH-4335 Laufenburg.

Schweizerische Verpackungsprämiierung. Seit 1957 jährlich veranstaltet von der Vereinigung Schweizerisches Verpackungsinstitut. Beurteilung durch je eine Jury nach grafisch-formalen und technisch-wirtschaftlichen Gesichtspunkten.
Vereinigung Schweizerisches Verpackungsinstitut, Verlag Max Binkert & Co., CH-4335 Laufenburg.

Prix national. Concours annuel, organisé depuis 1957 par l'Association Institut Suisse de l'Emballage. Deux jurys pour le jugement du point de vue conception technique/économique et conception graphique/forme.
Association Institut Suisse de l'Emballage, Ed. Max Binkert & Co., CH-4335 Laufenburg.

USA

National Folding Carton Competition. Annual awards, open to members only. Sponsored by the Paperboard Packaging Council, 1250 Connecticut Ave. N.W., Washington, D.C. 20036.

Nationaler Faltkarton-Wettbewerb, jährliche Preisverleihungen, nur für Mitglieder.
Paperboard Packaging Council, 1250 Connecticut Ave. N.W., Washington D.C. 20036.

Concours national pour des emballages pliants. Participation réservée aux membres. Organisé annuellement par le Paperboard Packaging Council, 1250 Connecticut Ave. N.W., Washington DC 20036.

The Packaging Institute's Annual Awards Program. Since 1957. Jury chosen from field of business management, education, publishing, government, etc., gives Corporate Award for applied packaging technology to product manufacturer. Jury from packaging and allied fields gives Professional Award to individual for contribution to packaging technology.
The Packaging Institute, 342 Madison Ave., New York, N.Y. 10017.

Seit 1957 verliehene Preise des Packaging Institute. Eine Jury (Vertreter aus Industrie, Regierung, Erziehungs- und Pressewesen) für Leistungen von Produzenten in angewandter Verpackungstechnik, eine zweite (aus Verpackungsindustrie) für Beiträge von Einzelpersonen zur Verbesserung der Verpackungstechnik.
The Packaging Institute, 342 Madison Ave., New York, N.Y. 10017.

Concours annuel, organisé depuis 1957 par le Packaging Institute. Un jury (représentants de l'industrie, de l'enseignement, de la presse et du gouvernement) attribue des distinctions aux fabricants pour la technologie d'emballage appliquée, un autre jury (industrie de conditionnement) aux personnes individuelles ayant contribué au progrès technique de l'emballage.
The Packaging Institute, 342 Madison Ave., New York, N.Y. 10017.

"Top Packaging Ideas of the Year." Annual contest sponsored by Packaging Design Magazine, 527 Madison Avenue, New York, N.Y. 10022.

«Top Packaging Ideas of the Year». Jährlicher Preis der Packaging Design Magazine, 527 Madison Avenue, New York, N.Y. 10022.

«Top Packaging Ideas of the Year.» Concours annuel, organisé par la revue Package Design Magazine, 527 Madison Avenue, New York, N.Y. 10022.

National Paper Box Association. Annual awards in four categories: general superiority according to end-use or common type, best surface design & execution, best in superiority of construction, best protective package.
National Paper Box Association, 231 Kings Highway E., Haddonfield, N.J. 08033.

«National Paper Box Association» (für Kartonverpackungen). Jährlich Preise in vier Kategorien: Beste Packung ganz allgemein oder im Hinblick auf Endzweck, beste in Ausführung und Design, beste Konstruktion, wirksamste Schutzpackung.
National Paper Box Association, 231 Kings Highway E., Haddonfield, N.Y. 08033.

National Paper Box Association. Concours annuel. Catégories: supériorité générale quant au domaine d'emploi, meilleur emballage du point de vue du design et de l'exécution, meilleur emballage quant à la construction, meilleur emballage de protection.
National Paper Box Association, 231 Kings Highway East, Haddonfield, N.J. 08033.

Paper/Papier: Papierfabrik Biberist — Biber GS SK3, blade coated, pure white, 125 gm² and Biber Offset SK3, pure white, machinefinished, 140 gm²/Biber GS SK3, hochweiss, satiniert, 125 gm² und Biber-Offset SK3, hochweiss, maschinenglatt, 140 gm²

Printed by/gedruckt von: Offset & Buchdruck AG, Zürich (Colour pages/Farbseiten), Stämpfli + Cie AG, Bern (Black and white/schwarzweiss).

Cover/Einband: Buchbinderei Stämpfli + Cie AG, Bern
Glossy lamination/Glanzfoliierung: Durolit AG, Pfäffikon SZ